THE LANDING OF WILLIAM PENN—1682

THE HISTORY
OF
PENNSYLVANIA

ARTHUR D. GRAEFF

Head, Department
Social Studies
Overbrook High School
Philadelphia

THE JOHN C. WINSTON COMPANY

Chicago	PHILADELPHIA	Toronto
Atlanta	Los Angeles	Dallas

INTRODUCTION

The History of Pennsylvania has been written for young Pennsylvanians, in order that they may better understand the important part played by their state in the past, the role it is taking in the present emergency, and the manner in which they, as citizens, will direct its future course. The story of Pennsylvania—for story it is, indeed, more vivid and exciting than a work of fiction—is one which the casual reader also will find of absorbing interest.

The study of Pennsylvania history is in reality a concentrated study of the nation as a whole. Here in Pennsylvania was a sanctuary for the oppressed from the Old World; here patriots struggled for the priceless blessings of liberty; and in Pennsylvania, as in the nation, many races and cultures were blended into the American pattern of life. The geographic placement of Pennsylvania as the keystone of the Union arch accounted in part for its military and industrial importance in the past; its wealth of natural resources and skilled workmen have helped to make Penn's woods today's cultural and industrial giant.

The student and the reader will, we believe, derive from a perusal of this textbook an appreciation of Pennsylvania's many contributions to the democratic way of life.

For classroom use, the history of Pennsylvania is presented in seven units of study. These units are designed to be integrated with the most widely used divisions or units of United States history. In this way we attempt to make the book serviceable either in a separate one-semester course, or as a supplement to a full year's course in United States history. Unit previews have been provided for the purpose of orienting the subject matter contained within the unit. They are designed to capture interest, focus attention, and give a perspective picture of the content and its relationship to the story as a whole. At the end of each chapter there are questions for review and further study. The suggested exercises, activities, and problems at the end of each unit may be adapted by pupils and teachers to meet local needs and interests. A carefully selected bibliography, grouped according to subject, is given for further reading.

The author wishes to use this opportunity to express his gratitude to the many individuals and societies which rendered assistance in the writing and construction of the book: Dr. William D. Mallam, now Lieutenant in the Army of the United States, for much of the preparation of the unit dealing with the War for the Union; to Dr. Elsie Murray of the Tioga Point Museum; to the American-Swedish Museum of Philadelphia; to the Carl Schurz Memorial Foundation; the historical societies of Berks, Bucks, Lancaster, and York counties; the Historical Society of Pennsylvania; the Philadelphia Museum of Art; the Pennsylvania Historical Commission; and the Landis Valley Museum.

The author is indebted to Barbara Wheaton Smith of London, England, for a critical reading of the unit dealing with the War for Independence; to David W. Harr, of the Frankford High School, Philadelphia, for valuable suggestions; to Dr. Mary E. Stewart of Philadelphia for editorial assistance; and to Honorable D. K. Hoch of Reading for the unfailing support and encouragement extended to the author throughout many years in pursuing the study of the history of the Commonwealth. The author alone is responsible for any errors that may have been made.

Arthur D. Graeff

A NOTE TO TEACHERS ON SOURCE READINGS

The published source readings dealing with Pennsylvania history are few, and most of them cannot be found in small libraries. The most readily available volume is *Pennsylvania History Told by Contemporaries*, edited by Asa Earl Martin and Hiram Herr Shenk, published by Macmillan, New York, 1925. Selected passages from *American History Told by Contemporaries* and *Source Readings in American History*, both edited by Albert Bushnell Hart, are also useful in the study of Pennsylvania history.

There are also published collections of manuscripts relating to Pennsylvania history, but, for the most part, these were published in limited editions and are not easily available. The sixty-six volumes of the *Pennsylvania Magazine of History and Biography* contain many diaries and letters. Bound copies of this valuable publication are frequently found in the libraries of local historical societies and large public libraries. Similar collections of manuscripts and documents may be found in the files of the *Western Pennsylvania Magazine* and in *Now and Then*, a small publication issued at various intervals since 1865 by the Muncy Historical Association. The journal *Pennsylvania History* (1933 to 1943), official publication of the Pennsylvania Historical Association, has appeared in ten volumes thus far. It contains authentic accounts of many phases of Pennsylvania history.

There are a number of county historical societies which publish historical journals dealing with local history. These should be used extensively. Not all of the material in these journals should be considered source material, however.

More difficult to locate are the published series of the *Pennsylvania Archives*, now in nine series, devoted largely to colonial history. The *Minutes of the Provincial Council of Pennsylvania*, commonly known as the *Colonial Records*, in sixteen volumes, were published more than a century ago, and full sets are rarely found outside of large libraries.

The fifty-three volumes of *The Proceedings of the Pennsylvania German Society,* from 1891 to 1944, are rich in their portrayal of the colonial history of eastern Pennsylvania. For folklore, the writings of Colonel Henry W. Shoemaker, State Archivist, are valuable but unfortunately are out of print. The seven volumes published by the Pennsylvania German Folklore Society are more easily accessible.

Teachers will find the special bulletins of the Pennsylvania State Department of Public Instruction of great value. The mimeographed essays, also published by the same department, have been found to be of value and interest to the various clubs of junior historians organized in many of the high schools of the Commonwealth. Much of this material may be obtained without cost by writing to the Department of Public Instruction, Harrisburg, Pennsylvania.

CONTENTS

UNIT ONE

DISCOVERY AND SETTLEMENT

UNIT TWO

COLONIAL PENNSYLVANIA

UNIT THREE

WINNING INDEPENDENCE

UNIT FOUR

DEMOCRACY MOVES FORWARD

UNIT FIVE

PENNSYLVANIA HELPS TO SAVE THE UNION

UNIT SIX

POLITICAL AND INDUSTRIAL DEVELOPMENT

UNIT SEVEN

MODERN TIMES

UNIT I

DISCOVERY AND SETTLEMENT

Three hundred years ago that part of the world we know as Pennsylvania was still a dense forest inhabited only by savage Indians and the wild animals of the woods. Today, the Commonwealth of Pennsylvania ranks high among the forty-eight states of the Union in wealth, culture, and population. How did this come about? Who were the early settlers and what led them to the New World where hardship and danger awaited them? Did they find the freedom they sought in Penn's Woods?

The land of Pennsylvania was first explored by the Dutch, and Dutch traders built their small posts along the Delaware River. Soon after, a band of hardy Swedish settlers founded a village at present-day Chester. For several years there was rivalry between the Dutch and Swedes for possession of the Delaware River and Bay region.

In 1664, however, the English won control of the region. It was William Penn's great dream to establish a haven for persecuted Quakers that led him to accept a grant of land in America from the English King, Charles II. Soon, Pennsylvania became a haven, not alone for English Quakers but for other persecuted religious groups of Europe as well. Germans from the valley of the Rhine and Scotch-Irish from the north of Ireland flocked to the colony. The industry, skill, and courage of these early immigrants soon made it one of the most prosperous colonies in the New World.

As our story unfolds we shall learn how the ideals of William Penn have shaped the history of Pennsylvania from his day to ours. We shall see that our heritage from the early settlers enriches the lives of the citizens of the Commonwealth today.

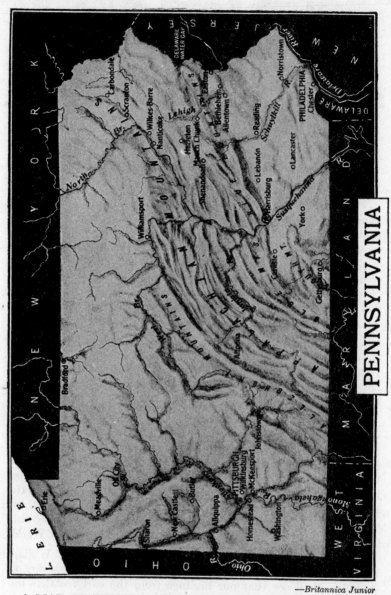

—*Britannica Junior*

A MAP OF PENNSYLVANIA SHOWING THE PHYSICAL
FEATURES

2

Chapter I

WHITE MEN ENTER PENNSYLVANIA

Before we begin the study of Pennsylvania we should have in mind the limits and characteristics of the region with which we will be concerned. The present area of Pennsylvania is 45,126 square miles. The state ranks thirty-second in size among the forty-eight states of the Union. The distance between the New York State line on the north and the Maryland-West Virginia line on the south is approximately 160 miles, while the east-west distance between the irregular boundary of the Delaware River and the Ohio-West Virginia line varies from 270 to 300 miles.

Measured in terms of population Pennsylvania ranks second only to her northern neighbor, New York. The Census of 1940 listed 9,900,180 persons as residents of the Keystone state, four and one-half million less than New York State.

PHYSICAL CHARACTERISTICS

In considering the physical features of Sylvania, the "Woods," let us examine some of the natural characteristics of the domain which William Penn found here. Mountains, rivers, lakes, and valleys do not change much with the passing of time. The Indians knew them then as we know them today, perhaps even more intimately than we do. Because physical geography has an important bearing on history, we need to know something about the great mountain walls that separate the valleys and the flowing streams that carried the red man's canoe, the settler's flat-bottomed boat, and later turned the wheels of great industries.

Mountains. Pennsylvania is ribbed by several series of mountain chains, all subdivisions of the great Appalachian range which extends from Maine to Georgia. As the branches of this range pass through Pennsylvania they run diagonally; that is, they cut across the state like lines forming bases of triangles whose apexes or tips may be marked at Philadelphia. Thus the

3

—*Aero Service Corporation*

THE DELAWARE WATER GAP

Blue Mountains, or Kittatinny Mountains as the Indians called them, cut southwest from the Delaware Water Gap, near Stroudsburg, through Northampton, Lehigh, Berks, Schuylkill, Lebanon, and Dauphin counties, where they are broken by the Susquehanna River. This chain continues southward and westward through Cumberland, York, Adams, and Franklin counties until it enters Maryland.

Farther west, in Bedford County and extending into Westmoreland County, begin the ranges of the towering Alleghenies with their many peaks, summits, and ridges. North of the Blue Mountains, and extending westward throughout most of the state, there are many steep mountains, cut occasionally by gaps through which streams of water escape to the rivers and fertile valleys.

Rivers. Three great rivers figure prominently in Pennsylvania history. They are the Delaware in the east, the Susquehanna draining the north and central portions of the state, and the Ohio and its tributaries in the west. The Delaware rises in New York State, flows southward along the eastern edge of Pennsylvania, and is joined by the waters of two other rivers, the Lehigh and Schuylkill, before it widens into the Delaware Bay south of the limits of Pennsylvania. The Susquehanna is

4

formed at the point where two of its branches, flowing from the west and northeast, meet at Sunbury. North of Harrisburg the Susquehanna is joined by the Juniata flowing from the west and northwest. From Harrisburg the Susquehanna flows in a southeasterly direction, entering Maryland before it empties into the Chesapeake Bay. In the western portion of the state two large streams, the Allegheny, flowing from the north, and the Monongahela, draining northward from Maryland, unite at Pittsburgh to form the mighty Ohio River, which, after a brief northward journey, bends at Beaver Falls to flow south, then west, into the Mississippi, and from thence to the Gulf of Mexico.

THE RED MEN

The Origin of the Indians. Lost in the obscurity of unrecorded history and confused by Indian legend and white man's conjecture is the true story of the origin of the American Indian. Students of Indian lore have advanced many theories to account for the presence of human beings on the American continent. These theories—in some cases they are little more than guesses—are of a wide variety. The most widely held theory is that the Indians came originally from Asia, crossing by way of the Bering Strait into Alaska. Some of the less plausible explanations suggest great land convulsions and drifting continents and the story of the lost tribes of Israel to account for the presence of the Indians.

Most historians seem to agree that the Pennsylvania Indians came from the west, and that the first tribe to inhabit the state was known as the Alligewe, from whom we derive the name "Allegheny." This tribe was conquered by two invading tribes, namely the Lenni-Lenape, later known to the English as the Delaware, and the Mengwe, called the Iroquois by the French. According to some Indian traditions, the two conquering nations divided the lands taken from the Allegewi, the Iroquois taking present-day New York State, while the Delawares occupied Pennsylvania.

Language Classifications. For the purpose of classification, the Indians east of the Mississippi may be divided into three groups: the Algonquian, Iroquoian, and Siouan, although the last-named will concern us very little. This classification is

5

based upon certain similarities of language found among the various tribes and not upon their places of habitation. The Delawares, among others, are classified as Algonquians and the Susquehannocks, as well as many other eastern tribes, make up the Iroquoian group. Only one important tribe of Siouan Indians lived within the limits of Pennsylvania—the Tutelos. This tribe lived in central Pennsylvania during the middle of the eighteenth century, having come here from North Carolina, tarrying a while along the Susquehanna, and then moving northward into what is now New York State.

THE ALGONQUIANS

The Delawares. When the English came to Pennsylvania, they found the Lenni-Lenape Indians settled on both sides of the river which an English explorer had named Delaware in honor of a governor of Virginia, Lord De la Warr. The name of the river was soon applied to these Indians; hence we shall speak of the Lenni-Lenape as Delawares.

The Delaware nation was subdivided into three tribes known in English as the Turtle, Wolf, and Turkey tribes. Soon after the arrival of the white men and the sale of some of their lands on the Delaware, these Indians moved their chief villages to the valley of the Susquehanna River, choosing the river forks at present-day Sunbury as their chief village. The name of that village was Shamokin (the place of eels). There is a city in Pennsylvania today named Shamokin in Northumberland County, but it is twenty miles east of the Indian village which once bore that name. Sunbury stands on the site of the Delaware capital of colonial times. As the tide of white settlers moved west, the Delawares, dispossessed of their lands, were forced to move from the Susquehanna to the Ohio, and finally out of the limits of Pennsylvania.

The Shawnee. There were other tribes of Indians in Pennsylvania which belonged to the large Algonquian group. The Shawnee, entering Pennsylvania from the south sometime after the arrival of William Penn, made their first villages in Lancaster County, then moved north to "Big Island," where Lock Haven now stands. When white men penetrated deeper into the woods the Shawnee sought refuge first on the Ohio and later in the western states.

6

The Susquehannocks. We are accustomed to think of the Iroquois Indians as residents of New York, but we must remember that several branches of that powerful nation established themselves within the present limits of Pennsylvania. It was the Susquehannocks who were the first Pennsylvania Indians to come in contact with white men. As early as 1608, one year after the settlement of Jamestown in Virginia, Captain John Smith explored the Chesapeake Bay and north along the Susquehanna River into the present limits of Pennsylvania. In describing the Susquehannocks, Smith wrote that they were ". . . great and well-proportioned men, for they seemed like giants to the English . . ."

Seven years later, in 1615, the French explorer, Samuel de Champlain, encountered Susquehannock Indians in the campaign in which he fought on the side of the Hurons against the Iroquois. While Champlain was preparing to attack the Iroquois near present-day Syracuse, New York, he learned that a group of Susquehannock Indians residing in a village named Carantouan wished to join his forces. He sent deputies to Carantouan to enlist their aid. This village was in northern Bradford County, on or near the present site of Spanish Hill. Champlain's deputy on this mission was one Etienne Brulé. In 1616 Brulé traveled the whole length of the Susquehanna River from its headwaters in New York, to its mouth in Maryland, thus becoming the first white man to traverse Pennsylvania from north to south.

The Susquehannocks were involved in many wars which reduced their numbers. In 1674, before the arrival of Penn, they were conquered by the Iroquois, and a remnant of their tribe

—Historical Society of Pennsylvania

THE LENNI-LENAPE INDIANS

Taken from an engraving in *Nya Swerige*, published in Stockholm in 1702.

7

—From a painting by Arthur A. Jansson.
Courtesy, American Museum of Natural History

HOME LIFE AMONG THE INDIANS

settled along the Conestoga Creek in Lancaster County. Thereafter they were known as the Conestogas.

The Tuscaroras. Other Iroquoian tribes resident in Pennsylvania were the Tuscaroras, the Wyandots, Eries, and Wenroes. Of these, the Tuscaroras were the most important. Early in the eighteenth century they migrated north from the Carolinas, resided for a time in the Juniata Valley, and then moved northward to New York. In 1714 they were admitted to the Five Nations Confederacy, the powerful Iroquois alliance, becoming the sixth of the historic Six Nations of the Iroquois. They lingered in Pennsylvania long enough to give their name to Tuscarora Summit and Tuscarora Valley in the Juniata region.

Cornplanter Reservation. It may come as a surprise to many students to learn that there are Iroquois Indians still living on a reservation within the limits of Pennsylvania today. A small tip of the Cornplanter Reservation extends from New York State into Pennsylvania near Warren. These Indians are a remnant of the Seneca Nation of New York. They eke out a living by tilling the soil allotted to them, much in the same way that their ancestors worked and lived.

LIFE AMONG THE INDIANS

Village Life. Pennsylvania Indians lived in villages usually located on the banks of a creek or river. Their dwellings were log huts, hewn from native timber, built without stone foundations. In considering the Indians, their way of life, their customs and beliefs, it is well to bear in mind that they were children of the forest, uneducated, facing an insecure future, torn by frequent wars, and almost wholly dependent upon nature to supply them with the needs of life. They did not understand private ownership of land; the tribe owned it, and the fowl and game there provided food for all.

The Indian was not thrifty. He did not store his harvests against future scarcities. Heavy snows in wintertime brought famine and pestilence because he was unable to hunt and fish for food, and there was no pantry or cellar on which to draw for stores which had been harvested during the preceding summer. Because their diet was unvaried, consisting chiefly of meats, nuts, berries, and corn when in season, often disease ravaged their communities.

The White Man's Influence. The white man's whisky, or "firewater," increased the misery of the Indians. Unrestrained by habits of temperance, they drank the "spirits" heavily, thus further weakening their health. In addition, the "firewater" frequently led them to commit crimes of many kinds. Indian law held that a drunken man could not be held responsible for his misdeeds because it was the "spirits," not the person, who had committed the crimes.

White traders trudged along the Indian trails in the mountains, carrying trinkets and glittering baubles with which they appealed to the vanity of these simple-hearted savages. The Indians were prevailed upon to part with treasures or pelts worth many times the value of the worthless goods the traders offered in exchange. Indian chieftains were influenced to sign deeds to vast tracts of land in exchange for such goods as shirts, mirrors, vermillion paint, ribbons, and similar items which soon were worn out. Resentment against such transactions frequently

9

led to bitter quarrels and to bloodshed between red man and white.

Cultural Contributions. Before the white man came, the North American Indian had reached a stage of development which was parallel to the New Stone Age of prehistoric times in Europe. Before civilizing forces had a full opportunity to improve this culture, the Pennsylvania Indian was forced to seek his quarters in regions far to the west. Consequently there are comparatively few survivals of Indian contributions to our present way of life. He taught us the use of some new foods, such as maize (corn), some herbal remedies for disease, and his knowledge of woodmanship. He blazed some of the forest trails which later became our roads, and when the colonies were young, he helped to build a prosperous trade in furs. We owe our greatest debt to the Indian for his artistic contributions, for his folk songs and dances, his skill in handicrafts such as weaving and pottery making, and for the beautiful decorative designs which we have borrowed freely.

Language. It was the language of the Indians, particularly that of the Delawares, that has left its clearest mark on our present life in Pennsylvania. Many of our figures of speech are translations of Delaware expressions, such as "to bury the hatchet," meaning to make peace; "you keep me in the dark," meaning you have not told me what I should know; and "the rivers run with blood," meaning that war rages in a country.

More lasting than borrowed phrases are the place names, especially the names of creeks that have retained their Indian names, such as Kittanning, "the main stream"; Pocono, "a stream between two mountains"; Wissahickon, "catfish creek."

EARLY DUTCH INTERESTS ON THE DELAWARE

Henry Hudson. The recorded history of Pennsylvania begins in the year 1609, when Henry Hudson, an explorer sent out by the Dutch East India Company, sailed his ship, the *Half Moon*, into the lower portion of the Delaware Bay. Five years later, in 1614, Captain Cornelis Jacobsen May explored the waters of the bay, drawing maps of creeks, inlets, and islands along his route. Cape May, New Jersey, was named for him. It is not known how far to the north his ship, the *Fortune*, sailed. The white man's interest in the Delaware was awakened.

Dutch West India Company. Two years later, 1616, another Dutch explorer, Cornelis Henrickson, reached the mouth of the Schuylkill River where it joins the Delaware below present-day Philadelphia. Soon thereafter was formed the Dutch West India Company which undertook to establish several trading posts along the Delaware, centering about the present sites of Lewes and New Castle, Delaware. Indian troubles combined with poor management of colonial affairs prevented the very early Dutch settlements from prospering. These first Dutch traders left a lasting mark in Pennsylvania by naming the Schuylkill. In the Dutch language the word means the "hidden river." It was so named because the first explorers had passed the mouth of the stream without seeing it.

NEW SWEDEN

The next European nation to attempt a settlement along the Delaware was Sweden. For a period of seventeen years (1638 to 1655) the Swedish West India Company sent a series of colonizing expeditions to the New World for the purpose of establishing trade and extending the domains of Swedish monarchs. Unlike the Dutch, the Swedes established permanent settlements and remained in Pennsylvania even after the Quakers came. Thus, they had a lasting influence on the history of the Pennsylvania.

Several of the men who had been connected with the early Dutch settlements along the Delaware left the employ of the Netherlands and turned to Sweden's king, the great Gustavus Adolphus, urging him to send an expedition to the New World. The most famous of these men was Peter Minuit, former governor of New Netherlands. These men pointed out the promise which the Delaware River and Bay offered for trade and colonization.

Peter Minuit. Peter Minuit led an expedition which landed on the shores of the Delaware Bay in 1638. In spite of protests from the English authorities in Virginia and the Dutch governors in New Netherlands, Minuit set himself the task of purchasing land from the Indians and founding a settlement where Wilmington, Delaware, now stands. He named the town Christina in honor of the Queen of Sweden. In the years that followed, the Swedish settlements were extended northward. In

11

1643 the first white settlement was established in Pennsylvania. It was known as Upland (up the river from Christina). Today Upland is a part of the city of Chester, Delaware County.

Tinicum Island. The period from 1643 to 1648 was the most prosperous one for New Sweden. An able governor, Johan Printz, established his capital on Tinicum Island between Chester and Philadelphia, and his wise administration caused the colony to grow and flourish for a time. Swedish settlements penetrated northward into the present limits of Philadelphia.

Type of Settlers. Not all of the settlers of New Sweden were Swedish nationals. Among those who came with the first group under the leadership of Peter Minuit were men from Holstein, Pomerania, and other Baltic states now a part of Germany. A large percentage of the later arrivals were Finns, for Finland was then a part of Sweden. In the earliest groups there were a number of undesirable men with criminal records; some were even kept in chains. Governor Printz put a stop to the immigration of such persons when he became governor, refusing to permit them to land from the ships.

In 1648 things began to go badly in New Sweden. For a time it appeared that the Swedish West India Company had lost interest in their far-off venture. In despair Governor Printz and some of his associates returned to Sweden in 1653, urging the Company to bestir itself in the interests of New Sweden.

A New Governor. In response to these pleas, the Swedish West India Company equipped a strong expedition in 1654 and sent it to strengthen the faltering settlement in the New World. This expedition was led by John Rysingh, newly appointed governor in the place of Printz.

Capture of Fort Casimir. Under the governorship of one-legged Peter Stuyvesant of New Amsterdam, Dutch troops had been sent to occupy Fort Casimir at New Castle, Delaware. When the Swedish expedition of 1654 sailed up the Delaware, Governor Rysingh took occasion to demand the surrender of the Dutch fort. Only twenty-two men were stationed at Fort Casimir and they were no match for the group of 350 persons that Rysingh brought with him. Accordingly, they surrendered without a fight. But the Swedish commander had not reckoned upon the stormy temper of Peter Stuyvesant, the governor of New Netherlands.

THE DUTCH SUMMONING FORT CASIMIR TO SURRENDER

THE DUTCH REGAIN THE DELAWARE

In August, 1655, two battleships and five smaller ships, carrying 300 men, set out from New Amsterdam, determined to recapture the Delaware region. They soon avenged the defeat at Fort Casimir and continued their way up the Delaware blasting the blockhouse at Naaman's on the border between present-day Pennsylvania and Delaware with cannon balls and compelling the complete surrender of New Sweden.

The Dutch control over the Delaware lasted for only nine years (1655 to 1664). During this time Holland might have had a chance to establish a permanent colony of Dutch settlers, but no serious effort was made in that direction.

THE ENGLISH CONQUEST

Basing his claims to the lands lying between New England and Virginia upon the early explorations of John and Sebastian

13

Cabot, Charles II granted these lands to his brother, James, Duke of York (later King James II). In 1664 an expedition was equipped and sent to the mouth of the Hudson where Peter Stuyvesant ruled over all of New Netherlands.

Even though Stuyvesant stormed and protested against the English demands for surrender, his soldiers would not attempt to fight the more powerful English forces, and all of the vast domains of present-day New York State, New Jersey, Delaware, and Pennsylvania became the property of the British Crown. English ownership of the territory was confirmed by the treaty which ended the second war with Holland in 1667.

In 1672, a third war flared between England and Holland. During this struggle, which lasted two years, the Dutch succeeded in recapturing the Delaware forts once more (1673), but when the treaty of peace was made in 1674, English possession was finally established and Dutch interests in North America were ended for all time.

QUESTIONS FOR STUDY AND REVIEW

1. Why is a knowledge of the geography of Pennsylvania necessary to the understanding of Pennsylvania history?

2. Why did the Indian tribes move from place to place instead of building permanent settlements?

3. How did the Indian's idea of land ownership differ from that of the white man?

4. Why were the early Dutch and Swedish settlers in Pennsylvania unable to found strong colonies?

5. How did England gain possession of the land which today forms Pennsylvania?

Chapter II

WILLIAM PENN AND THE QUAKERS

In 1681 the King of England granted a large portion of his recently acquired domains to William Penn, under whose wise leadership and inspiration colonization was undertaken earnestly and even zealously. Land was sold, trade established, towns and cities founded, a government formed, and the foundations laid for a great commonwealth. Penn's leadership was so direct and influential that the span of years between his arrival in America (in 1682) until his death thirty-six years later (in 1718) forms a distinct chapter for study.

THE SOCIETY OF FRIENDS (QUAKERS)

Intolerance. The kings of Europe three centuries ago did not allow their peoples to worship God as they pleased. There was no religious freedom as we know it today. The kings of Spain and France insisted that their people be Roman Catholics, and the princes of the various Germanic states compelled their subjects to adopt whatever form of worship they ordered, whether Roman Catholic or Protestant in form. In England, too, a state church was established, and measures to compel all Englishmen to conform to its doctrines were enforced. The Church of England, sometimes called the Anglican Church, was Protestant. English Roman Catholics and Protestants who refused to accept the Anglican faith were not imprisoned or persecuted as were those in the European states who refused to accept the established church, but often the non-Conformists, as they were called, were denied civil rights, were not allowed to take part in the government, and could not hold their meetings of worship in public.

We all know how the Puritans, followers of the teachings of the reformer, John Calvin, were "harried out of the land," as King James I expressed it. We know how the Pilgrims sought refuge first in Holland, then, in 1620 and thereafter, in New England. English Roman Catholics founded Maryland in 1634

15

as a home for those of their faith who could not accept the established Church of England. Among other groups restricted by English church laws was the Society of Friends, known popularly as Quakers and by other names.

Quaker Doctrines. Certain beliefs of the Quakers were at variance with English customs and laws. Their theological doctrines, in and of themselves, would not have brought about the hostility of the British government, for they taught peace, humility, and other fine virtues, and depended largely upon conscience, which they called the "Inner Light," to show them right from wrong. The outward evidences of their faith, however, were such as to draw the attention of outsiders, and frequently the professors of other faiths scoffed and scorned. Some of these practices were: unwillingness to take oaths in courts, to bear arms or aid directly in the prosecution of wars, or to remove their hats in the presence of persons of high authority. The story is related that the nickname Quaker was first applied to them on an occasion when the King summoned some of their leaders to explain why they did not doff their hats in His Majesty's presence. The spokesmen for the Society of Friends stood shaking nervously before the King, who laughed scornfully and said, "See them quaking there."

EARLY YEARS OF WILLIAM PENN

William Penn was born during the period of the Thirty Years' War (in 1644), and during most of his youth his country was engaged in a succession of wars. It is striking to note that the best portrait we have of him shows a young man in a suit of armor. We know that young Penn at the age of 22 engaged in a military expedition in Ireland one year before he was converted to the Quaker faith. William Penn was born of fighting stock. His father, Sir William Penn, Senior, was an admiral in the British Navy who distinguished himself by assisting in the capture of Jamaica from Spain in 1655. The family was wealthy, and young William was given the exceptional educational opportunities which were open to boys of his social standing.

Penn's Education. Although young Penn excelled in his studies, he did not like the religious restrictions imposed upon the students at Oxford. Rebelling against church and university authorities brought about his expulsion. The boy, aged sixteen, had been listening to Quaker teachings, and his resistance to authority can be attributed to the influence of such teaching. His expulsion led to a prolonged quarrel with his father and, after a time, he was sent to France. His father hoped that the gay life in Paris would divert young Penn from serious matters for a while. Instead, the son attended lectures teaching that war and Christianity were opposed to each other. Several years spent in France and Italy gave young Penn an opportunity to learn the French language and acquire an appreciation for the culture of continental Europe. In 1666 the young man was sent to Ireland to assist in managing some of his father's estates. It was during this period that he served for a short time as a soldier.

Conversion to Quakerism. In 1667 William Penn was definitely converted to the Quaker faith. He gave himself fully to the cause and was arrested and imprisoned several times for preaching Quaker doctrines, but the influence and wealth of his father secured his release from jail each time. The great inheritance which he received upon his father's death in 1670 gave William Penn an opportunity to put his ideals into practice in the wilderness of America.

THE KING OWES A DEBT

The King Was Poor. Charles II had spent his youth as an exile from England. The Revolutionists who had executed his father, Charles I, were in power from 1649 until 1660, when a weary English populace, tired of strict dictatorship under the Cromwells, invited Charles to return to England and take the throne. The restored King found himself badly in need of money, partly for his own extravagant needs and partly to finance the naval wars he carried on against Holland. During the first of these wars he had borrowed sixteen thousand pounds, or nearly $80,000, from Admiral Penn, William Penn's father, and never found enough money in the treasury to pay the debt in cash. More than ten years after the death of Admiral William Penn, King Charles II found a way to discharge his obligation to the heir, William Penn, Junior, through lands in America acquired by the Duke of York's conquest of New Netherlands. Penn had already shown an interest in founding Quaker settlements in the New World.

17

West New Jersey. After William Penn became a man of property in 1670 he found many influential friends at the royal court, including King Charles II and the King's brother James, the Duke of York. The Duke had given the territory which today forms New Jersey to two English gentlemen, Lord Berkeley and Sir George Carteret. These men sold the western half of their lands to two Quakers, John Fenwick and Edward Byllinge. A disagreement arose between Byllinge and Fenwick, however, as to the division of their lands, and in 1675 they referred their dispute to William Penn for arbitration. Penn decided in favor of Byllinge, granting him nine-tenths of all of west New Jersey, Fenwick receiving the remaining tenth.

Soon Byllinge fell into debt in England and was forced to transfer all of his possessions in west New Jersey to his creditors. The trustees for the creditors were Penn and two other Quakers named Gawen Laurie and Nicholas Lucas. For Penn and his associates, the New Jersey project became a land-selling venture which proved profitable when English Quakers began to emigrate from England to populate western New Jersey. Penn observed that North America was providing a place of refuge for the people of his faith.

Pennsylvania. Encouraged by the venture in western New Jersey, Penn became interested in the lands west of the Delaware River, which he believed would offer still more opportunities as a haven for his fellow Quakers. These lands had not been granted to anyone. King Charles II held the right to sell the area which is now Pennsylvania, and the Duke of York had the right to sell present-day Delaware. William Penn petitioned the King to have the King's debt to him of sixteen thousand pounds discharged by a grant from the royal lands in America. Penn also negotiated the outright purchase of Delaware from the Duke of York.

Charles II acceded to Penn's petition and granted him a charter on March 4, 1681. The document stated, ". . . and doe call itt Pennsilvania, and so from henceforth wee will have itt called . . ." William Penn would have preferred to name his colony "New Wales" or "Sylvania." He argued that it was not in accord with Quaker principles to show pride by using one's family name, but Charles II insisted and it was so named.

WILLIAM PENN RECEIVING THE CHARTER OF PENNSYLVANIA FROM CHARLES II

THE CHARTER OF PENNSYLVANIA

Boundaries. There were no maps to guide those who drew up the charter, and therefore the boundaries were vague and indefinite. The northern boundary was fixed at 43 degrees north latitude; that was clear enough. The eastern boundary was to be the Delaware River, provided the headwaters of the river extended northward as far as 43 degrees, north latitude; if not, then a straight line was to be drawn from the headwaters of the river due north to the line of 43 degrees north latitude. On the south, the boundary was complicated by the problem of fixing a definite line between Delaware, Maryland, and Pennsylvania. It was stated that an arc of a circle should be drawn using New Castle, Delaware, as the center, with a twelve-mile radius. All lands contained within the arc were given to Delaware, and all lands beyond it became Pennsylvania or Maryland. Note the arc in the southeastern corner of the state on present-day maps.

From the Province of Delaware westward, the southern boundary was set at the beginning of the fortieth latitude, due west to the western limits of the Province. This was to be the boundary between Pennsylvania and Maryland and, as we shall

19

see, the exact location of that line was the cause of many arguments later. The western limits of Penn's grant were stated in terms of longitude, 5 degrees west of the easternmost limits of the Province. Since no white man had penetrated the woods for such a distance westward, no one knew at the time exactly where that boundary was.

Proprietorship. There were three types of English colonies in America. Massachusetts and Connecticut operated under charters which granted certain rights and privileges to the local governments. New York and Virginia were royal colonies ruled by representatives of the King. The third type was the proprietary colony, in which the power to govern was given to the person who owned the grant. Lord Baltimore was the proprietor of Maryland; William Penn became the proprietor of Pennsylvania. Technically, of course, the colony still formed a part of the British Empire, and the charter which the King gave to William Penn required that a rental of two beaver skins should be paid each year in recognition of the higher authority of the King. Also, it was required that one-fifth of all the gold and silver found in the Province should be turned over to the royal treasury.

Conditions Imposed. All other profits and all powers of government were given to the proprietor except in such matters as navigation laws which were fixed by the British Parliament, and any other laws which affected all colonies equally.

THE HOLY EXPERIMENT

Objectives. Could men live together peacefully if they differed in their beliefs about God and the way to worship Him?

Could justice be administered by courts representing the people, and could prisons restore men to society as good citizens if the prisoners were taught an honest trade?

Could people of diverse nationalities, coming from nations that were hostile to each other, settle upon adjoining farms in the New World and get along as good neighbors? Could the savage Indian be appeased by fair treatment? Could the masses be trusted with liberty, allowed freedom of conscience and freedom of speech? Could war be abolished and men be encouraged to love one another according to divine law? Could noble ideals be translated into action?

Such were the objectives which the founder set for Pennsylvania. He, himself, was not sure that all or any of them could be achieved, but the attempt would be made. In his own words, Penn spoke of his venture as a "Holy Experiment." As the succeeding years unfold we shall see how this experiment worked in practice.

The Measure of True Greatness. William Penn was a rare combination of an idealist and a realist. Unlike many idealists before and since his day, Penn was a practical man— willing to face and to attempt to solve problems, able to plan and carry his plans into action, inspired but patient, devout and pious yet tolerant. Strong himself, he was always sympathetic and ever aware of human frailties. In short, he met the requirements of true greatness.

FORMING A GOVERNMENT

While the Proprietor was still in England he had laid his plans for governing and populating his faraway "Woods." Soon after he received the charter from the King, Penn appointed his cousin, William Markham, as his deputy and sent him to America with instructions for governing the new possession. Markham arrived in Pennsylvania in June, 1681, sixteen months earlier than the Proprietor. During the time before Penn's arrival, the deputy attempted, in vain, to settle a boundary dispute with Lord Baltimore of Maryland, purchased some lands in what is now Bucks County from the Indians, and set up a temporary provincial government with headquarters at Upland.

Arrival of Penn. With high purposes and high hopes, William Penn set out from England in September, 1682, to visit his possessions in America. The good ship *Welcome* carried him and one hundred persons who intended to settle in America. The first stop of the *Welcome* was at New Castle, Delaware, where Penn greeted the people of another of his newly acquired possessions.

Penn Lands at Chester. On October 29, 1682, Penn landed at Upland in present-day Pennsylvania for the first time. The name of Upland was promptly changed to Chester, in honor of Chester, England. Lingering at Chester for only a short time, and after conferring with some of the local officers, including persons of Swedish descent, he resumed his journey northward

21

to the site of his capital city, Philadelphia, the City of Brotherly Love.

First Frame of Government. In April, 1682, six months before Penn arrived in the colony, the first written constitution for the government of Pennsylvania was introduced. The document was called the Frame of Government, although now it is always referred to as the First Frame of Government, to distinguish it from the second and third frames adopted later. The First Frame provided for a Governor, who was to be William Penn or someone appointed by him, a Provincial Council, or upper house, and a Great Assembly. Both bodies were to be elected by the people. The powers of the lawmaking body were limited; the Assembly at that time was little more than a debating society under the terms of the First Frame. While the First Frame served as the basis of government for the Province of Pennsylvania for a short time, it was never ratified by the people and soon was replaced by the Second Frame of Government, which was more democratic in its provisions.

The Forty Laws. The First Frame of Government was concerned only with the functions of the executive and legislative branches of the government. The judicial branch of the

WILLIAM PENN HOLDING A CONFERENCE WITH THE COLONISTS

government was provided for in a set of "Forty Laws Agreed upon in England." The most important provisions of the Forty Laws were those which sought to protect all persons from unfair trials; to guarantee the rights of property; to punish crimes; to provide for the education of children; to provide laws regulating marriage, the establishment of Sunday as a day of worship; and the protection of the peace and the safety of the public.

The Great Law. The First Frame and the Forty Laws served as a temporary government for Penn's possessions. Soon after Penn arrived in Pennsylvania, he summoned an assembly to meet at Chester in December, 1682, to help in establishing a permanent government for the two provinces of Pennsylvania and Delaware. The delegates of the three Delaware counties, Kent, Sussex, and New Castle, met with the representatives of the three newly formed counties of Pennsylvania—Philadelphia, Chester, and Bucks. After a brief session of four days, the "Great Law" was formulated. It included most of the provisions of the Forty Laws. Significantly, the first provision of the Great Law established religious liberty, the only exception being that officeholders must be Christians and believers in God the Father and Christ the Son. This provision deprived Unitarians, Jews, and atheists of some privileges, but it did not interfere with their freedom of worship.

The Second Frame of Government. Soon afterward, the Assembly approved of the Second Frame of Government which gave more real power to the legislative branch. The Second Frame of 1683 remained in force for thirteen years.

Markham's Frame of 1696. In 1696, while Penn was in England, his Deputy Governor, William Markham, was forced to agree to the demands of the Assembly for a new Frame of Government. The Third Frame, Markham's, was still more democratic than its predecessors. It permitted persons whose religious beliefs prevented them from taking oaths to make statements of affirmation instead of oaths, and judges were charged that "thou shalt do equal right to rich and poor, to the best of thy knowledge." William Penn permitted Markham's Frame to remain in force until 1701, when, during his second stay in Pennsylvania, he granted the Charter of Privileges which replaced all former instruments of government and remained in force until the Revolutionary War.

23

The Charter of Privileges. Because Penn's Charter of Privileges became the fundamental law of the Province for many years, we should examine some of its provisions. The first provision guaranteed religious liberty and stipulated that this section could never be changed. All other provisions in this and previous Frames could be amended with the consent of the Governor and six-sevenths of the votes of the General Assembly. In this way Penn and his colleagues saw to it that no future body of lawmakers could deny this priceless freedom to the people of Pennsylvania.

Toward Democracy. Another important change under the Charter of Privileges was placing all law-making power in the Assembly, which was elected by the people. The Provincial Council continued to exist as an advisory body to the Governor, but members had no power to pass or reject laws. The Governor retained his power to veto laws passed by the Assembly, but this power was balanced by a provision that the Governor's salary was to be paid by the Assembly. Therefore, if a Governor became too stubborn, the Assembly could bring him to terms by withholding all or a part of his salary.

LAND TRANSACTIONS

Purchases from Indians. We have seen that Penn secured his domains in the New World by purchasing Delaware and accepting Pennsylvania instead of money owed to him by the King. In ordinary business transactions these arrangements would appear to be final, establishing Penn's proprietorship without doubt, and giving him the right to sell or lease his property as he willed. There was another factor to be considered, however. The Indians still regarded nearly all of these lands as their own. In order to secure clear land titles for his settlers and at the same time retain the good will of the red men, Penn adopted the policy of buying lands which were already his under the terms of his charter from Charles II. Numerous Indian treaties were arranged by Penn and his agents for the purpose of securing deeds from the Indian chiefs who acted as agents for their tribes. True, the money value of the goods exchanged for these lands was usually far less than a sum which a European would regard as a fair purchase price, but the Indians were satisfied, and that was the real purpose of the transactions.

Indian Deeds. The purchase of land from the Indians usually called for a great deal of ceremony: a public distribution of the treaty purchase goods, the application of the Great Seal of the Province to a formal document drawn up to record the purchase by pressing it into molten wax, and attaching the signatures of white men and Indians making the treaty. The red men could not write, so they made their marks. Some made crude drawings of animals or birds, others used symbols, and still others merely made scratches with a quill. It was always wise to secure the signatures of several young braves to a deed, lest at some future time the tribe would refuse to be bound by the signs made by old chiefs who had died.

The Treaty Elm. Before Penn's arrival, his deputy, William Markham, had made a number of purchases of lands in and near Philadelphia. Penn himself made four such purchases during his first visit to his colony. The story of the Elm Tree Treaty in Kensington, Philadelphia, has become a part of Pennsylvania's tradition, even though there are no definite records to prove that it was ever held. Penn may have met with Chief Tammany and his tribe of Delawares to form a treaty of friendship.

—Hildreth Collection and Index of Historic Prints

VOTING IN COLONIAL TIMES
Only propertied men were permitted to vote.

25

**WILLIAM PENN INSPECTING DEEDS DURING SURVEYING OPERA-
TIONS LEADING TO THE ESTABLISHMENT OF PHILADELPHIA**

Sale of Lands. In selling his lands to settlers, Penn offered huge tracts at very low prices. To some persons—adventurers who wished to invest in lands and transport settlers to occupy them—Penn offered as much as 5000 acres for one hundred pounds (about $500), plus an annual ground rent of a shilling (about 25¢) for every hundred acres. To renters he offered blocks of land of 200 acres for the nominal rent of a penny an acre a year. To servants he promised fifty acres when their services had repaid their masters for transporting them to America. These terms appear to be very generous, as the possessor of 45,000 square miles could afford to be, and yet the terms were very shrewd because, out of each parcel of land sold to settlers, Penn held onto some lands in those sections for himself. As the colony grew, the Penn tracts rose rapidly in value because as towns and cities developed all lands became more desirable. This was especially true of certain building lots in Philadelphia.

PENN'S RETURN TO ENGLAND

Difficulties. In 1684 William Penn returned to England to set in order some of his affairs there. Lord Baltimore had gone to London to put the question of the Maryland-Pennsylvania boundary dispute before the King, and other matters needed attention. When Penn departed, he probably had no idea that fifteen years would pass before he would visit his colony again. During his absence the affairs of the Province were entrusted to the Council whose President was then Thomas Lloyd.

Loss of Proprietorship. Penn's friend, James II (the former Duke of York), was now King in place of Charles II. In 1688 James II was overthrown in the "Glorious Revolution." After that, Penn no longer had powerful friends at court. His friendship for the deposed King, led to his persecution by the new rulers, King William and Queen Mary. Several times Penn was arrested on charges of plotting to restore James to the throne or of plotting against the new rulers. Each time he was cleared of the charges against him, but in spite of this, his enemies were able to persuade William and Mary to revoke Penn's charter to Pennsylvania. The royal Governor of New York was ordered to take charge of the Province of Pennsylvania. These were dreary days for the Holy Experiment.

Restoration. Fortunately for Penn, Benjamin Fletcher, the Governor of New York, was his friend, and Fletcher appointed Markham, Penn's cousin, as Deputy Governor of Pennsylvania, realizing that Markham would protect Penn's interests. In 1694 Penn's possessions in America were returned to him

THE TRIAL OF WILLIAM PENN

because influential friends had been able to persuade the King and Queen that he was loyal.

Additional Troubles. Even though his possessions had been restored to him, Penn's troubles were far from over. The British authorities in London were not pleased with his conduct of the colony in America. During King William's War, 1689 to 1697, the Quaker Assemblies in Pennsylvania had failed to raise money or to equip military expeditions for England's aid. Quaker principles were opposed to aiding a war effort. Reports were reaching London that crime was unchecked by the provincial authorities in Pennsylvania, and there were hints that officials there were corrupt. William Penn was summoned before the Board of Trade in London to explain or answer these charges. As a result of these investigations, the Board ordered Penn's Deputy Governor, William Markham, to be dismissed. Hoping to straighten out matters in his domains, Penn set out from England late in 1699 and arrived in Pennsylvania for his second visit in December of that year.

Delaware Becomes a Separate Colony. Establishing his residence at Pennsbury Manor in Bucks County, the Proprietor set himself to the task of governing his colony. It was during this period that Penn granted the Charter of Privileges discussed earlier in this chapter.

One other noteworthy achievement of Penn during his short stay was to make possible the separation of Delaware and Pennsylvania as distinct colonies, each with their own separate legislatures, but both having the same governor. This separation was not brought about until 1703, although Penn had consented to it in 1701 shortly before he returned to England for what proved to be the last time.

PENN'S LATER YEARS

Tragic Years. Having followed the movements of the founder of Pennsylvania rather closely, we cannot terminate our story with his departure for England in 1701. He continued to live for seventeen years more, passing from this life at his home, the Jordans, in England, in July, 1718. The closing years of his life were tragic. In 1711 he testified that the Pennsylvania venture had cost him 50,000 pounds, or a quarter of a million dollars more than he had received from it. For nine months the impoverished old man languished in a debtor's prison in London. In 1712 Penn tried to sell his holdings in America to the English Crown, asking only 12,000 pounds, less than the amount owed to him for which he had acquired the Province. Before negotiations for the transfer of these lands back to the Crown could be completed, Penn was the victim of a stroke of paralysis which affected him mentally, and the sale was never completed. During the six years that he lingered as a helpless invalid, his affairs were administered by his wife, the former Hannah Callowhill. For William Penn, in his own day, the Holy Experiment had brought him little personal reward.

QUESTIONS FOR STUDY AND REVIEW

1. Why were the Quakers persecuted in England?

2. What influences in William Penn's life led him to become a Quaker?

3. What is an experiment? In what sense was William Penn's colony in America an experiment? Can you name any other experiments which have been made in government? Are any being made today?

4. Why were boundary lines fixed in terms of degrees of latitude and longitude in the early provincial charters?

5. Why was it necessary to change the Frame of Government of colonial Pennsylvania so frequently during the days of William Penn?

6. Why did Penn purchase lands from the Indians which had already been granted to him by the King?

Chapter III

THE SETTLERS COME

In less than one hundred years after Penn's landing, Philadelphia was the largest city in all of the English colonies, and Pennsylvania, although ranking only sixth in area, was third in population, exceeded only by Virginia and Massachusetts. Whence came these immigrants? And why? This chapter will try to answer these questions.

INVITATION BY WILLIAM PENN

Mennonites. Several years before he became Proprietor of Pennsylvania, William Penn paid two visits to the Rhineland areas of Europe. His mother was of Dutch extraction and there were other ties, too, which drew his attention to the people of the Netherlands and to the rich agricultural areas of the south German states and Switzerland. In Holland and southward along the Rhine River the teachings of Menno Simons had won many followers. These people, called Mennonites, practiced a religion which in many respects resembled that of the Quakers. They were opposed to war; they would not take an oath in court; they would not wear articles of personal adornment. They were being persecuted in their countries, more severely than were the Quakers in England.

Penn's Advertisements. In the months between receiving the grant from the King (1681) and Penn's departure for his possessions (1682), he published and distributed glowing advertisements in the form of pamphlets and posters in the English, Dutch, and German languages, describing the great promise that his new venture held. He described the abundance of fish, game, and wild fruits; he praised the fertility of the soil, declaring that crops yielded far more bountifully in Pennsylvania than elsewhere. He promised religious freedom to the persecuted and a new start in life for the despairing.

Settlement of Germantown. The first continental group to respond to Penn's invitation was a congregation of

MENNONITES PLANNING TO COME TO AMERICA

Dutch and German Mennonites led by Francis Daniel Pastorius, a brilliant scholar. After purchasing 15,000 acres of land, this group sailed from Europe in July, 1683, in the ship *Concord*, arriving at Philadelphia in October of the same year. At first there were no houses in which to live; temporarily, they sought shelter in caves which they dug into the banks of the Delaware River. Later, lands were allotted to them and they built the community which was and is known as Germantown. Not all of these settlers were Germans, however. There were a number of Dutch as well. The group had come from along the Rhine River, which flows through both Germany and Holland.

Within a few years of their settlement in Germantown, skilled weavers established a textile industry there. William Rittenhouse built the first paper mill in the colony, and the gardens of Germantown were selling their surplus foods in Philadelphia. The variety of garden products available in the Philadelphia area was one of the factors in the city's rapid growth. Vegetable gardening was not practised to any great extent in England before the eighteenth century, hence English settlers knew little of this form of culture.

31

First Protest against Slavery. The Germantown settlers are worthy of mention in many ways, but there is one notable deed for which they must be given credit at once. In 1688, five years after they had landed in America, having shared in the blessings of the Holy Experiment, they took a bold action. In a document addressed to the Quakers, the men of Germantown, led by Pastorius, issued the first protest against Negro slavery ever made in the New World.

Other Settlers. Meanwhile, English Quakers continued to pour into the Province, most of them establishing themselves in trade in the growing towns or settling upon farms in the three original counties of Bucks, Chester, and Philadelphia. Welshmen brought their families, first settling on the west side of the Schuylkill in Montgomery County, and later in Berks and the northern counties. The great tide of Irish, Scotch-Irish, and Palatinate (German) immigration did not develop during William Penn's lifetime.

THE PALATINE GERMANS

Wanderers in the Wilderness. Sir William Keith was Deputy Governor at the time of the death of the Proprietor and continued in that office until 1726. In 1722 Keith attended a conference of colonial governors at Albany, New York. There he learned of the sad plight of thousands of German settlers from the Palatinate who were being forced off of their farms in the rich Schoharie Valley, near Schenectady, New York, because rich Dutch farmers wished these lands for themselves. These poor settlers had already suffered much, and they faced a dismal future with nowhere to find homes. Fully aware that the Mennonite farmers were proving to be of help to the Province, Keith invited the distressed Palatines to come to Pennsylvania, where good lands were to be had along the Tulpehocken and Swatara creeks.

Down the Susquehanna. In 1723 a vanguard of thirty-three families followed some Indian guides to the headwaters of the Susquehanna River. Near present-day Binghamton they constructed rafts, placed their belongings on them, and floated down the Susquehanna to what is now Middletown at the mouth of the Swatara Creek. They moved up the Swatara, crossed the Blue Mountains, and thus entered the valley of the

Tulpehocken. Soon other groups migrated from New York by the same route and settled large portions of Berks, Lebanon, Schuylkill, and Dauphin counties.

Mass Immigration. Letters went back to relatives and friends living along the Rhine River. Here was religious freedom! Here was the same limestone soil they had worked for centuries! Here was plenteous game! Here were gurgling springs in peaceful meadows, unlike the fields of their homelands torn by clashing armies. Then the rush began. Thousands of Germans crowded the port of Rotterdam, Pennsylvania bound. English authorities, fearing that Pennsylvania might become a German colony, tried to send them to other colonies—New York, New Jersey, Maryland. But no sooner had they landed than these hopeful immigrants asked how to get to Pennsylvania. The colony was like a magnet, drawing homeless, persecuted peoples to a new life.

Oaths of Allegiance. No advertising was needed now. Instead, the provincial authorities became alarmed lest the coming of so many foreigners might mean the Germanization of Pennsylvania. Accordingly, in 1727 a law was passed requiring those immigrants who were not English to swear allegiance to the British Crown. Consequently, we now have records of all German immigrants who entered through the port of Philadelphia between 1727 and 1776. This number alone was more than 68,000. But this figure does not include those who entered the Province from neighboring colonies, those who came before 1727, or the natural increase of nearly a hundred years.

Expanding Settlements. Through the gates of Philadelphia they poured, spreading fanwise to the north to settle the new counties of Northampton, Berks, and Lancaster. In the Lebanon Valley the newcomers met the settlements of the Palatines who had migrated from New York; in Lancaster County they met with the older Mennonite groups. The tide spilled over the Susquehanna into the counties of York and northern Cumberland.

OTHER CONTINENTAL GROUPS

French Huguenots. Not only the Rhine areas of Holland and Germany provided settlers for Penn's Woods. French Protestants, known as Huguenots, many of them from Alsace

NAMING OF BETHLEHEM, CHRISTMAS EVE, 1741

Celebrating the first Christmas Eve vigil, in 1741, the original group of Moravians hailed their little town by the name of Bethlehem, in honor of the other Christmas city.

and Lorraine in France, who had been denied religious liberty, set out for the New World, finding new homes in Philadelphia and in the Oley Valley of Berks County.

Schwenkfelders. In the fertile rim of the old Austrian empire lies the state of Silesia, which Empress Maria Theresa called the brightest jewel in her crown. There the devout followers of Caspar Schwenkfeld suffered religious persecution. They decided to move to Pennsylvania, and in 1735 began their mass immigration, moving northward from Philadelphia to settle the northeastern townships of Montgomery County. They brought with them their devotion to education, their knowledge of the fine arts, and their capacities for leadership. Like the Quakers and Mennonites, they were opposed to war on general principles, but unlike these groups they were willing always to fight in self-defense.

Moravians. In far-off Moravia the Christian Brothers, followers of the teachings of John Huss, who lived in Bohemia in the late fourteenth century, were being denied religious rights. An intense desire to spread the teaching of Christianity to the heathen led many of them to come to Pennsylvania. They migrated by congregations and settled in separate communities in Pennsylvania, at Bethlehem and Nazareth in Northampton County, Gnadenhutten in Carbon County, Lititz in Lancaster

34

County, and Heidelberg in Berks County. Of all European groups that came to the English colonies they were the most successful missionaries to the Indian tribes. Their love of fine music soon made Bethlehem the musical capital of America, and their insistence upon education for all built the first seminary for girls in the New World, the Moravian Female Seminary, in 1742.

Swiss Refugees. From Switzerland came other survivors of religious persecution. The tortures inflicted upon the followers of Jacob Ammon, known to us as the Amish, and upon members of other self-effacing, peaceful groups, such as Dunkards and Mennonites, form a sorry picture in the history of the miseries of mankind. A record of these deeds is preserved in a huge book entitled *The Martyr's Mirror*, first published in Holland and then republished several times in America. This book recounts for posterity the sufferings of those who had the courage of their convictions in the Old World. Generation after generation of Mennonites, Dunkards, Amish—called the "Plain Sects" of Pennsylvania—have learned from this book how sweet was the liberty their ancestors found here and how bitter indeed was life under tyrants. The next time you see a bearded Amish man wearing his broadbrimmed, black hat, or a woman dressed in somber gray, her head covered by a little white prayer cap, remember that their odd attire is a convincing symbol of the great boon their people found here—the priceless liberty to worship God as they chose. Their headpieces are the crowns that free men wear.

Jews. Mixed among the settlers of Philadelphia and Lancaster in colonial times were numerous Jews. Many came from the German states. The only distinctly Hebrew settlement, however, was made at Schaefferstown in Lebanon County by a group of Portuguese Jews who came to trade with the Indians as early as 1723. Very little is known about that early settlement, and historians are not agreed upon many matters concerning it. The only evidence remaining today that it ever existed is the Hebrew cemetery, which still can be seen in Schaefferstown, and the family traditions of people still living in the neighborhood.

The Pennsylvania "Dutch." All of these immigrants had one thing in common. They all came from continental

Europe and nearly all of them spoke a Germanic language. English settlers not concerned about keen distinctions applied a general term to characterize all of them, calling them Pennsylvania Dutch. More careful students, however, have preferred to use the term Pennsylvania Germans, designating a language classification and not a political one. Neither term is quite correct historically. Today both terms are used—Pennsylvania Dutch in popular usage and Pennsylvania German in scholarly language.

THE SCOTCH-IRISH

Migration to Ireland. The term Scotch-Irish is used to describe those people who were Scotch in origin but who lived in Ireland before coming to America. In the sixteenth century, Queen Elizabeth of England induced thousands of Scottish Protestants to move to Ireland, hoping that their influence would help to convert the Irish to the Protestant faith. The Roman Catholic Irish had long been bitterly opposed to the Protestant rulers of the British Isles. The Scotch who moved to Ireland were just as firmly Protestant as the Irish were devoted to their Roman Catholic faith. The two groups would not mix. The Scotch settled in northern Ireland, where some have remained down to the present day. Always their presence in Ireland has been resented by the Irish.

When they were persuaded to move to Ireland, the Scotsmen were promised by Queen Elizabeth that they would be allowed to worship according to their Presbyterian faith without interference, and that any goods which they might sell to England and Scotland would not be taxed. The successors of Queen Elizabeth failed to keep her promises. Attempts were made to force the Scotch-Irish to accept the Church of England. Duties were placed on the wool which they shipped to English ports, and other economic measures prevented their developing their industries and agriculture as they had hoped.

Scotch-Irish Immigration. The quarrel between the Scotch-Irish and the rulers of Britain led to armed rebellion on the part of those who remained in Ireland. Many of the group, however, decided to move to America, where they would be far-removed from the authority of the British Crown. Early in the eighteenth century they began to come to the New World.

Their stern Presbyterian faith had taught them rigid self-discipline, rugged individualism, and belief in democratic principles. Asking only to be left alone with God and their consciences, these sturdy pioneers erected their cabins along the frontier from Massachusetts to Georgia, making their homes on the outposts of civilization and forming a bulwark between the Indians and the farms and cities on the seaboard. Expert woodsmen, they cleared forests, killed off the wild beasts, and without too many twinges of conscience, drove the Indians deeper and deeper into the interior. The reward they worked for was liberty and a democratic order. Certainly these virile men were a tremendous asset to any colony.

Scotch-Irish in Pennsylvania. It is estimated that there were 80,000 Scotch-Irish living in Pennsylvania at the time of the Revolutionary War. They were second in numbers only to the settlers of German origin. We cannot determine the exact numbers because as British subjects they were not required to take the oath of allegiance as were the immigrants from continental Europe. We do know, however, where they built their settlements in the early years. A few lingered in Philadelphia, but the great majority of them moved to the farthest

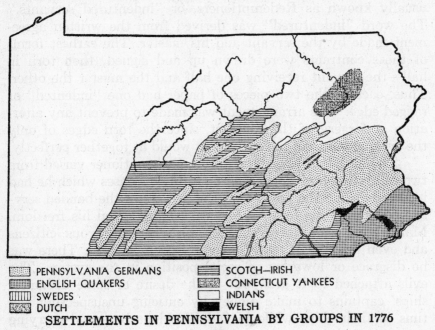

PENNSYLVANIA GERMANS	SCOTCH-IRISH
ENGLISH QUAKERS	CONNECTICUT YANKEES
SWEDES	INDIANS
DUTCH	WELSH

SETTLEMENTS IN PENNSYLVANIA BY GROUPS IN 1776

frontiers. So impatient were they that sometimes these Scotch-Irish pioneers built their cabins on lands that had not yet been purchased from the Indians. Often this led them into conflict with the red men.

Among the earliest settlements of Scotch-Irish were Donegal in Lancaster County and Paxton in Dauphin County. The first county to be predominantly Scotch-Irish was Cumberland with Carlisle as the principal town. Later these dauntless pioneers continued to move on westward, extending the line of settlement west of the Alleghenies.

INDENTURED SERVANTS

Many poor people in Europe did not possess the money for their transportation to America. For these, a special arrangement was made whereby they could be brought here free of charge, provided they agreed to be bonded to some master for a certain number of years until they had worked out the money for their passage. The captains of the ships which brought these people reimbursed themselves by selling their human cargo to wealthy settlers for cash, the settler contracting for the service period of the immigrant. The servants were usually known as Redemptioners, or "indentured servants." The word "indentured" was derived from the written agreement made by the servant and his master. The earliest forms of these contracts were drawn up and signed, then torn in half—the servant receiving one half and the master the other. Thus, each of the two pieces of paper had one "indented" or ragged edge. This arrangement was made to prevent any alteration or forgery of the contract, since the torn edges of only the original pieces of the agreement would fit together perfectly.

The length of time served by a Redemptioner varied from two to seven years, depending upon the expenses which he had incurred during the voyage to America. After the bonded servant completed his term of service, he was given his freedom. Many bond servants eventually became prosperous citizens and even masters of newly-arrived Redemptioners. There was no disgrace or lowering of social position in the system. The evils attached to it grew out of the desire of some dishonest ships' captains to make money by enticing unsuspecting victims to their ships while in Old World harbors and carrying them to the New World by force. Often these unfortunate victims were forced to live in horribly cramped and unsanitary conditions while aboard the ship during the voyage. Young children rarely survived the long trip.

A large number of indentured servants were brought to the port of Philadelphia, where wealthy farmers, iron manufacturers, and city merchants bought their services. Men and women from all the states of northwest Europe came as Redemptioners in the hope of beginning a new life in America.

NEGROES

The Negro population of colonial Pennsylvania was about 6000 at the time of the Revolutionary War. Some of these Negroes were slaves, persons who spent their entire lives working for masters without pay, but there were also many free Negroes in the Province. It was the custom of Quaker gentlemen to make provisions in their wills for the freedom of their slaves, and the idea of enslaving other human beings was hateful to the liberty-loving Germans and Scotch-Irish who lived in the interior of the Province. Furthermore, the system of slavery was not profitable anywhere but in the southern colonies where plantations could make use of the labor of unskilled men, women, and children. The growing industries of the northern colonies called for skilled or semi-skilled labor which could be secured only by hiring free men. The farms in Pennsylvania were small enough to be operated by the farmer and his immediate family with perhaps the occasional help of hired hands. The chief use of slave labor in colonial Pennsylvania was in domestic service in the homes of wealthy city dwellers and as laborers in some of the early iron furnaces of the Province.

THE MELTING POT

Pennsylvania was settled by people of many nations. Under the liberal rule established by William Penn, the distressed peoples of the Old World found shelter and a new life in the broad valleys north and west of Philadelphia. More than any other colony, Pennsylvania was the proving ground for the blending of nationalities and the bringing together of cultures. Here, on a small scale, was conducted the great

39

experiment in human relations which was to characterize the history of all America, the assimilation of men of many creeds and customs, welding all of them into a new nationality—the American nationality. Truly, Pennsylvania was a melting pot in which the desirable elements of all cultures remained and the ugly hatreds of the Old World were burned away. Penn's Holy Experiment had begun to pay dividends.

Thus we have seen how Pennsylvania came into being. From a dense, uncharted forest it became an English colony under the proprietorship of the Penns. We have observed the aims which the founder set for himself in establishing his colony here and the framework of government which was set up to rule the Province. By learning from what parts of the world the early settlers came we can better understand the various racial, religious, and cultural differences that we find among Pennsylvanians today. Also we have had conclusive proof that it is possible for people of different national origins to get along in peace and happiness under democratic forms of government.

QUESTIONS FOR STUDY AND REVIEW

1. Why did William Penn induce settlers to come to his Province? What gain was there for him?

2. Why did the various groups from continental Europe flock to Pennsylvania rather than scatter among the other English colonies?

3. Who are the Pennsylvania "Dutch"? Why did they come to Pennsylvania? Where did they build their settlements? What are some of their contributions to American life?

4. What qualities possessed by the Scotch-Irish settlers were highly desirable in building a new country?

5. Explain why it was that Pennsylvania did not employ many slaves? Give several reasons.

6. What is meant by calling Pennsylvania a "melting pot"?

7. Why is Bethlehem, Pennsylvania, called the Christmas City?

PROBLEMS AND ACTIVITIES

1. List the names by which your local creeks and rivers are known. If these names are not English in origin, explain where the names came from. (See Espenshade, *Pennsylvania Place Names*, or Donehoo, *A History of Indian Villages and Place Names in Pennsylvania*.)

2. Where were the first houses built in your community? Who were the first white settlers? What are some of the oldest buildings which are still standing? Are the descendants of the first families still living in your community?

3. Can you find Indian legends which are still told in your community?

4. Prepare an imaginary diary such as Etienne Brulé might have written during his trip through Pennsylvania. What do you think he would have seen?

5. Prepare a brief sketch of the adventures and achievements of one of the following men: John Smith, Henry Hudson, John and Sebastian Cabot, Peter Minuit, Peter Stuyvesant, Samuel de Champlain. (Use an American History text for your report.)

6. Plan a class visit to the nearest museum, historical society, or historic spot. Write an account of your trip in your notebook.

7. Some schools may be able to prepare an exhibit of Indian relics for the school library or museum. Do you know of any private collections of Indian arrowheads, spears, axes, or similar relics which the class might see?

8. Perhaps some students will be interested in constructing a model of a ship like the *Half Moon*, an Indian canoe, a Dutch trading post. Other students may wish to draw scenes of an Indian village, landing of the Quakers, or of any other event in the early history of the Province.

9. Organize the class as an Indian tribal council. Discuss some problem which would have been a matter of concern to the Indians in early Pennsylvania. One of the following is suggested: the food supply, the coming of the white man, the sale of lands to the settlers, the goods brought by white traders to the village.

10. Choose passages from William Penn's charter to be read to the class. (See *Bulletin*, No. 506, issued by the Department of Public Instruction, or Martin and Shenk, *Pennsylvania History Told by Contemporaries*, pp. 5–6. Also notice the interesting letter which William Penn wrote to a friend on page 7.)

11. In a standard textbook on European history you will be able to find additional information about the persecuted religious groups such as the Quakers, Puritans, and Huguenots. Perhaps you can add to your knowledge about the Moravians by reading about John Huss, or the Mennonites by learning something about Menno Simons. Share what you find with your classmates.

12. The class may wish to prepare a list of place names—streets, towns, streams—and business firms which have been named for William Penn or his family.

13. Using a text on American history, make a list of the thirteen original colonies showing which ones were royal, proprietary, and charter colonies in 1776.

14. Dramatize a treaty with the Indians showing the white men purchasing the land which forms the county in which you live.

15. Can you name some counties or communities which were settled mostly by German immigrants in colonial times. (See *The Pennsylvania Germans*, edited by Ralph Wood, Chapter I.)

16. Can you show any reasons why many of the descendants of the German settlers who came here more than two centuries ago still speak Pennsylvania Dutch even though most other national groups have forgotten the language of their mother country after a few generations in America?

17. Can you explain why the Scotch-Irish were usually the ones to settle on the frontiers? Can you name some outstanding leaders in United States history who were of Scotch-Irish descent?

18. In what ways did the life and work of an indentured servant differ from that of a slave? Do you think the indenture system was democratic?

SUGGESTIONS FOR FURTHER READING
Geography

George H. Ashley, *The Scenery of Pennsylvania*, Harrisburg: Department of Internal Affairs; Francis B. Brandt, *The Majestic Delaware, the Nation's Foremost Historic River*, Philadelphia: Brandt and Grummere Co.; R. E. and Marion Murphy, *Pennsylvania, A Regional Geography*, Harrisburg: Pennsylvania Book Service; *Pennsylvania: An Inventory of Human and Economic Resources of the Commonwealth*, Harrisburg: Department of Public Instruction; H. H. Russell, *The Geography of Pennsylvania*, New York: Macmillan; A. F. Stokes, *Geography and History of Northeastern Pennsylvania*, Scranton: International Text Book Co.; Harry Emerson Wildes, *The Delaware* (Rivers of America Series) New York: Farrar and Rinehart.

Indians

George P. Donehoo, *A History of Indian Villages and Place Names in Pennsylvania*, Harrisburg: Pennsylvania Book Service; J. G. E. Heckewelder, *History, Manners, and Customs of the Indian Nations Who Once Inhabited Pennsylvania and the Neighboring States* (Pennsylvania Society Memoirs, Vol. 12) Philadelphia: Historical Society of Pennsylvania; C. Hale Sipe, *Indian Chiefs of Pennsylvania*, Butler: the Author; C. Hale Sipe, *Indian Wars of Pennsylvania*, Harrisburg: Telegraph Press; Gladys Tantaquidgeon, *A Study of Delaware Indian Medicine Practice and Folk Belief*, Harrisburg: Pennsylvania Historical Commission.

Swedish and Dutch Settlements

Adolph B. Benson and Hedin Naboth, *Swedes in America*, New Haven: Yale University Press; Emma C. Dowling and A. A. Rapp, *Early Pennsylvania Settlers*, Appleton, Wis.: Nelson Publishing Co.; Sidney George Fisher, *The Making of Pennsylvania*, Philadelphia: Lippincott; Amandus Johnson, *The Swedish Settlements on the Delaware*, 2 vols. Philadelphia: University of Pennsylvania; Walter Lefferts, *Settlement and Growth of Pennsylvania*, Harrisburg: Pennsylvania Book Service; *Pennsylvania's Swedish Heritage*, compiled by the Work Projects Administration of the State of Pennsylvania, Harrisburg; Christopher Longstreth Ward, *Dutch and Swedes on the Delaware*, Harrisburg: Pennsylvania Book Service; John H. Wuorinen, *The Finns on the Delaware*, New York: Columbia University Press.

William Penn and the Quakers

Mabel Richmond Brailsford, *Making of William Penn*, New York: Longmans; Sidney George Fisher, *Making of Pennsylvania*, Philadelphia: Lippincott; John Fiske, *Dutch and Quaker Colonies in America* (Historical Works, vols. 7–8) New York: Houghton Mifflin; W. I. Hall, *William Penn and the Dutch-Quaker Migration to Pennsylvania*, Swarthmore College, Swarthmore: the Author; Arthur Pound, *Penns of Pennsylvania and England*, New York: Macmillan; C. E. Vulliamy, *William Penn*, New York: Scribners.

Pennsylvania Germans

William Beidleman, *The Story of the Pennsylvania Germans*, Easton: Express Book Print; Oscar Kuhns, *German and Swiss Settlements of Pennsylvania*, New York: Henry Holt; Ralph Wood (ed.) *Pennsylvania Germans*, Princeton, N. J.: Princeton University Press.

Fiction

Edna Albert, *Little Pilgrim to Penn's Woods*, New York: Longmans; Hezekiah Butterworth, *Wampum Belt*, New York: Appleton; Marguerite de Angeli, *Elin's Amerika*, New York: Doubleday; Frances M. Fox, *Quakers Courageous*, New York: Lothrop, Lee and Shepard; Ann Hark, *The Story of the Pennsylvania Dutch*, New York: Harper, Mark R. Harrington, *Dickon Among the Indians*, Philadelphia: John C. Winston Co.; Clifton Lisle, *The Lenape Trail*, New York: Harcourt; Jacob J. Sessler, *Saints and Tomahawks*, New York: Pyramid Press; Ella Mae Seyfert, *Little Amish Schoolhouse*, New York: Crowell; Elsie Singmaster, *The Long Journey*, New York: Houghton Mifflin; Elsie Singmaster, *Stories of Pennsylvania, 1616–1781*, 4 vols., Harrisburg: Pennsylvania Book Service; Joseph W. Yoder, *Rosanna of the Amish*, Huntingdon: Yoder Publishing Co.

UNIT II
COLONIAL PENNSYLVANIA

The years before the United States won its independence from England were important years in the state and national history. Just as youth is the period of learning and development for boys and girls, so too the colonial period of American history was the period when foundations were laid for the great state and nation of today.

The colonial settlers were made up of many peoples from many different lands. During the early years of the Province they learned how to live with each other as good neighbors. Occasionally there was friction among groups of colonists within the Province and quarrels with the settlers from other colonies.

The framework of democratic government established by William Penn was strengthened as the early Pennsylvanians learned the workings of democratic machinery. The machinery creaked and groaned at times, as the colonial governors did not always get on well with the Provincial Assembly.

The colonists learned other things, too. The bitter conflicts with the Indians and the struggle between France and England for the control of the Ohio country furnished valuable lessons in waging war. These lessons were to mean much in the later struggle for independence.

When they came to America, the colonists brought with them their own traits of character, their ways of working, their customs and beliefs. These had to be adapted to the demands of life in a new and strange country. The people of colonial Pennsylvania found their new home a great treasure house of natural resources which they gradually learned to use. In these early years we can trace the beginning of that industrial development which was to bring the state wealth and renown.

44

Chapter IV

COLONIAL STRUGGLES

The early history of the Province of Pennsylvania is a record of peaceful progress. There was little if any trouble with the Indians of Pennsylvania. As long as William Penn lived, and for a number of years after his death, the relations between red men and white men were friendly. However, this happy state of affairs was destined to change, and we shall see how dreadful became the frontier warfare during the later years of the Province.

The disputes which plagued the people of Pennsylvania between 1718 and 1776 were not confined to quarrels with the Indians; in many cases the settlers quarreled among themselves. The Province grew so rapidly that it felt the "growing pains." Conflicts with neighboring provinces developed over boundaries; within the Province disputes arose from the attempts of various groups to gain political power; and always there were prolonged debates between the deputy governors and the provincial assemblies.

BOUNDARY DISPUTES

The boundaries of Penn's lands in America had been fixed by the charter. However, the terms of the charter conflicted with other charters granted to neighboring colonies. As a result, throughout the colonial history of the Province, the location of the boundaries plagued the provincial authorities. In fact, it was not until after the Revolutionary War and the formation of a national government that the disputes were finally settled.

The Southern Boundary. The dispute between William Penn and Lord Baltimore over the proper boundaries of their respective domains began soon after Penn secured his grant, and it was not settled during the lifetime of either proprietor. Their heirs carried on the long-drawn-out quarrel until 1763, when the boundary between Pennsylvania and Maryland was

45

finally surveyed. During the intervening years, the settlers of the southern counties—Chester, Lancaster, York, Adams—could never be certain to which province they owed allegiance.

The issue at stake in the Penn-Baltimore argument grew out of the confused language of their charters. Baltimore's grant in 1632 gave him the land "which lies under the fortieth degree of northern latitude." Penn's charter fixed the boundary "on the south by a circle drawn at twelve miles distance from New Castle, northward and westward, unto the beginning of the fortieth degree of northern latitude, and then by a straight line westward. . . ." The wording of this charter raised doubts as to who owned the land between the thirty-ninth and fortieth degree; both proprietors claimed it.

If Penn's claims had been established, the city of Baltimore, Maryland, lying north of the thirty-ninth degree, would today be in Pennsylvania, and if Lord Baltimore had gained all that he claimed, then Philadelphia and a wide strip westward along the southern counties of the state would today form a part of Maryland.

The Mason and Dixon Line. The dispute was carried on in a series of trials in English courts, and it was not until 1750 that a decision was handed down in favor of the Penns. The actual surveying of the dividing line was begun ten years later, when commissioners were appointed to locate the boundaries, and David Rittenhouse, the Philadelphia astronomer, was engaged to make the surveys. The line between Pennsylvania and Maryland was to be fixed at thirty-nine degrees, forty minutes. Working with crude instruments of his own making, Rittenhouse located the circle separating Delaware from Pennsylvania and Maryland. In order to get the work done more quickly, the proprietors engaged two English surveyors to check upon and complete the work done by Rittenhouse. The names of these men were Charles Mason and Jeremiah Dixon. They worked for four years, extending the line almost two hundred and thirty miles westward when they were forced to stop because the Indians interfered with their work. The remainder of the line was run by other surveyors.

The Southwest Boundary. It will be remembered that the western limits of Pennsylvania were fixed by the charter at five degrees longitude west of the Delaware River. This was generally understood to mean five degrees measured from the easternmost point of the Delaware. Maryland did not extend westward as far as Penn's grant; therefore, the southern boundary between Pennsylvania and Virginia remained undetermined even after the Mason and Dixon Line was approved. There were still other difficulties in dealing with the royal Province of Virginia because of the peculiar wording of Virginia's charter.

Virginia's Charter of 1609. With grand flourishes of the pen, the Stuart kings of England had granted charters in high-sounding terms, partly because exact knowledge of American geography was lacking. Virginia's charter of 1609 granted her a strip of land two hundred miles in width, stretching from "sea to sea" (ocean to ocean), "west and northwest." According to Virginia's interpretation of this phrase, the southwestern corner of present-day Pennsylvania belonged to her. Pennsylvania's western limits were still undetermined at this time. Virginia gentlemen formed the Ohio Land Company to sell lands in the Ohio Valley. During the middle of the eighteenth century, the King of England lent his support to the plans of the Ohio Land Company because English colonization would serve to prevent French occupation of the Ohio region.

Virginia Assumes Control. Young George Washington was sent by the governor of Virginia to warn off the French who were building forts near present-day Pittsburgh and along the Allegheny River. Although some of the provincial authorities of Pennsylvania realized that the western limits of the Province extended beyond the junction of the Monongahela and Allegheny rivers at Pittsburgh, Pennsylvania did little or nothing to establish her claim to the region at that time. The reason for this neglect lay in the unwillingness of the Quaker-controlled Assembly to vote money to build and equip forts which were needed to hold the territory. The Quakers were unwilling to engage in any warlike activity.

The defense of the territory fell largely to the Virginians until 1756, when Pennsylvania joined with Virginia in furnishing men and supplies to wrest the Ohio country from French control. After the French were driven out, both Pennsylvania and Virginia sold lands in the region and both formed their own governments in the southwestern corner of Pennsylvania.

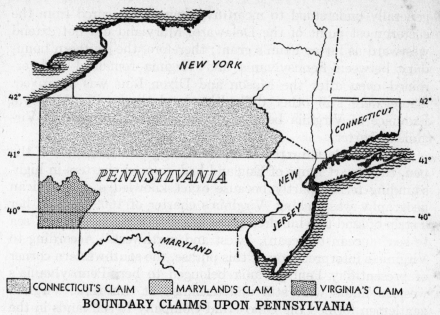

CONNECTICUT'S CLAIM   MARYLAND'S CLAIM   VIRGINIA'S CLAIM

BOUNDARY CLAIMS UPON PENNSYLVANIA

Settlement of the Virginia Boundary. In 1779, during the Revolutionary War, an agreement between Virginia and Pennsylvania gave Pennsylvania more land than the original charter had provided. It was agreed that the Mason and Dixon Line should be extended five degrees west of its beginning point. At the western end of the Mason and Dixon Line a line was to run due north to Lake Erie, thus establishing the present western boundary of Pennsylvania. These surveys were completed in 1786. Generously, Virginia yielded her claim to the lands, asking only that Pennsylvania should ratify all land titles issued by the Virginia government to settlers.

The Northern Boundary. The northern boundary of Pennsylvania was contested by the colonies of New York and Connecticut. There was very little argument between Pennsylvania and New York, however, for the forty-second degree latitude was readily agreed upon as the boundary. Penn's charter had fixed the boundaries of his possessions at the forty-third degree. This was interpreted as the beginning of the forty-third degree. In other words, the Province claimed all of the land between the forty-second and the forty-third degrees. In 1788 the question was settled when Pennsylvania agreed to accept the forty-second degree as the northern boundary.

The Erie Triangle. The Erie Triangle, or the chimney-shaped peak in the northwestern corner of the state, was purchased by the Commonwealth of Pennsylvania in 1792. This section was claimed by New York and Massachusetts during colonial times. Massachusetts based her claim on her "sea to sea" charter. In 1781 New York withdrew her claims in favor of the United States government, and five years later Massachusetts did likewise. Then Pennsylvania purchased these 202,187 acres of land from the United States government for about 75 cents per acre, or $151,540.25.

Connecticut's Claims. The dispute between Pennsylvania and Connecticut was far more serious. It grew out of Connecticut's original charter which granted her lands within certain latitudes from "sea to sea" unless those lands were already possessed by other colonies. New York and New Jersey were already settled when Connecticut's grant was made in 1662, but by leaping over these areas, the Province of Connecticut claimed that her charter was valid again west of the Delaware River, because Penn's charter of 1681 had been granted much later than her own. These claims were not made at the time of Penn's grant, and it was not until 1750, almost seventy years later, that enterprising Yankees began to settle in the Wyoming Valley in Luzerne County on lands which were sold to them by the Susquehanna Company, a land company organized in Connecticut.

At first neither the colonial government of Connecticut nor of Pennsylvania paid much attention to the Yankee settlements along the eastern branch of the Susquehanna. The Pennsylvania Assembly was unwilling to raise a military force to turn off the trespassers, and the heirs of William Penn were unable to employ enough magistrates and sheriffs to force the Connecticut people from the lands in Pennsylvania. Between the years 1769 and 1784 there were three armed conflicts between Pennsylvania settlers and the determined men from New England. These contests were known as the Yankee-Pennamite wars.

The Yankee-Pennamite Wars. These "wars" were local in character, and the authorities of both provinces avoided taking any official part in the struggle. The contests were bitter and blood was shed. The first "war" (1669 to 1771), fought near

Kingston, Luzerne County, succeeded at first in driving the Connecticut people out of the Wyoming Valley, but they returned in great numbers, so that by 1771 they were once more in possession of the Wyoming region. The area was formed into a New England "town," named Westmoreland, and delegates were elected to the Connecticut Legislature. The second "war" was fought at Muncy in present-day Lycoming County, in 1775.

The uprisings of civil strife came to the attention of Continental Congress during the Revolutionary War. In 1782 a commission was appointed by that body to settle the issue between Pennsylvania and Connecticut. This commission met at Trenton, New Jersey, and, acting as a special court, listened to the claims of both groups. The decision, known as the Trenton Decree, was unanimous in confirming Pennsylvania's ownership of all of the disputed areas. Even though the officials of the government of Connecticut accepted the verdict of the commissioners, the New England settlers in Pennsylvania were not satisfied. In 1784 another uprising, known as the Third Pennamite War, disturbed the peace in the northeastern counties of Pennsylvania. The issue was finally settled by a series of acts passed by the Pennsylvania Legislature granting Pennsylvania titles to the lands which the settlers had previously held under Connecticut grants.

The most lasting effect of the attempt to extend the boundaries of New England into Pennsylvania was the extension of New England culture into the diverse pattern of Pennsylvania's many peoples from many lands. The northern counties reflect the New England influence in their way of life today.

POLITICAL STRIFE

Problems of the Governors. The life of a deputy governor of Pennsylvania was far from pleasant. In his relations with his employers and with the stubborn assemblies of the Province, it was the governor's duty as an employee of the Penns to see that the Indians should be kept friendly by frequent payments or gifts. Lands had to be purchased from the red men; frequently the same land had to be bought from different tribes at different times. The Province had to be defended against attack, and during periods when England was at war, the Province of Pennsylvania was expected to do its share in raising and supporting armies. All of these duties required money which had to be raised by taxation or by issuing paper bills of credit. The raising of revenue was a right jealously guarded by the Assembly, which was elected by the people and therefore was not, like the governor, responsible to the Penns.

William Penn's sons, John, Thomas, and Richard Penn, were not members of the Quaker faith, and the men they sent to govern the Province were not Quakers. But the Provincial Assembly was controlled by the Quakers. Even though the Quakers formed a minority of the population of the Province, they always managed to elect a majority of representatives to the Assembly until this power was overthrown in 1756. This Quaker power was due to two things: First, the "Old Counties"—Bucks, Philadelphia and Chester, the counties in which most of the Quakers lived—had a larger number of seats in the Assembly than did the newer counties of Lancaster, Northampton, Berks, and Cumberland. Second, the huge German vote prior to 1756 was always cast in favor of Quaker candidates. The Germans regarded the Quakers as the rightful rulers of the Province and were in sympathy with the peace policy of the Assembly. In addition, it meant lower taxes on their lands. This vote was usually powerful enough to tip the balance in favor of the Quakers in all counties except Cumberland, where the Scotch-Irish opposed the policy of the Quakers.

The Quaker-controlled Assembly was always unwilling to raise money for military expeditions, and more than one deputy governor was exasperated to find himself torn between the demands for guns, ammunition, and soldiers, and the attitude of the pacifists in the Assembly, who were unwilling to raise funds for warfare.

Political Parties. In 1740, however, Governor George Thomas found himself almost at his wit's end in trying to coax the Assembly into raising money for King George's War, known in Europe as the War of the Austrian Succession. Two political parties were formed at this time. One party, known as the Governors' Men, supported candidates for the Assembly who promised to "strengthen the governor's hand" in providing troops for the defense of the Province. The other party, known as the Sticklers, favored the Quaker policies of non-resistance. From 1740 to 1756, the Sticklers won.

Raising War Funds. Quaker opposition to raising revenue for war was based upon the argument that such funds ought to come out of the Proprietor's purse and not from taxation. No one likes to pay taxes if the same good can be achieved without doing so. Therefore, the Quaker position found favor with many persons who otherwise had no sympathy for their doctrines. The trouble was that the Proprietor's purse was frequently empty, and even if it were filled, the Penns were unwilling to part with the funds gained from the sale of their lands and the income from their private estates.

A much easier way to raise money was to print it. Orders to issue paper money had to come from the Assembly. This could be done without resorting to direct forms of taxation, but there was always the danger that the paper money would become worthless if too much of it were issued—or if not entirely worthless, then less desirable than the paper money issued by neighboring provinces. Paper money must always be based upon some form of security. Several times the Assembly printed money, based upon nothing other than the credit of the Province of Pennsylvania, but whenever this was done the governor was forbidden to spend it for military undertakings.

The recruiting of soldiers presented no great problem if the money were available to hire them. Although the Quakers, Mennonites, and Schwenkfelders were conscientious objectors against the bearing of arms, there were many Irish indentured servants who wanted to buy their freedom by enlisting, Scotch-Irish who clamored for a stern policy in dealing with the Indians, and Palatine Germans who had seen extensive military service in their homeland before coming to Pennsylvania; all of these were available to fill the ranks and man the forts if funds could be supplied.

INDIAN AFFAIRS

James Logan. William Penn's kind treatment of the Indians set an example which his successors followed. The conduct of Indian affairs was entrusted to James Logan, a brilliant scholar, who had come to Pennsylvania as a young man in 1699 as William Penn's personal secretary. When Penn returned to England he entrusted the management of his land interests to Logan. After Penn's death, Logan continued to serve the sons

52

of Penn as their chief representative in the Province. He continued to hold this position until his retirement in 1750, acting as president of the Provincial Council, advising the various deputy governors sent by the Penns, and directing Indian affairs.

Pennsylvania's Indian Policy after 1736. The basis of Pennsylvania's Indian policy after 1736 was to regard the Delawares and other resident tribes as ruled by the powerful Six Nations Confederacy whose headquarters were in New York Province. The Six Nations of the Iroquois had conquered the Pennsylvania Indians and had established an Oneida chief named Shikellimy to govern their "cousins," the Delawares and Shawnees. In 1736 a large delegation of Six Nations Indians journeyed to Philadelphia to arrange the sale of some lands just south of the Blue Mountains. On this occasion the Pennsylvanians entered into a treaty of friendship with the Six Nations. This treaty was regarded by the red men as an alliance with Pennsylvania, and, whether the Quakers liked it or not, the Six Nations fully expected Pennsylvania to aid them in their wars.

Conrad Weiser's Service. Fortunately for all concerned, Logan employed a very able interpreter and agent to negotiate

THE HANDLOOM IN A COLONIAL HOME

treaties and transact business with the Iroquois. This man was Conrad Weiser, a German immigrant who had come to Pennsylvania from New York and followed the route of the Palatines to the Tulpehocken region of Pennsylvania. As a boy, Weiser had lived with the Indians in their villages in New York, learned their language and customs, and won their complete confidence. For a quarter of a century this brave man traveled among the Indian villages of Pennsylvania and other provinces, carrying messages of peace and smoothing out difficulties which arose.

The Walking Purchase. One of the disgraceful pages of colonial history is the story of the "Walking Purchase" of 1737. In the days of William Penn, in 1686, the Indians had given a deed to Penn releasing certain lands along the Delaware River. The wording of this deed was probably understood by both Indians and white men at the time it was agreed upon. Fifty-one years passed before the heirs of William Penn undertook to have the survey made. The men who originally wrote the deed were no longer alive in 1737. Therefore, the only basis for determining the extent of the purchased lands was the deed itself.

The deed fixed a beginning point west of the Delaware River from which a line was to be run northward as far as a man could "go in a day and a half." To the Indian, the word "go" meant to walk at a normal pace, or a distance of approximately twenty miles a day. The Delawares thought that the lands involved would not extend north of the Lehigh Hills, or a distance of thirty miles from the beginning point which was near Wrightstown, Bucks County.

The methods employed to "walk" the purchase line were far different from the original intent of the Delaware Indians. On September 19, 1737, the day set to "go," three white men began to run as fast as they could. The Indians who had come to "walk" with them soon realized that they were being cheated. Two of the white men were soon exhausted, but one, Edward Marshall, succeeded in keeping his pace from dawn to darkness, then rested for the night and ran again the following day, covering a distance of sixty-five miles instead of only thirty.

The Indians contended that the transaction was a fraud, not only because the white men ran instead of walked, but because the route taken did not follow the course of the river. Instead of running parallel to the river, the runners ran inland to Mauch Chunk in Carbon County and cut a line eastward to the Delaware. This action cost the Minsi tribe of Delawares all of the land which today forms Pike, Monroe, Carbon, and a part of Northampton counties. When the Minsi were driven from their possessions, they moved westward where they joined with Shawnees who also were smarting under wrongs inflicted by the settlers of Pennsylvania. These tribes came under the influence of the French after 1749, and in 1755 they returned to eastern Pennsylvania to wreak savage vengeance on helpless settlers along the foothills of the Blue Mountains.

THE FRENCH AND INDIAN WAR

The French Forts, 1749 to 1754. In 1748, Conrad Weiser, the Pennsylvania Indian agent, carried a message to the Indians at Logstown near Ambridge in Beaver County. On this visit he "ran up a little Flagg" to signify that the country belonged to England. The following year a French officer planted some leaden plates along the Allegheny and Ohio rivers. These plates bore inscriptions in the French language claiming the lands for France. Now the race for control began.

The French were far more active in asserting and protecting their claims than were Pennsylvania and Virginia. They erected a chain of forts leading southward from Lake Erie to the junction of the Allegheny and Monongahela rivers. Some of these forts were ar Presque Isle, where the city of Erie now stands; LeBoeuf, at Waterford in Erie County; Machault, later named Venango and now the site of the city of Franklin in Venango County.

Virginia Takes the Lead. In 1753 Governor Dinwiddie of Virginia sent George Washington to warn the French that they were trespassing. When this gesture failed, Virginia attempted to fortify the forks of the Ohio, but the French quickly expelled them in April, 1754, and built their own fort, Fort Duquesne. Additional Virginia troops were then sent to wrest the control of the territory from the French. George Washington built fortifications near present-day Uniontown, and later built Fort Necessity in the same region. In July of 1754, the forces under Washington were attacked by the French. The result of this contest was a defeat for the Virginians, who now decided to wait until Great Britain could help them.

DEFEAT OF GENERAL BRADDOCK

The Braddock Expedition. The British government was alarmed by the French encroachments in the Ohio country and in 1755 decided to send a military expedition to help the Virginians. General Edward Braddock arrived in Alexandria, Virginia, with 1000 soldiers in the spring of 1755. A conference of governors of neighboring provinces was summoned to find ways to transport Braddock's army across the mountains to Will's Creek (Cumberland, Maryland). Attending this conference was Benjamin Franklin, Postmaster General of the colonies. Franklin suggested that horses and wagons should be engaged from the farmers of Pennsylvania, because they could supply sturdy animals and well-built Conestoga wagons. Accordingly, Franklin was empowered to contract for the teams. Pennsylvania wagons and their drivers carried Braddock's men westward over rough roads and towering mountains.

Disaster. The Braddock expedition met with complete disaster. In July, 1755, the British soldiers and colonial militiamen were advancing northward along the Monongahela, ten miles south of Fort Duquesne, when they were attacked by the French and Indians who poured gunfire into the ranks of Braddock's men from all sides. The Indian allies of the French crouched behind rocks and trees, taking aim and firing at will, while the British forces attempted to keep their formations intact. The result was utter defeat for the British forces. General Braddock was wounded fatally, and his men were forced to retreat. Colonel Thomas Dunbar reassembled the battered forces and marched them eastward to Philadelphia, leaving the entire frontier unguarded and an easy prey for marauding Indian bands which followed the retreating British forces and inaugurated a reign of terror from the southern borders of Cumberland County, northeastward to the Delaware.

The Massacres. It is impossible to describe in detail the horrors of Indian warfare against the helpless settlers during the late summer and autumn of 1755. The first raid struck at a settlement in Penn's Creek in Snyder County. Soon attacks spread east and southwest; settlers were murdered in Tulpehocken in western Berks, and at the forks of the Delaware near present-day Stroudsburg. A group of peaceful Moravians at Gnadenhutten, now Weissport in Carbon County, were attacked and slain while they were eating their evening meal.

—*Hildreth Collection and Index of Historic Prints*

THE MASSACRE OF CONOCOCHEAGUE, PENNSYLVANIA

During the French and Indian wars the Indian anger was directed against the remote settlements of the Conococheague Valley.

The tomahawk and firebrand ruled the frontiers of Pennsylvania. Local militiamen collected hurriedly in an effort to prevent these atrocities, but their forces were poorly organized and for the most part their efforts were unavailing, except that their presence prevented the Indians from carrying their raids deeper into the settled areas.

Passing a Militia Act. While all of these horrors were taking place, the provincial authorities debated and wasted precious time. In November, 1755, a large group of irate citizens marched to Philadelphia to demand action in defense of their homes. Most of these marchers came from the counties immediately north of Philadelphia—Berks and Northampton. Governor Robert Hunter Morris met the angry citizens and promised that the Province would pass a Militia Act and provide the funds necessary to build a chain of forts along the foothills of the Blue Mountains.

The Frontier Forts. In 1756, the building of the frontier forts was begun. Benjamin Franklin supervised the construction of the forts between the Lehigh River and the Delaware. The chief forts built in that region were Fort Allen, built upon the ruins of the murdered Moravian settlement, and Forts Franklin,

—*Culver Service*

BENJAMIN FRANKLIN EXAMINING THE BUILDING OF THE
STOCKADE AT GNADENHUTTEN, FORT ALLEN

58

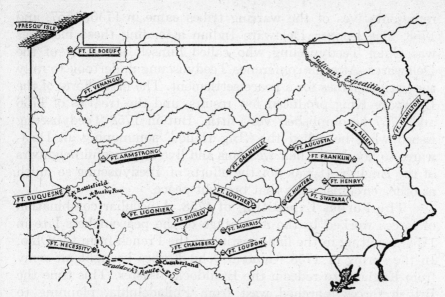

MAIN COLONIAL FORTS IN PENNSYLVANIA
Note Braddock's Route, Bushy Run, and the route followed by Sullivan
in 1779.

Norris, Hamilton, and Penn were added to the chain east of the
Lehigh River. Meanwhile, Conrad Weiser supervised the building of the chain of forts westward from the Lehigh to the Susquehanna. Fort Henry, near Bethel in Berks County, was the
key fort in this chain; others were Fort Northkill, at present-
day Strausstown, Forts Swatara, Manada, and Fort Hunter, six
miles north of present-day Harrisburg. Later other forts were
built at strategic places throughout Pennsylvania.

These frontier forts did not put an end to Indian raids because they were too far apart to guard every mountain pass,
but they did serve to prevent any large-scale Indian or French
invasion from the north and west. The settlements near Philadelphia were never again subjected to Indian atrocities.

Treaties of Easton. Not all of the Indians joined in the
slaughter of the white settlers. There were several friendly Indians who moved back and forth between Philadelphia and the
Indian villages carrying messages which sought to restore
peace. In 1756 the Quakers organized a group of men known
among themselves as the Friendly Association. The purpose of
the association was to negotiate for peace with the Indians. A
series of treaties and conferences were held in Easton to which

59

representatives of the warring tribes came in 1756, 1757, and 1758. The leading Delaware Indian attending these meetings was Chief Teedyuscung who called himself the King of the Delawares. At each conference Teedyuscung undertook to rally the various tribes for a peace settlement. The first efforts of the Delaware King produced few results, and the treaties of 1756 and 1757 accomplished very little. But in 1758 Teedyuscung issued what he called the "Big Hello," summoning all Delawares to lay down their weapons and live as peaceful neighbors of the English. It was not the efforts of Teedyuscung so much as other circumstances that brought peace.

The Forbes Expedition of 1758. A peculiar combination of forces worked to the advantage of the peacemakers late in 1758, resulting in the final ousting of the French from the Ohio. In the spring of 1758, General John Forbes brought an army from England to redeem the Braddock disaster. This time the British forces marched west from Philadelphia, planning to cross the southern portions of Pennsylvania to reach their objective at Fort Duquesne. The route of this army led westward along a newly constructed road, some sections of which later became the Lincoln Highway. Raystown, now the city of Bedford, became the main depot of the forces which advanced as far as Fort Ligonier, where wagons and cannon bogged down hopelessly in the mud as a result of autumn rains. For a time it appeared to Forbes and his men that winter would trap them in the mountains of Pennsylvania, and that nature would inflict upon them a worse defeat than Braddock's army had suffered three years earlier.

The French Abandon the Ohio. One day late in November a dull thud was heard by the advanced patrols of Forbes' army. The French had blown up Fort Duquesne to prevent it from falling into British hands and had abandoned their positions in western Pennsylvania. What had happened to change the course of events so suddenly? A Moravian missionary, Christian Frederick Post, had dared to visit the Indian tribes which were allied with the French. Combining his missionary activities with an assignment from the Governor of Pennsylvania to inform the western Indians of the peace made at Easton, and with no weapon other than a Bible, Post succeeded in doing what all of Braddock's army had failed to do

WASHINGTON RAISING THE BRITISH FLAG AT FORT DUQUESNE
This fort was renamed Fort Pitt.

and what Forbes was despairing of doing. From village to village, Post had spread the word of the peace made at the Easton meeting and of the "Big Hello" that Teedyuscung had issued. In this way he prevailed upon the Indians to desert the French, and, without the support of their Indians, the French were unable to hold Fort Duquesne. The Quakers, men of peace, Conrad Weiser as the chief negotiator of the Easton Treaty, and Christian Frederick Post, a pious man of God, had saved the Ohio country for the British Crown while Forbes and his army were stuck in the mud at Ligonier. In this instance, at least, it would appear that the ways of peace availed far more than the use of the sword.

Fort Pitt. The British rebuilt the fort at the forks of the Ohio, naming it Fort Pitt, in honor of the British Prime Minister, William Pitt. For a few years, 1759 to 1763, there was a period of comparative peace in the Ohio country west of the Allegheny mountains. During this period a small village began to form in the neighborhood of the fort, the beginning of Pittsburgh. But in 1763 a new Indian threat appeared from the west.

Pontiac's War. After the French troops abandoned their forts in western Pennsylvania, those Indian tribes that had always been loyal to the French were unwilling to accept the English as their masters. These tribes were the Miamis, Wyandots, Ottawas, all of them living west of the Ohio River. Moreover, the tribes were alarmed over the growing numbers of white settlers. Chief Pontiac, an Ottawa, succeeded in drawing these tribes into an alliance to destroy all of the English settlements on the frontiers of Virginia and Pennsylvania. Some Delawares and Shawnees also joined in the plan. The Senecas, the westernmost branch of the Six Nations, sent some of their warriors to aid Pontiac. The alliance was known as Pontiac's Conspiracy. The plot was to attack a number of English outposts at the same time.

To protect her frontiers against this threat, Pennsylvania organized a military expedition, led by Colonel Henri Bouquet, a Swiss. The provincial forces met the Indians at Bushy Run, near present-day Jeannette in Westmoreland County. There, the white soldiers won a decisive victory over Pontiac's men, which saved Fort Pitt and proved that the western lands could be held for the English. The battle of Bushy Run was not the last conflict between Indians and white men within the borders of Pennsylvania, but it was the most decisive victory in provincial warfare. The power of the Indians was broken.

The brunt of the Indian raids had been borne by the Scotch-Irish and German settlers whose clearings were exposed to their attacks. The frontier settlers hated the red men and they were bitter against the Quakers, whose policies were always directed toward the peaceful settlement of all difficulties. The hardy frontiersmen were unwilling to deal gently with their foes. A glaring example of the extreme measures occasionally taken by the settlers is the incident known as the "Conestoga Massacre."

The Conestoga Massacre. In 1764 some Indians attacked a schoolhouse in Franklin County, near Greencastle, killing Enoch Brown, the teacher, and eleven of his pupils. The Scotch-Irish settlers of the region were enraged. They retaliated by wiping out the remnants of the Conestoga tribe of Indians living upon lands set aside for them by William Penn in 1701.

These Indians were harmless—a few old men, women, and children were the only ones left at Conestoga, near Safe Harbor in Lancaster County. Their desire to destroy all Indians whetted, the vengeful band of white men threatened to deal in the same way with another group of friendly Indians farther to the east which were known as the Moravian Indians.

The Paxton Boys. In Northampton County, the Moravians had given shelter to Indians converted to Christianity who chose to live near the white settlements. Because these Christian Indians came from many different tribes, they were known generally as the Moravian Indians.

Alarmed by the threats of the angry men from the Scotch-Irish settlement at Paxton, the provincial authorities had the Moravian Indians transferred to Philadelphia under armed guards. Not daunted by this move, the "Paxton Boys" marched toward Philadelphia, threatening to seize the Indians, even if it meant fighting against their Quaker protectors. Great excitement prevailed in Philadelphia as citizens waited for the "invasion," and even Quakers looked curiously at gun sights as they took weapons into their hands to resist if necessary.

The invading men from Paxton could not cross the Schuylkill at Philadelphia because all boats had been taken to the eastern side of the stream. Undaunted by this, they crossed the river above the city and entered Germantown. There they were prevailed upon to reconsider their wild plans, and during the conference better judgment won.

Let Us Be Fair. We have seen that the Indian could be cruel in his methods of fighting; we know that the early settlers suffered much at the hands of the red men. Quite properly we are proud of the courage of our ancestors, and yet a spirit of fair-mindedness prompts us to look at the Indian's side of the story. They felt that the land was theirs. The coming of the white man pushed the tribes farther and farther westward as the settlements grew. True, the white men bought these lands, giving in exchange Indian trinkets, shiny mirrors, and other pretty things which soon were broken or worn out, but the land was gone. The wild animals which the red man hunted to provide food for his family became scarce. Sometimes the white fur traders cheated the Indians or took sides in the wars which Indian tribes fought among themselves. Because the Indian was not a coward, he tried to avenge these wrongs by the only method the savage mind knew. That was by fighting.

In warfare the Indian was brave but cruel. He fought with the weapons he had—the tomahawk, scalping knife, and the fire-brand; he crept stealthily upon his foe, striking without warning and showing no mercy. According to white men's standards, these tactics were shameful, of course, but the red man knew no better. We can see, therefore, why the Indians molested the settlements and also why the white people on the frontier were bitter against the Indians.

PETITION FOR A ROYAL CHARTER

New Political Parties. The Quakers and Scotch-Irish were opposed to each other on a political issue that reshaped party lines between 1757 and 1765. The new parties were the Proprietary party, whose members favored keeping the Province under the proprietorship of the Penns, and the Anti-proprietary party, whose adherents wished to have Pennsylvania become a royal province under the direct administration of the King. Those who favored the royal control believed that the King would provide better protection against the Indians and against unlawful proceedings such as the march of the "Paxton Boys." In this controversy the Quakers, aided by Benjamin Franklin, advocated royal control, while the Scotch-Irish, remembering the tyranny of the Stuart kings, were against subjecting themselves to the Crown of England. The Germans, who held the balance of power in this controversy, were divided. Some of them, still loyal to the Quakers, signed petitions favoring a royal charter, while others made common cause with the Scotch-Irish. Those Germans living near the frontiers no longer were willing to support the Quakers, feeling that the Quakers had neglected them during the Indian wars.

John Penn, Governor. In 1763 the rule by deputy governor came to an end when John Penn, a grandson of William Penn, came to govern in his own right. One of the difficulties that always confronted the deputy governors was caused by the definite instructions of their employers who lived in England. The deputy governors were not free to change these instructions to meet the needs of the times. It was hoped that John Penn, making his own decisions right on the spot, could govern more wisely than had his immediate predecessors, Robert Hunter Morris and William Denny. But John Penn proved to be just as arbitrary and selfish as the absentee proprietors, his father, Richard Penn, and his uncle, Thomas Penn, had ever been.

Benjamin Franklin Waits. Benjamin Franklin began the movement to secure a royal charter when, in 1757, he published a series of charges against the proprietors under the title of *Heads of Complaints*. In 1764 he published a pamphlet entitled *Cool Thoughts* in which he renewed his attacks against the Penn heirs. The Provincial Assembly then sent Franklin to London with petitions to the King to give Pennsylvania a royal charter. Franklin was instructed, however, not to present the petitition unless he thought it wise to do so. As we shall see, events taking place in America aroused the suspicions of those favoring a royal charter, and they soon decided that rule by the King might not be so desirable after all. New instructions were sent to Benjamin Franklin to hold the petition. It was never presented. When Pennsylvania finally adopted a new form of government it was as an independent state.

QUESTIONS FOR STUDY AND REVIEW

1. Why is it necessary to fix exact boundary lines between states and counties? What principles should be followed in drawing the boundary lines between European nations to maintain peace?

2. Why did the colonial governors quarrel with the Assembly? What provisions do we have in our state and national government today. which prevent such deadlocks? Do you think colonial Pennsylvania would have been better off under a royal governor instead of one appointed by the Penns?

3. Why was the Ohio country so valuable to both the French and the English that they fought for it? Why did most of the Indians join with the French in the colonial wars?

4. How much protection was given the settlers by the frontier forts of Pennsylvania?

5. Why was the Forbes Road built? What part did this road play in the later development of Pennsylvania?

6. Why was the Battle of Bushy Run one of the important events in the history of Pennsylvania?

Chapter V

COLONIAL LIFE IN PENNSYLVANIA

The summer of 1770 was an unforgettable one for John Evans, a boy of fourteen, who lived on a farm in Berks County. John had worked hard on his father's farm all summer helping with the harvests and doing the tasks about the barn such as feeding the cattle, milking the cows, hunting eggs, and keeping the stables clean. During the early part of August, John was especially diligent helping to thresh the grains of wheat out of the bundles, or sheaves, which had been harvested from the fields in July. It was hard work striking the tips of these sheaves with a flail made by tying two sticks together, end on end. As soon as a wagonload of wheat was threshed it would be hauled to the grain market in Philadelphia.

This year John's father had promised him that he would take him on the journey to Philadelphia. They would visit John's cousin, Charles Hughes. Charles had written such interesting letters about the wonderful things to be seen in the city. Now John would see them for himself.

The big four-horse wagon rumbled over the rutted roads leading from John's home in Cumru Township in Berks County, through Reading and Pottsgrove (now known as Pottstown), to Philadelphia. As they passed through the village of Trappe, John's father stopped to pay his respects to the great Lutheran pastor, Reverend Henry Melchior Muhlenberg. They did not tarry long, however, because the day was almost gone, and the tavern where they planned to spend the night was still one mile to the east on the edge of the Perkiomen Creek.

At the tavern the horses were stabled in a large barn, and the wagon was covered with a canvas cloth to protect the bags of grain from possible rain during the night. At dinner they joined the other guests in the dining room on the first floor. All of the guests were seated at one long table on which were placed steaming dishes of boiled potatoes, beans, and other vegetables. Among the guests were several travelers who told interesting tales of their adventures. One man described his escape from the Indians while he was trapping wild animals in the mountains and valleys of western Pennsylvania; he was now on his way to Philadelphia to sell his pelts. Another guest spoke of the fine music he had heard in the Moravian settlement in Bethlehem. A wagoner on his way to Reading was transporting a load of axes, saws, plowshares, and other tools which had been brought to Philadelphia by ship from England.

Early the next morning John and his father crossed the Perkiomen Creek at a ford. This was always a dangerous undertaking because

RULES OF THIS TAVERN

Four pence a night for Bed
Six pence with Supper
No more than five to sleep in one bed
No Boots to be worn in bed
Organ Grinders to sleep in the Wash house
No dogs allowed upstairs
No Beer allowed in the Kitchen
No Razor Grinders or Tinkers taken in

—Courtesy, Barron Collier

A TAVERN SIGN IN COLONIAL TIMES

there were no bridges, and the horses had to pull the heavily-loaded wagon through the water. This morning the horses performed nobly. In a short time the horses, wagon, and travelers were on dry land again and climbing a gentle slope of the road which led to Germantown and from there to Philadelphia.

Late that afternoon they would reach Philadelphia, thought John. Anticipation grew keener as the end of the journey grew near. John thought of the many things that Charles had written in his letters. He would see the large ocean-going ships that came from far-off places bringing goods to the wharves and docks in Philadelphia. Perhaps he would see a ship being built. He would certainly see the State House, the place where the laws of the Province were made. Perhaps on Sunday he would attend services at Christ Church. That must be a very old church, he reasoned, for he remembered hearing his grandmother speak of attending it when she was still a young woman. Charles had mentioned in one of his letters that it had been built in 1727.

Philadelphia. The city that John was to visit was the largest city in North America during the eighteenth century. From a population of only 4000 in 1700 it grew to more than 50,000 when the first census was taken in 1790. Several factors led to this rapid growth. We have already seen how the generous offer of religious freedom by William Penn brought many of the distressed peoples of the Old World to Pennsylvania. Even though most of the newcomers did not remain long in the city but moved on to the north and west to settle on farms, their arrival helped to create a flourishing business at the port on the Delaware.

Because only a few articles were manufactured in America many things had to be brought from Europe. The ships that brought the settlers brought goods as well. Merchants imported tools, utensils, cloth, and other manufactured articles from Europe to sell to the settlers in the back country in exchange for products from the farms. Fur traders bought or bartered pelts from the Indians in exchange for imported mirrors, blankets, velvet, and trinkets which they purchased from Philadelphia merchants. In their turn the merchants exported the furs and

—Culver Service

THE STATE HOUSE, NOW INDEPENDENCE HALL, PHILADELPHIA

—From drawings based on Historic Dress in America
  by Elizabeth McClelland
—From Harper's Weekly
  and Godey's Lady Book

THE STORY OF WOMEN'S COSTUMES FROM THE SEVENTEENTH TO THE TWENTIETH CENTURY

1600's   1700's   1800's   1900's

farm products which poured into Philadelphia over the mountain trails and roads which led to the city from the north and west.

The wharves and docks along Philadelphia's waterfront hummed with activity. Eager citizens gathered along Dock Street to greet the white-winged messengers which brought letters from friends and relatives in the Old World and newspapers reporting the latest political developments and advertising new styles in clothing. The city taverns were crowded with sailors from all parts of the world, and many a salty tale was told as sea-going men vied with the fur traders in telling breathtaking stories of adventure.

John would be a part of the hurrying city life which was so different from the life on a farm. He would visit the houses of the city dwellers and accompany his cousin to see the school he attended. He would learn about the colleges where men were taught to be doctors, lawyers, preachers, or teachers. The music, plays, and dances; the libraries, art studios, and publishing houses; the markets, harbor, and ships—John would see or learn about these and many more enterprises, all of which had helped to make Philadelphia the cultural and business center of the colonies.

**A FAMILY ARRIVING AT THE ARCH STREET MEETING HOUSE,
PHILADELPHIA**

Houses in Colonial Philadelphia. The visitor to colonial
Philadelphia found a well-planned and prosperous city. The
principal streets were laid out in parallel lines running north
and south and east and west. The main street, now called
Market Street, was then known as High Street. The business
life of the colonial city centered nearer the Delaware River than

it does today. Second Street was the busiest street in colonial times.

The houses in colonial Philadelphia were built after the Georgian style of architecture. This style of architecture was named for the four Georges, Kings of England from 1714 to 1830. Houses built in this style formed a plain rectangle, with plain sides and back, unadorned by any fancy woodwork or masonry. Sometimes there was a roofed porch at the front of the house, but usually the front door was shielded by a hood supported by columns and was entered from the street level. Public buildings such as the State House and Carpenters' Hall were more pretentious in appearance. So, too, were some of the mansions built by the wealthier residents on the outskirts of the city.

Some colonists brought their furniture with them when they came from Europe, but most of the tables, chairs, bedsteads, and other wooden pieces were made in this country. Philadelphia was the center of the colonial furniture industry. The first Windsor chair was made in Philadelphia in 1699, although it was not known by that name at the time it was made. There is a story that King George I of England was attracted by one of these chairs which had been taken overseas to Windsor Castle in England; hence the name.

Cultural Leadership. The size of colonial Philadelphia, combined with her central location in relation to the thirteen colonies, placed Philadelphia in a position of leadership not enjoyed by any other city in the New World. Thus, Philadelphia early became the center of cultural life in America. Here the great portrait painters set up their studios; musicians found eager audiences; distinguished clergymen expounded their doctrines; scientists explored the mysteries of earth and sky; the best physicians attended the sick; social workers experimented with new institutions for the unfortunate; and inspired educators founded institutions of learning which have served many generations of seekers of truth.

The Junto. One of the most influential groups in colonial Pennsylvania was the organization known as the Junto. The word, junto, means a group of men united in a common purpose. The purpose of the Junto of colonial Philadelphia was to advance the knowledge of its members. The group was organized in

1727 by Benjamin Franklin, who gathered together a number of young printers and mechanics with interests similar to his own. The members promised "not only to love truth for truth's sake, but to receive it impartially themselves and to communicate it industriously to others." In their Friday evening meetings these young men debated all sorts of questions, ranging from morals to metaphysics. But they did more than talk. The questions which they raised prompted many of them, including Franklin himself, to study and experiment with many problems.

For forty years this group encouraged scientific research and built an enviable record for Pennsylvania in the field of science. Today there are three world-famous institutions located in Philadelphia which are direct outgrowths of the activities of the Junto. They are the Franklin Institute, the American Philosophical Society, and the Academy of Natural Sciences.

Leaders in Science. A member of the Junto, John Bartram, became one of America's greatest botanists. He traveled in many parts of the New World bringing back seeds and young trees for his botanical garden. Some of these trees are living today and can be seen in Bartram's Garden in Philadelphia. In 1743 the Junto supplied some of the money which made it possible for Bartram to explore the forests of inland Pennsylvania and to study the plants and flowers that grew in Penn's Woods.

Benjamin Franklin, the organizer of the Junto, was one of the greatest scientists of his time. We all know how, in 1752, he flew his famous kite and discovered that lightning and electricity were related. This experiment resulted in the equipping of many houses and barns with lightning rods. In addition to his studies in electricity and his activities as a publisher and statesman, Franklin was the inventor of the first iron stove and the founder of the first fire company in Philadelphia and the first fire insurance society. He aided in founding the Philadelphia Library Company, the Pennsylvania Hospital, the University of Pennsylvania, and Franklin College, now Franklin and Marshall.

David Rittenhouse was a great mathematician and astronomer. He surveyed the boundary between Pennsylvania and Delaware and made the original surveys for the Union Canal. Few men have had as much influence upon succeeding generations as Rittenhouse had.

With crude instruments of his own making, he measured the transit of the planet Venus in 1769. David Rittenhouse inspired other Pennsylvanians from generation to generation which led eventually to the building of the famous Lick Observatory in California. James Lick, a native of Fredericksburg, in Lebanon County, became interested in astronomy through his friendship with James Davidson. Davidson, who made the first geodetic survey of the Pacific coast, had received his education in the Central High School, Philadelphia. This high school had an astronomical observatory placed there through the efforts of a Philadelphia school director who as a boy had known and admired David Rittenhouse.

Medicine. From colonial times to the present, Philadelphia has been the medical center of America. Some of the finest hospitals of the country and many of the most highly skilled doctors are in the city now, as they have been all through American history. Some of the noted physicians of colonial times were Dr. Thomas Bond, who took the lead in founding

BENJAMIN FRANKLIN EXPERIMENTING WITH ELECTRICITY

ANTHONY BENEZET INSTRUCTING COLORED CHILDREN

the Pennsylvania Hospital, the first institution of its kind in America; Dr. Thomas Cadwalader, who published the first medical book in Pennsylvania; and Dr. Benjamin Rush, in honor of whose medical achievements the Rush Memorial Hospital was named.

The first medical school in the American colonies was established in 1765 as a part of the College of Philadelphia which has since become the University of Pennsylvania. Doctors William Shippen and John Morgan, both natives of Pennsylvania and educated in European schools, were the first American teachers of medicine in systematic courses. Later the Philadelphia Dispensary, the first institution for the medical care of the poor, was established.

From the beginning of the history of the Province, the Quakers had provided relief for the poor people, but when a huge fire destroyed many of the homes in the city it became necessary to care for many persons who had lost everything in the disaster. It was then that an almshouse was built which was known as the Philadelphia Hospital.

Schools. Public education as we understand the term today was not provided for the children of Pennsylvania during the colonial period. The Quakers provided private schools for those who could pay tuition. For a boy or girl to learn to read or write cost one dollar and a half each year; one dollar was charged if only reading was to be learned. The cost of learning arithmetic was fixed at two dollars a year. If a student lived outside of Philadelphia, he was required to pay forty dollars for his board and lodging for the term. In addition to these schools, there were many private tutors who taught the children of parents who could afford to pay for their services.

One of the most successful teachers of Philadelphia children was Anthony Benezet, a French Huguenot, who began teaching in Philadelphia in 1742 and continued until his death in 1784. During the last two years of his life he organized and taught a school for Negroes which was sponsored by the Quakers. Benezet was widely known as a public-spirited man. When in 1755 a group of French Canadians, known as Acadians, was

—Dallin Aerial Surveys and William Penn Charter School

WILLIAM PENN CHARTER SCHOOL TODAY

brought to Philadelphia from Canada, it was Anthony Benezet who looked after them and tried to ease their suffering. This group of exiles was described by Henry Wadsworth Longfellow in the beautiful poem "Evangeline."

Higher Schools. There were no high schools as we know them today in colonial times. There were a number of private schools which were similar to our high schools, or secondary schools. The first of these was conducted by Christopher Taylor on Tinicum Island as early as 1684. The Friends Public School, organized in May, 1689, operated under a series of charters granted by William Penn. As time went on this school came to be known as the William Penn Charter School, as it is still called today. Two outstanding teachers of the school in its earliest years were George Keith and Thomas Makin.

The University of Pennsylvania dates its beginning from 1740 when Reverend George Whitefield established a school which in 1753 took the name of Academy and Charitable School. Two years later, in 1755, the word "College" was added to the charter of the institution. Benjamin Franklin was interested in the early development of the institution. During the Revolutionary War the charter of the college was withdrawn because the state Assembly believed that some of the heads of the school were not in sympathy with the war against Great Britain. The school continued to operate, however, under the name of University of the State of Pennsylvania. After the war, the original charter was restored, and in 1791 the title was officially made the University of Pennsylvania.

Newspapers. The newspapers of colonial Philadelphia usually were issued once each week. They contained very little local news, probably because the publishers realized that their readers were more interested in news from Europe, which to them was news from home. It was assumed that everyone already knew the local news. Editorial comment seldom appeared. The advertisements in the colonial newspapers are interesting to us today. There were few pictures of any kind; those which did appear were rough drawings. The advertisements contained detailed descriptions of runaway indentured servants, letters from persons who were separated from their families, and the latest announcements of goods brought to Philadelphia by ships. Occasionally there were advertisements by teachers of

76

dancing or music, by medical practitioners offering to cure all sicknesses, and descriptions of articles of livestock lost, strayed, or stolen.

The first newspaper to be published in Pennsylvania was Andrew Bradford's *American Weekly Mercury*, begun in 1719. This was the third newspaper to be published in the American colonies. In 1728 Samuel Keimer began the publication of the *Pennsylvania Gazette*. It was this newspaper which Benjamin Franklin purchased in 1729 and continued to publish under the same name until 1766. After Franklin retired, other publishers continued to publish the *Gazette* until 1815. In 1739 Christopher Sauer began his publication of *Die Germantauner Zeitung*, the first German-language newspaper in America. Many other

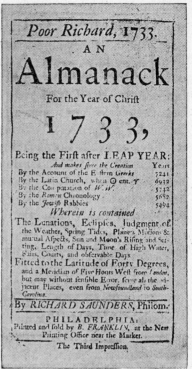

—*Franklin Institute*

POOR RICHARD ALMANACK
Title page of Benjamin Franklin's almanac, published in 1733.

newspapers were published during the period from 1740 to the Revolutionary War, but most of them lasted but a short time.

Travel in Colonial Pennsylvania. The first road constructed by the white settlers of Pennsylvania was the Queen's Road which extended from Chester to Philadelphia. Old York Road, leading from Philadelphia to New York, was opened in 1711. A road from Philadelphia to Lancaster was begun in 1733. This road was extended to Harrisburg and connected with a road leading through Cumberland County to Maryland. Later, a series of roads known as the King's Highways were built in the eastern counties. None of these roads were paved, and in the summer months they were dusty, while during the rainy seasons in the spring and autumn they were almost impassable. These main roads leading out of Philadelphia are still in existence today, but they have been surfaced with macadam

77

or concrete and widened and graded to take care of modern methods of transportation.

There was very little traveling for pleasure in colonial Pennsylvania. Carriages were a luxury which only the rich could afford, and most people traveled from place to place on horseback. In 1756 a regular stagecoach line was established between New York and Philadelphia. Ten years later another line was organized between Philadelphia and Baltimore. A regular schedule of wagon travel was maintained between Bethlehem and Philadelphia as early as 1763. But travel at its best was slow and wearisome. Wayside taverns provided food and shelter for horses, drivers, and passengers. These taverns were not always clean and often were poorly equipped. Very few comforts could be had by a person whose journey was more than forty miles, which was as far as one could hope to travel in a day.

THE HOMEWARD JOURNEY

John Evans was thrilled by the many things he saw in Philadelphia. However, in his mind was always the thought that, while life in the city was much easier than it was in the country

A TOLL GATE ON A PRIVATELY BUILT ROAD

RECEPTION ROOM, SISTERS' HOUSE, EPHRATA CLOISTERS
Visitors to the Ephrata Cloisters write their names on a book placed on this desk. Notice the plank floor, the low ceiling, and the unadorned windows.

where he lived, city people did not have as much pleasure. He told this to his cousin Charles one day, but Charles was unwilling to believe it. Day after day the boys argued about this question at the dinner table, until finally John's father declared that there was a way to settle it—Charles should go home with them and spend a few weeks in the country. School would not open until late September, and there were a few more weeks of vacation.

We shall learn about some of the things which the city boy saw when he visited rural Pennsylvania in colonial times. Perhaps we can decide whether John was right in his argument.

John Evans' father decided to return to the farm along a different route from that which had been followed to reach Philadelphia. Grandmother Evans wanted a new hymn-book and her heart was set upon owning one printed at the Ephrata Cloisters on Cocalico Creek in Lancaster County. Ephrata, or Dunkerstown as it was then known, was several miles west of

Cumru Township, Berks County. John's father planned to set out from Philadelphia along a westward route and pass through Ephrata on his homeward journey. This road leading west from Philadelphia was known as the Lancaster Road, now the Lincoln Highway. At Downingtown, almost a day's journey from the city, the three travelers, Charles, John, and John's father, stopped for the night at a tavern. On the following day they set out again, this time turning northward on another road which led through excellent farming country to the Ephrata Cloisters.

Charles saw bearded farmers at work in their fields and small children whose clothes were cut in the same patterns as those of their parents. This was the part of the country in which the Plain People lived—the Amish, Dunkards, and Mennonites. John explained to his cousin that these people had a way of worship which was different from most religions. The Amish had no churches. They met in private homes for divine worship. The Dunkards, or Brethren as they were known, believed in baptising grown persons by immersion in country streams. The Mennonites, explained John, were greater in numbers than the other Plain Sects. They too were very devout and believed in plain dress and frugal living but were not quite as strict as the Amish about worldly things.

John's father listened to the discussion for awhile and then asked his nephew, Charles, whether he knew anything about the Seventh-day Baptists who lived at the Ephrata Cloisters. This religious group was new to the city boy. Of course, he knew about the Lutheran churches that had been founded in early Pennsylvania by the Swedish immigrants; many of his neighbors in the city were Quakers; his own family attended the Episcopalian Church, and among his schoolmates there were some Presbyterians and a few Methodists. When he explained this to John's father, the man decided he would pass the time while they traveled by telling the boys about the various religious groups that had settled in Pennsylvania to enjoy the religious freedom promised by William Penn.

There were the Moravians, scattered through several counties, north and west of Philadelphia. Their graveyards could always be distinguished from others because their tombstones were placed flat upon the ground instead of standing upright; there were the Schwenkfelders in Montgomery County, the

Baptists in Bucks County, and the Presbyterians scattered in nearly all sections of the Province.

Mr. Evans made a special point of telling the boys about the early Catholic church in eastern Berks County. It was as if he were trying to teach a lesson. When a group of German Catholics settled in Goshenhoppen, now Bally, Berks County, they needed help to build their church. They had no tools with which to work, no horses to haul the logs, and only a few skilled workmen in their midst. The Mennonite farmers in the neighborhood came to their assistance, furnishing the Catholics with material and labor to build their church. He explained how this illustrated the working out of William Penn's ideals of religious life as it should be lived in the New World.

The travelers had reached the Brothers' House at the Cloister. A bearded brother approached them, asking in a mild tone what errand had brought them. John's father stated that he wished to purchase a hymn-book. Obligingly the brother moved

—Luke Swank
Philadelphia Museum of Art
ENTRANCE HALL, SISTERS' HOUSE, EPHRATA CLOISTERS
The low ceilings, the rough stone floors, the doorways which compel one to stoop when entering, are all reminders of the humble and useful lives led by these devout people.

81

off in the direction of a building which was marked as the printing shop.

There were a number of buildings, two of which were much larger than the others. One of these was the Brothers' House in which the male members lived; the other was the Sisters' House. The doors entering the houses were built very low so that grown people were forced to stoop when they entered, and the ceilings of the rooms or "cells" were low. This was their way of teaching humility.

Conrad Beissel, a baker who came to Pennsylvania from Europe, had founded the religious sect that worshipped in the Cloisters. The lives of his followers were devoted to work and worship. The brothers tilled the fields, operated a paper mill, a printing press, a flour mill, and a bakery. The sisters prepared the food, did household chores, and spun the flax and wool into thread from which clothing was woven in the weaving mill. In this way the worshippers lived together, providing for the needs of the entire group and devoutly worshipping God as their consciences directed them.

These things John's father explained while they waited for the brother to return with the hymn-book. Both boys realized that they had learned something of the meaning of religious freedom in Pennsylvania.

LIFE IN THE COUNTRY

The Frontier. The outer limits of the white man's settlements bordering on lands still held by the Indians were considered the frontier. The Pennsylvania frontier differed from the settlements nearer to Philadelphia in several ways. There the lands were still covered with thick forests, broken here and there by some pioneer settler's log hut and an occasional store built for the purpose of trading with the Indians. Frontiersmen made their living by hunting and trapping wild animals. They lived a lonely life, far from neighbors and friends. Only occasionally did they travel to the settlements to exchange the pelts of the animals that they had taken in the woods for supplies at the markets in the settlements. Our interest lies chiefly in the settled areas of the Province, in the farms and villages where the white man's civilization was being firmly established. To these early settlers we owe a great debt.

BEAUTIFUL DESIGNS ON A PENNSYLVANIA GERMAN BARN

The Settlements. Life in rural Pennsylvania was greatly different from the life of comparative ease and comfort that could be found in the city of Philadelphia. There was difficult work to be done. Forests had to be cleared; seeds planted and crops harvested; ores mined and smelted; goods had to be transported over rough roads to reach the markets; and for those who lived near the frontiers there was constant danger from Indian raids. Nevertheless, we shall see that the country people of colonial times had many excellent rewards for their labor.

Because rural Pennsylvanians were not brought into close daily contact with English-speaking people as they were in the city, their way of life was not molded into a pattern. The rural people preserved the culture they had brought with them from the Old World and adapted it to their new life in America. Thus traces of the original cultures can be observed even today by travelers who visit the Pennsylvania countryside.

Their Buildings. When these settlers built their houses they reproduced the types which they had known in Europe. Some sections of the colony reflected the early Dutch influence in their low, squatty buildings. Early travelers in the colony noted that the houses of the German settlers could be distinguished from other houses because the chimney was placed in the center of the house rather than near the ends of the roof. The Swiss barn even today is a distinctive feature of the Pennsylvania countryside.

Their Attire. Too frequently we are accustomed to picture colonial people as dressed in silks and satins, the men in tightly fitted knee breeches and colored waistcoats with a fluff of lace at the sleeves, their heads covered with heavy wigs; the women, hair in curls, in dresses made with snugly-fitted bodices, wide skirts, and ornate trimmings at the necks. Such was the attire of the leisure class, but the working people knew and cared little about such frills. Their garments were made of coarse cloth, either of homespun flax or wool or imported duffel, or kersey. Their boots were made of home-tanned leather. For the frontiersmen, buckskin trousers were very serviceable, and if headgear was needed, the pelt of a racoon or otter would serve to keep the ears warm in winter weather.

Their Furniture. The furniture of a Pennsylvania farmstead of two centuries ago had to be made from materials at hand. The chairs were not upholstered, but they were sturdily built. The cabinetmaker working with rough tools constructed chairs, tables, chests, and wooden beds, applying his own skill to his work. There were no planing mills or furniture factories to turn out highly polished household furniture.

—Hildreth Collection and Index of Historic Prints

A KITCHEN IN A COLONIAL FARMHOUSE
Here are shown the iron kettle, the bellows, the indoor Dutch oven, the bed warmer, the corn grinder, and the candle molds. How many other things can you identify?

—*Philadelphia Museum of Art*

PENNSYLVANIA GERMAN ART

Here are two samples of the art the Pennsylvania Germans brought with them from their homeland. At the left, the dower chest, embellished with birds and tulips; at the right, the decorative plate, gay with dancing couples, is known as sgraffito pottery.

Cooking utensils were made from cast iron. The meals were cooked over open fires in huge fireplaces which were built into one wall of the kitchen. Only iron pans and other utensils with long handles attached could be used. Baking was done in outdoor ovens specially built for that purpose, or in the famous Dutch oven placed in front of the fireplace. Bed coverings were all made in the home. A canvas bag filled with chopped straw served as a mattress, and comforters filled with the down of birds provided a luxurious covering. Diligent housewives quilted lighter bed coverings, incorporating attractive designs into the pattern and producing multicolored quilts, which helped to brighten the otherwise drab interior of bedrooms whose walls were of rough boards with no brightly colored wallpaper to give the room beauty.

Fractur Art. In the field of art, Pennsylvania has made a unique contribution in the *fractur schriften*, or the illuminated writings, of the Pennsylvania Germans. From the Old World they brought the skill of decorating objects they treasured. Angels, birds, flowers, geometric designs, and symbols were drawn on the borders of birth certificates, baptismal certificates, and other important documents. Chests, chairs, and other furniture were painted with these picturesque designs—always in brilliant shades of red, yellow, green, and blue. These designs, especially the heart and tulip motifs, had deep symbolic meaning for the people of the Old World. In the process of transplanting the culture to America the designs lost their significance as symbols. They were retained because of tradition and because they were attractive.

Clearing Farms. The chief occupation found in the interior of Pennsylvania in colonial days was farming. The process of clearing land, planting crops, and building a home out of the wilderness was long and difficult. The first lands to be cleared for farms were those surrounding Philadelphia. These were quickly occupied by settlers. As people continued to come to Pennsylvania from Europe, they pushed deeper into the interior of the Province.

—*Hildreth Collection and Index of Historic Prints*
CLEARING THE LANDS IN PENNSYLVANIA
The inset shows the head of the special ax devised by the frontiersmen of Pennsylvania.

Two methods were employed in the process of clearing the forests. One method, a very wasteful one, was to girdle the trees; that is, to cut away the bark from the trunk of the tree, thus causing it to die for want of sap to nourish it. When all of the trees were dead and dried, the forest was set afire. This was a foolish waste of timber and destruction of wild life that lived in the woods. Frequently the ground was seared and robbed of some of its fertility. The second method, used chiefly by the German settlers, was to cut down the trees, using the timber for lumber and firewood. Then the stumps and roots were dug out with painstaking care to clear the land.

Much of the land in Pennsylvania was rocky, especially in the southern belt which had been on the edge of a prehistoric glacier and was therefore littered with glacial deposits of rocks and stones. Often neighbors organized fence-building parties, in which many persons joined in carrying the stones to the edges of the field, arranging them into stone fences. Stones were also used in building houses and for foundations for barns.

The Crops. The chief crop of the colonial farm was wheat. Grist mills were built very early to grind the grain and extract the flour. These mills were built along creeks which provided the waterpower to run the mill wheels. The surplus of wheat and other grains was hauled to Philadelphia in huge canvas-covered wagons drawn by sturdy horses. Rye and barley were grown in large quantities for the distilling and brewing industries. Corn, or more correctly, maize, was second only to wheat as the principal crop in colonial Pennsylvania. Potatoes and tobacco were not grown in large quantities during the colonial times. The wheat crop was menaced late in the colonial period by an insect known as the Hessian fly, a plague which still besets wheat growers today. According to tradition, the larvae of the Hessian fly were brought to this country by Hessian soldiers in the straw-filled bags which they used as mattresses and pillows. Whether or not this is correct, it does account for the term, Hessian fly.

Livestock. Farm animals were first brought to Pennsylvania by the Swedes. Later, horses, cows, and hogs were brought from England. Very little attention was paid to careful breeding during colonial times, and consequently the original stocks degenerated until more scientific methods were introduced during the nineteenth century. Only one distinct breed of animals was improved in colonial Pennsylvania; this was the Conestoga horse. The German and Swiss farmers of Lancaster County took better care of their animals than did most of the settlers on the frontier, and they were proud of their Conestoga horses. Oxen were used for plowing; horses for draying; cows produced milk for dairy products, but the amount of milk the average cow produced would dismay a modern dairy farmer. Beef cattle were raised and fattened for the Philadelphia market; sheep provided mutton and wool; hogs provided lard and pork products. As time went on, the farms of Pennsylvania produced a surplus of grain and meats which Philadelphia merchants exported to the West Indies and to Europe.

Farming Methods. The land in Pennsylvania is as rich today as it was two centuries ago. The farms have kept their fertility through two hundred years of cultivation because of the methods used by Pennsylvania farmers. From the beginning, farm animals were stabled in barns and the manure gathered from the stables and carried out to the fields. This form of fertilizer gave the soil humus needed for plant life. The crops were rotated so that the growing elements in the soil were not used up by planting to the same crop year after year. By these methods the soil was continually restored.

Farming was especially hard work in colonial times. Grain had to be cut with a curved blade known as a sickle and threshed with a flail; hay was mown with a scythe, raked by hand, and hauled to the shed in small wagonloads. All dairying was done by hand—milking, separating the cream, and churning butter. The colonial farmer had to be a "jack of all trades," ready to repair a building, to know how to slaughter and butcher, and to be ready to lend a hand in helping to build a barn at a neighbor's farm.

Colonial industry. Farming was not the only occupation in rural Pennsylvania. Already the foundations were being laid for the industrial development which makes the state one of the great manufacturing centers of the nation today. By far the most important industry in colonial days was that of iron manufacture.

Iron. The iron industry which today constitutes one of the greatest industries of Pennsylvania was begun in early colonial

—*The Bettmann Archive*

AN IRON FURNACE DURING COLONIAL TIMES
Find the furnace; the cart in which the iron ore was carried; the bellows;
the molten iron. What kind of fuel was being used? What will be the fate
of the huge trees shown here?

times. The first iron works was established in 1716 when Thomas
Rutter built a forge at Manatawny, near present-day Pottstown.
Soon other furnaces were built at Coventry and at Warwick in
Chester County, Colebrookdale in Berks County, and Durham
Furnace, on Durham Creek in northern Bucks County. The first
stove built after the plans of Franklin's invention was manufac-
tured at Warwick in 1742. Near Brickerville in Lancaster
County, Johan Huber built the Elizabeth Furnace which later
was operated by his son-in-law Heinrich Wilhelm Stiegel.

Pennsylvania iron ore was of superior quality, and the inland streams of the Province provided the waterpower needed
to drive the hammers of the forges. The Cornwall mines, near
Lebanon, produced the best ore in America, and a furnace was
built at Cornwall in 1742. From 1730 to 1750 the iron industry
grew rapidly. Shortly after the Revolutionary War there were
fourteen furnaces and thirty-four forges in operation in Pennsylvania. As early as 1750 the Province had become the leader of
the American colonies in the production of iron.

In colonial days the iron ore was mined and carried to furnaces where it was melted and poured into rectangular forms known as pigs. Pig iron is so named because of the appearance of the molten iron. As the metal was smelted from the ore it flowed into a trough which was called the "sow." At various intervals along the sides of the "sow" there were small rectangular vats into which the liquid ore flowed. When the mass cooled, these protruding rectangles, which resembled little pigs suckling at the mother pig, were broken from the long mass known as the "sow." The small rectangles could be handled readily, but the long strip of raw iron was thrown back into the furnace to be remelted because the "sow" was too heavy to be handled before the days of modern power machinery.

In the days when horseback was the only means of transportation, the iron pigs were forged into bars six feet long and then bent into the shape of a letter "U" so that they could be turned over a horse's back and carried from the place of manufacture to their destination. The pig iron was then taken to a forge or slitting mill to be forged into the shape of desired goods such as stove plates, pots, axes, wagon wheel rims, and other metal objects. Frequently the forges had their own furnaces, and some of the establishments known as furnaces also made castings as well as slabs of pig iron.

The iron furnaces used charcoal as fuel. The consumption of timber for this purpose was so rapid that farms in the neighborhood of iron furnaces were valued on the basis of timber still uncut, rather than on the fertility of the fields or the condition of the buildings. Great charcoal pits dotted the countryside where the logs were piled on end, tent-like, while a fire burned inside the enclosure, charring the timbers into black coals. The charcoal was then placed in the fire box of the furnace, furnishing the fuel for smelting iron ore.

Glass. The glass industry was one of the first and one of the most extensive of colonial manufactures in Pennsylvania. One year after the first English settlement in Pennsylvania, in 1683, Joshua Tittery opened a glass house in Philadelphia. In 1707 glass bottles were produced at Schwenksville, along the Perkiomen Creek in Montgomery County. In 1739 a Philadelphian named Caspar Wistar built a glass factory in New Jersey. The most important colonial glass works was built in Manheim,

Lancaster County, in 1763, when Heinrich Wilhelm Stiegel combined the manufacture of glass with his activities as an iron-master. Stiegel is frequently referred to as "Baron" Stiegel, not because he was a titled nobleman, but because of the grand style in which he lived. Stiegel glass is prized by collectors today because of the excellence and beauty of the glassware he and his workmen manufactured. Stiegel's factory made all of the service needed for the table, such as tumblers, bowls, pitchers, vases, salt cellars, cruets, and all sorts of dishes.

Travel in Rural Pennsylvania. We have already seen how travel from one place to another was extremely hazardous and difficult in colonial days. At best the roads leading from one city to another were often almost impassable. In the interior of the Province the roads were often little better than wagon tracks through the forests. The earliest roads followed Indian trails which were footpaths through the woods. White men could follow the trails on foot or on horseback, but they were not wide enough for wagons.

When General Braddock led his expedition against Fort Duquesne in 1755 it was necessary to build a road across the Alleghenies in order that his wagon trains might travel with the marching men. Most of Braddock's route led through Maryland, following much the same course of the modern national highway, United States Route 40. Braddock's road turned northward into Pennsylvania and ran through Washington County. Three years later General Forbes led a second expedition against Fort Duquesne, this time following a route which led through Pennsylvania all the way. From Raystown in Bedford County a new road was built westward toward what is now Pittsburgh. This road came to be the most direct east-west highway, long after its military importance was ended.

Conestoga Wagons. Nothing is more symbolic of the American scene than the covered wagon. It was the ship of inland commerce for two centuries, rolling along rutted roads carrying produce from farm to city and later carrying American civilization westward across the plains, over rivers, deserts, and mountains until the Pacific coast was reached. The name Conestoga comes from the place where these vehicles were first built, along the Conestoga Creek in Lancaster County. Their construction was begun in the middle of the eighteenth century.

A CONESTOGA WAGON ARRIVING AT THE EAGLE TAVERN

Inland Water Transport. In an unsettled country the waterways often were a safer and more comfortable means of travel than the rutted roads and narrow trails by which land travel had to be made. Thus, the rivers of colonial Pennsylvania soon became important routes through which goods reached the cities and harbors on the seacoast from which they could be exported. Durham boats built at the Durham iron furnace carried the traffic on the Delaware River. These boats were very long, sometimes sixty feet, narrow, and light of draft. Open in the center, with high decks on either end, they resembled huge canoes. Each boat was manned by three men who poled it upstream and allowed it to drift down. Loads as heavy as fifteen tons could be carried downstream to Philadelphia. Similar boats were used on the Schuylkill carrying goods from Reading to Philadelphia. It is said that Durham boats carried Washington's men across the Delaware River on Christmas night in 1776.

On the Susquehanna the canoe was used for small loads, and rafts carried huge loads of lumber from the forests north of Sunbury. The canoe was the favorite type of vessel used on the Ohio River before the Revolutionary War.

Social Life in Rural Pennsylvania. The people who lived on the farms and in inland towns extracted from life a rich harvest of pleasure, most of which they made for themselves. There was the quilting bee, the sleigh ride, the husking bee, the thrill of hunting and fishing, the comradeship of group labor on the farm at threshing time, in mowing hay, at barn raisings, at butchering time, when neighbors and relatives gathered to work and chat. There were other gatherings at public sales, at county fairs, at weddings and funerals, at church services, and at harvest home celebrations. Then, as now, friends and neighbors met at the shooting in of the New Year, a custom which originated in colonial Pennsylvania and which still survives.

Religious Life. The guarantee of freedom of worship brought many religious sects to Pennsylvania, especially to the inland counties. Many new sects were formed when members of old denominations differed amongst themselves, some of them withdrawing to form new church bodies of their own. Consequently, the number of sects became large, too large to discuss all of them here.

The German Churches. We have already mentioned a number of the religious groups which came to Pennsylvania from the German-speaking states of Europe—the Plain Sects, as they are called. However, those mentioned thus far were relatively small in number when compared with the large numbers of Lutherans and Reformed Church people.

The Lutherans and the Reformed Church members had much in common during the colonial period in Pennsylvania. They settled side by side in the same communities, and the German language was spoken by adherents of both churches. Out of this common interest grew a unique feature in church history, the Union Church, where the two denominations worshipped together in the same building which they had erected by their joint efforts. Usually they held services alternately; that is, on one Sunday a Lutheran clergyman would conduct the services, and on the following Sunday a Reformed pastor would occupy the pulpit. Many of the fine stone churches which these groups built before the Revolutionary War still stand today, serving the spiritual needs of the seventh and eighth generations of the descendants of the founders of the churches.

93

Schools in Interior Pennsylvania. Prior to 1750 the task of providing schools for children was carried on by the churches in the form of parochial schools. Each denomination provided schools for its own young people. This was not always a satisfactory arrangement, however, because often congregations were too poor to support a good school or to engage a good teacher. There were no laws requiring children to go to school, and many families lived too far from the settlements to send their children to the church schools. Consequently many children grew to adulthood unable to read or write.

Three Types of Schools. After 1750 several new types of schools were organized. One of these was the Neighborhood School, organized by leading citizens of the community. They were supported by charging the pupils tuition fees. Parents paid approximately eight dollars a year to send their children to these Neighborhood Schools.

The second type of school, organized in eastern Pennsylvania in 1754, was known as the Charity School and was established in the German-speaking districts of the Province—Reading, Tulpehocken, Lancaster, York, and elsewhere—for the purpose of teaching the English language to the children of German parents. Most of the financial support for the Charity Schools came from wealthy settlers who were interested in the undertaking. The word "charity" was used to indicate that no fees were charged; it did not mean that the students were regarded as paupers. The Charity Schools were unpopular among the Germans who resented the effort to teach their children the English language, and after 1758 the schools were discontinued.

The Free School was a third type of school established in the Wyoming Valley a few years before the Revolutionary War. The settlers from Connecticut brought with them their ideas about education. They believed that all children should receive at least an elementary education at public expense. The Free School in colonial Pennsylvania was limited to the few New England settlements.

Course of Study. The first schools of colonial Pennsylvania provided only an elementary education. They specialized in teaching the three R's, "Reading, 'Riting and 'Rithmetic." Spelling was taught as a part of the reading exercises. Geography and social studies were not taught. Most of the arithmetic taught was "mental arithmetic"; that is, learning to solve problems without the use of writing materials. Promotion took place when the student was qualified to study a more difficult reader than he had used before. This did not mean that the student owned or used graded textbooks. Because books were expensive, often the teacher had the only book, from which he read aloud while the students wrote what they heard. Writing was done with pens made of goose quills, and every teacher had to be an expert in making and mending such quills. In the church schools much time was devoted to learning hymns, prayers, and other religious subjects.

School Houses in Colonial Times. The first schools which were not held in the churches were log cabins similar in outward appearance to the homes of settlers.

THE HORN BOOK OF COLONIAL SCHOOLS

The horn book was not a book at all, but a frame in which the teacher put the day's lesson and held up for all to see.

The interior usually consisted of a hallway leading into one large room in which all students were gathered and where they remained for the full day's session regardless of grade or age. They were seated on long, rough benches hewn from logs from the nearby forests. Sometimes there were a few stools which served as movable seats. Nearly always there was the dunce stool placed somewhere in the front of the room on which a misbehaving child was forced to sit as punishment, wearing a dunce cap as an additional bit of humiliation.

The teacher's desk was usually in the center of a raised platform at the front of the room. From his elevated position, the schoolmaster controlled the behavior of his pupils, usually maintaining strict discipline. The younger children remained in their seats engaged in writing or drawing, while the older students stood or seated themselves in rows in front of the teacher and recited their lessons to him. After a class had completed its recitation, the members took seats in the rear while the next class came forward to recite. Lessons were usually memorized in those early days; that is why a class period came to be known as a recitation period. There were no blackboards, no slates, no lead pencils, and very few textbooks. The building was heated by an open fireplace or stove, and drinking water was kept in a bucket in the rear of the room.

The Teachers. Most of the schoolmasters of the colonial schools were not highly qualified for the positions they held. The pay was poor, and the position was not held in high esteem by the people of the community. Consequently, very few persons of ability were attracted to teaching. There were some fine teachers, however, and a few of these should be remembered. Enoch Flower taught the first school established in Pennsylvania. Francis Daniel Pastorious, the founder of Germantown, wrote *A New Primmer*, the first schoolbook used in Pennsylvania for the teaching of English. Christopher Dock, a Mennonite schoolmaster at Skippack, wrote the *Schul Ordnung* dealing with schoolroom methods. Dock taught the children of the Skippack School. He is known in Pennsylvania school history as the "pious schoolmaster." Each day after school was dismissed it was his custom to kneel and pray for his students. One evening the pious teacher was found dead, still kneeling with his arms propped upon his desk, his class roll before him.

Academies and Colleges. The Moravians built schools in which their young people could study advanced courses. They founded Linden Hall in Lititz in 1749 and Moravian Seminary in Bethlehem in the same year. Both of these were boarding schools for girls. In 1759 Nazareth Hall in Nazareth was founded by the Moravians as an advanced school for boys. The Presbyterians founded Log College in Warwick Township, Bucks County, as early as 1726. Log College became Princeton University. Other Presbyterian academies organized during colonial times were Dobbin's Academy near Gettysburg, Adams County; the New London Academy and the Chestnut Level Academy, both in Chester County.

In addition to the University of Pennsylvania, mentioned earlier, two other colleges were founded in Pennsylvania before the close of the century. Dickinson College was founded in Carlisle in 1783 and four years later, 1787, Franklin College, now Franklin and Marshall College, was established in Lancaster for the education of the German youth. Benjamin Franklin was one of the founders of the college in Lancaster.

Music. Pennsylvania was also the musical center of the American colonies. There were large immigrant groups traditionally devoted to music. The Irish, Welsh, and Scotch-Irish brought with them their folksongs. The Moravians at Bethlehem and Lititz wrote and produced hymns and sacred music. As early as 1748, the Collegium Musicum was formed in Bethlehem. In his *Autobiography*, written in 1756, Benjamin Franklin wrote of a visit to the city, saying that he was "entertained with good music, the organ being accompanied with violins, hautboys, flutes, clarinets." Bethlehem is a great musical center even today.

COUNTRY AND TOWN IN COLONIAL PENNSYLVANIA

Charles Hughes returned to his home in Philadelphia in time to attend the opening sessions of his school. There he told his classmates what he had seen in the country. He described the surveyors carrying chains to measure the land so that the owners could know the exact limits of their farms. He told of a public sale where farmers purchased cattle, furniture, and implements by bidding at auctions. He remembered that he had watched iron ore being smelted, glass being blown, dishes and tableware molded out of clay, sheep being shorn, flax being spun, and spinning wheels whirring in a corner of the kitchen of the Evans home. Bread was baked in outdoor ovens, and butter was churned in cylinders shaped like tubs. Somehow, Charles thought, the food tasted much better on the farm, especially the vegetables which were cooked soon after they were brought in from the garden.

Charles' classmates agreed that life in the country must be a lot of fun, but John knew that the work was hard. Both boys saw how the people of the city and the people of the country depended upon each other. The merchants of Philadelphia needed the goods the farmers produced, and the country people needed the articles which were for sale in the city. One could not prosper without the other.

Some Guide-posts. We have seen that Pennsylvania's boundary disputes were solved, for the most part, peaceably; that the disputes between the governor and the Assembly gave rise to political parties through which people gave expression to their views. This is the democratic process. In the white men's dealings with the Indians there were some cases of injustice, and the Pennsylvania frontier was ravaged by angry red men in alliance with the French who were enemies of Great Britain. But wiser counsels prevailed and peace was restored.

There were some clashes between groups of settlers, but gradually the many national groups learned to live side by side as friendly neighbors, all helping to build a great state and nation. Perhaps some day the nations of the world will learn to live together and join in building a better world for all of us.

Life in colonial times was very different from life today. We can see how many of the fine things we enjoy today were begun by the sturdy pioneer settlers of colonial times. As we move forward from the present into the future, life will become richer and fuller for everyone if we in our turn continue to build new institutions, invent new machinery, and add to the cultural values we have inherited from the past.

QUESTIONS FOR STUDY AND REVIEW

1. Why did Philadelphia become the largest city in the American colonies?

2. Tell how the Junto lived up to the ideals which it set for its members.

3. What educational advantages would a city boy living in Philadelphia during colonial times have as compared with a boy from the country? What advantages would the country boy have?

4. Which of the following items would have been found in colonial Philadelphia? Which ones then in use would not be found today?

a. Street lamps	d. Fire plugs	g. Coal yards
b. Church bells	e. Street criers	h. Snuff boxes
c. Gymnasiums	f. Hitching posts	i. Powdered wigs

5. What tools or implements would the colonial farmer have used to perform the following tasks:

a. Mow a field of wheat	c. Make cream into butter
b. Thresh a bushel of wheat	d. Haul produce to market

6. In what industries other than farming could a man have found employment in rural Pennsylvania in colonial times?

PROBLEMS AND ACTIVITIES

1. Prepare a list of Pennsylvania towns which would today be in Maryland if Lord Baltimore had gained the boundaries he claimed.

2. Perhaps some members of the class who have crossed the Mason and Dixon Line can report on markers they saw. By what signs and markers can a tourist know when he is crossing from one state into another?

3. Using a standard textbook in American history, prepare a report on Virginia's claims to the Ohio country. How were these claims finally settled?

4. Give an account of George Washington's mission to Fort Le Beouf; the fight at Great Meadows; the building of Fort Necessity. (Suggested source: C. H. Sipe, *The Indian Wars of Pennsylvania*, Chapter V, or any of the biographies of George Washington which are in your school library.)

5. Assume that you are a deputy governor of colonial Pennsylvania during the French and Indian wars. Write a letter to Thomas Penn, the Proprietor, explaining the difficulties that you must meet.

6. Why were the Germans inclined to support Quaker candidates for election, rather than members of their own group? (See *The Pennsylvania Germans*, Ralph Wood, ed., Chapter I, pp. 9–10.)

7. What dangers may be present when paper money is used? What is meant by inflation today? Can you think of any nations whose currency became valueless? What are we doing to prevent such a disaster in our country?

8. Read Benjamin Franklin's advertisement for wagons during the French and Indian War. (Martin and Shenk, *Pennsylvania History Told by Contemporaries*, pp. 43–45, or Franklin's *Autobiography*.)

9. Report on events which took place in your locality during the French and Indian wars. Local historical societies will be pleased to help you. County libraries may contain some interesting stories.

10. Organize the class as a meeting of commissioners and decide on the boundary claims of Pennsylvania and Connecticut. Have some members present the disputed claims and then ask the commissioners to render a decision.

11. Write a diary such as you might have kept if you had lived in Philadelphia in colonial times; if you had lived on a farm; if you had lived on the frontier.

12. Construct models of colonial buildings. Suggestions: a frontier fort, a log cabin, or settler's hut; the State House, or Independence Hall; a colonial schoolhouse; an early iron furnace.

13. Prepare a list of questions which you think the Junto would discuss if it were meeting in your classroom.

14. Perhaps your school newspaper will publish the best essay by a class member on some topic dealing with the colonial history of Pennsylvania.

15. Students who can draw well may be interested in making posters showing colonial costumes; maps showing the early settlements in your county; illustrations of imaginary scenes of colonial days.

SUGGESTIONS FOR FURTHER READING

Boundary Disputes

Wayland Fuller Dunaway, *A History of Pennsylvania*, New York: Prentice-Hall, Inc.; Robert Fortenbaugh and H. J. Tarman, *Pennsylvania: the Story of a Commonwealth*, Harrisburg: Pennsylvania Book Service; Asa Earl Martin and H. H. Shenk, *Pennsylvania History Told by Contemporaries*, New York: Macmillan.

Indian Problems

George Dallas Albert (ed.), *Frontier Forts of Pennsylvania*, 2 vol., Reading: Eagle Press; D. B. Brunner, *The Indians of Berks County*, Reading: Eagle Press; A. B. Hulbert, *The Braddock Road* (Historic Highways of America, vol. 4), Cleveland, Ohio: Arthur Clark; A. B. Hulbert, *The Old Glade Road* (Historic Highways of America, vol. 5), Cleveland, Ohio: Arthur Clark; Francis Parkman, *The Conspiracy of Pontiac*, 2 vol., Boston: Little, Brown; Winthrop Sargent, *History of the Braddock Expedition*, Philadelphia: The Historical Society of Pennsylvania; Chester Hale Sipe, *Fort Ligonier and Its Times*, Butler: the author; Chester Hale Sipe, *Indian Wars in Pennsylvania*, Butler: the author; Charles Thompson, *The Causes of the Alienation of the Delaware and Shawnee Indians*, London: J. Wilkie; Joseph Solomon Walton, *Conrad Weiser and the Indian Policy of Colonial Pennsylvania*, Philadelphia: G. W. Jacobs.

Life in Colonial Times

A. M. Archambault (ed.) *A Guide Book of Art, Architecture, and Historic Interests in Pennsylvania*, Philadelphia: John C. Winston Co.; Arthur C. Binning, *Pennsylvania Iron Manufacture in the Eighteenth Century*, Harrisburg: Pennsylvania Historical Commission; Carl and Jessica Bridenbaugh, *Rebels and Gentlemen: Philadelphia in the Age of Franklin*, New York: Reynal; Edward Potts Cheyney, *History of the University of Pennsylvania, 1740–1940*, Philadelphia: University of Pennsylvania Press; John T. Faris, *Old Church and Meeting Houses in and around Philadelphia*, Harrisburg: Pennsylvania Book Service; John T. Faris, *Old Roads out of Philadelphia*, Philadelphia:

Lippincott; William Chauncey Langdon, *Everyday Things in American Life*, vol. 1, New York: Scribner's; Charles L. Maurer, *Early Lutheran Education in Pennsylvania*, Philadelphia: Dorrance and Co.; *Philadelphia: A Guide to the Nation's Birthplace*, compiled by the Work Projects Administration of the State of Pennsylvania, Harrisburg; *Pennsylvania in Music*, Harrisburg: Department of Public Instruction.

Biographies

Ethel Arnes, *Nancy Shippen, Her Journal Book*, Philadelphia: Lippincott; G. S. Brooks, *Friend Anthony Benezet*, Philadelphia: University of Pennsylvania Press; Ernest Earnest, *John and William Bartram: Botanists and Explorers* (Pennsylvania Lives) Philadelphia: University of Pennsylvania Press; Bernard Fay, *Franklin, the Apostle of Modern Times*, Boston: Little, Brown; Nathan Goodman, *Benjamin Rush: Physician and Citizen, 1746–1813* (Pennsylvania Lives) Philadelphia: University of Pennsylvania Press; G. L. Heiges, *Henry William Stiegel: Life Story of a Famous American Glass-Maker*, Manheim: the Author; Walter C. Klein, *Johann Conrad Beissel* (Pennsylvania Lives) Philadelphia: University of Pennsylvania Press; Lily L. Nixon, *James Burd: Frontier Defender, 1726–1793* (Pennsylvania Lives) Philadelphia: University of Pennsylvania Press.

Fiction

J. A. Altsheler, *Rulers of the Lakes*, New York: Appleton; Thomas Boyd, *The Shadow of the Long Knives*, New York: Scribner's; Elizabeth H. Buck, *Moccasins in the Wilderness*, Philadelphia: Penn Publishing Co.; Elizabeth H. Buck, *The Powder Keg*, Philadelphia: Penn Publishing Co.; Elizabeth H. Buck, *Rifles Beyond Fort Pitt*, Philadelphia: Penn Publishing Co.; Hezekiah Butterworth, *True to His Home*, New York: Appleton; Amanda M. Douglas, *A Little Girl in Old Philadelphia*, New York: Dodd Mead; Amanda M. Douglas, *A Little Girl in Old Pittsburgh*, New York: Dodd Mead; E. R. Gregor, *Jim Mason, Scout*, New York: Appleton; Joseph Hergesheimer, *Tubal Cain*, New York: Knopf; John Jennings, *Next to Valor*, New York: Macmillan; Mildred Jordan, *One Red Rose Forever*, New York: Knopf; R. W. Kauffman, *The Ranger of the Susquehannock*, Philadelphia: Penn Publishing Co.; Charles McKnight, *Old Fort Duquesne; Or, Captain Jack, the Scout*, available through Pennsylvania Book Service, Harrisburg; S. Weir Mitchell, *Far in the Forest*, New York: Century Co.; Edwin L. Sabin, *With George Washington into the Wilderness*, Philadelphia: Lippincott; Elsie Singmaster, *A High Wind Rising*, New York: Houghton Mifflin; Neil H. Swanson, *The Judas Tree*, New York: Putnam's.

UNIT III

WINNING INDEPENDENCE

In 1763 at the close of the long struggle with France for control of North America, the colonists were loyal subjects of the British Crown. Twenty years later, they were citizens of an independent nation. In this unit we shall see how this change occurred.

Pennsylvania joined with the other colonies in the War for Independence. The new nation was born in the State House in Philadelphia, and on the hills of Valley Forge, American soldiers met their severest test and proved their devotion to the ideals of liberty. Citizens of the new Commonwealth served in the army of General Washington. Skilled craftsmen made rifles and cannon for the patriots. From Pennsylvania fields and farms came food for the soldiers.

In the midst of their struggle for freedom, Pennsylvanians were able to create a government for themselves and to help in the building of a national government. While the war was still in progress, the Commonwealth made a settlement with the Penn proprietors and undertook the difficult task of providing revenue for the state to carry on its share of the war. In 1785 the final purchase of lands from the Indians was made.

The first attempts at democratic government were not completely successful, but in 1787 the leaders of the young republic, their faith in the ideals of democracy undimmed, set about the task of constructing a new constitution for the United States. In the Whisky and the Fries rebellions, the constitution was challenged on Pennsylvania soil and found worthy of its high purpose of holding the nation together.

The Commonwealth of Pennsylvania followed the lead of the national government and adopted a new state constitution in 1790.

Chapter VI

THE REVOLUTIONARY WAR

Each of the thirteen original colonies shared in the glory of the struggle for independence which gave birth to our nation. The part which Pennsylvania played in that memorable conflict should bring a glow of natural and proper pride to every Pennsylvanian. The greatest national shrines are here: Independence Hall with the Liberty Bell, in Philadelphia, and Valley Forge where the Continental Army spent the crucial winter of 1777–1778. This was the home of Benjamin Franklin, "Mad" Anthony Wayne, John Dickinson, Robert Morris, Haym Salomon, Arthur St. Clair, and many other leaders in the cause of freedom. Momentous gatherings of men from all of the colonies met in Philadelphia. They united in drawing up petitions for redress of grievances, in declaring independence, and finally in establishing a new nation under the constitution of the United States.

STRAINED RELATIONS WITH THE MOTHER COUNTRY

Preliminaries of the Revolution. The successful conclusion of the French and Indian War brought with it a marked change in Britain's colonial policy. In an effort to appease the Indians, the British Ministry issued the Proclamation of 1763, reserving all the territory west of the Allegheny Ridge from Quebec to Florida, for the Indians. White men were forbidden to settle or to purchase land in this territory. The Proclamation Line, therefore, was designated as running northeast to southwest, along the Allegheny watershed. This seemed a sincere effort on the part of Great Britain to solve the Indian problem in the American colonies. The Scotch-Irish settlers of Pennsylvania, however, interpreted the Proclamation as a check upon their westward-expanding settlements.

The costs of the war with France had placed a heavy burden upon the British treasury, and the British Ministry reasoned that henceforth the colonies should be obliged to pay

**A BRITISH
STAMP**

some of the expenses connected with the defense of the empire. In carrying out this policy, it was decided to make another attempt to collect taxes which the colonists had been avoiding before by smuggling goods into the country.

In 1765 an act was passed by Parliament requiring all newspapers and all legal papers to bear a stamp purchased from British agents stationed in the chief cities of the colonies. This was known as the Stamp Act. The cost of the stamps was not great, but the colonists objected to the principle of taxes which were levied without their having a vote in passing such measures. They were willing to pay taxes levied by their own representatives in provincial assemblies but were unwilling to submit to taxation imposed upon them by a Parliament which, in their view, did not represent them. This attitude clashed with the theory maintained by British leaders that all members of Parliament represented all of the people of the Empire. To the American colonists, however, representation meant a direct voice in choosing their own representatives to their own provincial assemblies; hence their protest, "Taxation without representation is tyranny."

The Stamp Act in Pennsylvania. The Stamp Act was passed by Parliament in March, 1765. On October 5 of that same year the British ship *Royal Charlotte* entered the port of Philadelphia bringing the hated cargo of stamps. The church bells were tolled in the city, and all ships in the port hung their flags at half-mast in protest. The law was to go into effect on November 1. On the last day of October, *The Pennsylvania Journal* appeared in broad black borders, as if in mourning for the dead. Beneath a skull and crossbones appeared the words "Expiring: In Hopes of a Resurrection to Life Again." The German newspaper *Staatsbothe* printed the deaths'-head with a legend which said, "Here is the place for the stamp." Actually there were no stamps to be had because the agent who had charge of selling them was forced by the aroused citizens to put them back into the ship.

Repeal of the Stamp Act. To make their protests to the British government even more effective, Philadelphia merchants passed resolutions declaring that they would buy no

104

goods from England so long as the Stamp Act was in force. Many orders which had already been placed were canceled. Merchants in other colonies adopted similar measures. As a result the boycott of English goods became so effective that English merchants became alarmed and put pressure on the British Parliament to remove the tax. In March, 1766, the Stamp Act was repealed. The news of the repeal of the Stamp Act was greeted with cheers and bonfires, and a special celebration was held in the State House.

The Townshend Duties. The repeal of the Stamp Act served to quiet the disturbances for a time, but in 1767 Great Britain tried another tax, this time on a list of specific articles as they were imported into America. These taxes were known as the Townshend Duties. Paper, painters' colors, lead, glass, and tea were named as taxable goods. The issue of taxation without representation was revived, and the colonists were just as stubborn as before. In the colonies, the merchants renewed their non-importation agreements, and social pressure was brought to bear against persons who served tea on their tables or purchased other articles on the list. The most effective protests against these taxes came from the pen of a Pennsylvanian, John Dickinson. In a series of articles entitled *Letters from a Farmer in Pennsylvania*, Dickinson pointed out the threat to American liberty inherent in Britain's claim to the power of

A PROTEST AGAINST THE STAMP ACT

levying taxes. Dickinson's *Letters* were widely printed in newspapers and read in many colonies.

Once again, as in 1766, British exporters felt the loss of trade resulting from the refusal of Americans to buy their goods. Once again they requested Parliament to remove the taxes. As a result, all the taxes except the one on tea were repealed in 1770. This was retained by Parliament to uphold the principle of her *right* to tax.

The Tea Tax. In 1773 the issue of taxation was revived when the great East India Company tried to dispose of a huge surplus of tea by offering it to the Americans at a price lower than it was in England. They did this by removing the duty always paid by the tea merchant when his ship stopped at England on its way from the Orient to America. The colonists had steadfastly refused to buy the tea and pay the tax, even though it was a real sacrifice for them to give up the tea-drinking habit. It was hoped in London that Americans would forget their scruples about taxes to avail themselves of this bargain price. Unfortunately, the East India Company had also secured the right to sell the tea directly to buyers instead of to tea shops. This enraged the colonial shopkeepers, who saw in it a dangerous precedent which might, if applied to other articles imported from abroad, ruin their business.

Four shiploads of tea were sent to the American colonies—to Boston, New York, Philadelphia, and Charleston. We know the story of the Boston Tea Party and how patriots in that city, dressed as Indians, dumped the tea into the waters of the harbor. In Philadelphia, the tea ship *Polly* was treated more gently. When it was known that the *Polly* and her cargo were sailing to Philadelphia, a group which called itself the "Committee on Tarring and Feathering" warned Delaware River pilots not to act as guides to pilot the ship into port. On Christmas Day, 1773, the *Polly* arrived at Chester. A committee of patriots met the captain of the tea ship at Gloucester Point, New Jersey, and prevailed upon him to come to Philadelphia. There he attended a mass meeting of citizens who convinced him that he should turn the ship back to England without trying to unload his cargo. The captain realized that the Pennsylvanians meant business.

Attitude of the Farmers. Up to this point the quarrels between Great Britain and her colonies had not greatly disturbed the masses of the population of Pennsylvania living outside of Philadelphia. Because the Stamp Act was never actually put into effect, it did not disturb most farmers and frontiersmen, who had little occasion to use legal documents. The German settlers would have found the provisions of that act particularly objectionable because it provided that all papers written or printed in any language other than English were to be taxed doubly. The editors of the German newspapers were bitter in their opposition to the Stamp Act, but there is little evidence that the farmers of Lancaster, Berks, and Northampton counties were much excited about the issue.

So, too, the Townshend taxes did not greatly vex the farmers, who were almost self-sufficient, using the products of their own farms instead of buying imported goods. Although the British government had passed regulations against the manufacture of finished products such as glassware, axes, and metal goods, these were never enforced against the inland industries of Pennsylvania. Consequently, the farmers of the inland counties were able to buy many of the wares they needed from local manufacturers. They could paint their fences and buildings with a whitewash made from slaked lime, and instead of imported teas they drank brews of herbs found in their own meadows and mountains, or brewed a kind of coffee from roasted grains of rye or acorns.

The Scotch-Irish settlers, traditionally opposed to the British, joined in the protests against the tyranny of the King, but the non-English groups were reluctant to appear ungrateful to the nation that had befriended them and their parents in providing a new home with liberty and freedom of worship.

The Boston Port Act. This attitude was changed, however, when in 1774 the British government passed a series of acts, known sometimes as the Coercive, or Intolerable, Acts. These were planned to punish the people of Massachusetts, and especially the people of the city of Boston, for taking the lead in defying the authority of Great Britain. One of the Coercive Acts closed the port of Boston. Even the peaceful German element in Pennsylvania saw in this act danger to the liberty which had been sought and found in the New World.

Committees of Correspondence. Meanwhile, the people of Massachusetts were active. As early as 1772, Samuel Adams had organized a Committee of Correspondence which established a headquarters and operated much like a post office, so that men riding on horseback could quickly spread news from town to town and from colony to colony. Similar committees were organized in other colonies, including Pennsylvania. In May, 1774, Paul Revere, the man who later became the hero of Lexington and Concord, came to Philadelphia to ask the aid of Pennsylvania in protesting against the treatment of Boston and Massachusetts.

In every county of Pennsylvania, organizations were formed to protest against the Boston Port Act and to send relief to the people of the New England city. Because the port was closed, the people of Boston could not secure firewood, food, and other supplies unless their neighbors aided them. Pennsylvania joined in the effort to relieve their distress by raising money.

First Continental Congress. So widespread was the discontent with British policy and so unified were the sentiments of Americans that all colonies were invited by the Virginia

THE HORSE "AMERICA" THROWING HIS MASTER
A contemporary cartoon published in England.

108

House of Burgesses to send representatives to Philadelphia in September, 1774, to form a group which later came to be known as the First Continental Congress. Representatives of twelve of the thirteen colonies attended. Georgia alone failed to send deputies. The meetings were held in Carpenters' Hall because the Pennsylvania Assembly was in session in the State House. Peyton Randolph of Virginia presided; George Washington, Patrick Henry, John Adams, Samuel Adams, and many other famous men attended. Among those representing Pennsylvania were John Dickinson, Joseph Galloway, and Charles Thompson, the latter serving as the clerk of the Congress.

The group drew up a "Declaration of Rights and Grievances," a petition to the King of England, and addresses to the people of England and Canada. A trade boycott against English goods was agreed upon. The members agreed to meet again if their petitions were not answered and if the wrongs of which they complained were not set right. These men were united in their opposition to the acts of Parliament, but they differed among themselves as to how far the colonies should go in resisting British authority. Some wanted to fight it out; others wanted to wait for developments before taking strong measures. John Dickinson and Joseph Galloway advocated the latter policy.

Tories. At this period new political terms came into use. Those who wished to go to the support of Boston with arms, if necessary, were known as Whigs, while those who advocated loyalty to the British Crown were known as Tories. These words were borrowed from the names of the two political parties in England—the Whigs who were opposed to the extension of the King's power and the Tories who favored the King's policies. Many who were Tories in 1774 became patriots in the American cause once war actually began.

HOSTILITIES BEGIN

When the First Continental Congress adjourned, it was agreed to meet again the next year, fixing the date as May 10, 1775. Many events took place before that date arrived, events which plunged the colonies into actual warfare with Britain. The battles of Lexington and Concord were fought in April, 1775, and men's minds were turned toward providing the means to continue armed resistance. In Pennsylvania a recently arrived Englishman named Thomas Paine turned his skilful pen to writing his pamphlet, *Common Sense*, in which he argued that the time had come to make a bold move toward independence. Committees of Safety were formed in all sections of Pennsylvania for the purpose of recruiting military units; groups known as Associators organized into military companies for the protection of the Province. Benjamin Franklin, who had recently returned from England, and John Dickinson took the lead in forming such units.

Washington Takes Command. The Second Continental Congress met as scheduled on May 10, 1775, this time using the State House on Chestnut Street in Philadelphia as its headquarters. One of its early acts was to appoint George Washington as Commander in Chief of the Continental Army. Traveling through Pennsylvania on horseback, the new Commander journeyed to Cambridge, Massachusetts, there to take command of the troops which had fought at Lexington, Concord, and Bunker Hill.

Pennsylvania Riflemen. One of Washington's first acts was to issue a call for companies of riflemen. The first groups to respond to this call were two rifle companies from Pennsylvania, one from Berks County and the other from York County. Washington had observed the effectiveness of the rifled guns used by the Pennsylvania militia serving in the campaigns against Fort Duquesne during the French and Indian wars. He knew that rifles were effective at much greater distances than the smoothbore musket type of guns which New Englanders carried. The British soldiers did not have rifled guns because the skill and craft of rifling was to be found only on the continent of Europe at that time. It was the continental Europeans—the Germans, Swiss, and French—who had brought those skills with them to America. Groups of these people had long been making rifled guns for their own use. The creeks in their localities furnished the power to turn their lathes. The fact that Washington had men who could shoot with rifles was one very convincing argument which prevailed upon the British to evacuate the city of Boston in the spring of 1776 and sail to Halifax, Nova Scotia, to await the arrival of Hessian mercenaries who were equipped with rifled guns.

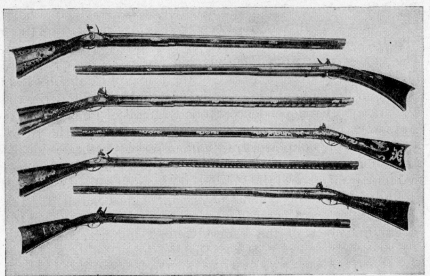

—*Courtesy of the Philadelphia Museum of Art*

PENNSYLVANIA RIFLES

Pennsylvania rifles were one of the most important factors in helping to win our independence. These rifles are also called "Kentucky" rifles because Daniel Boone took them with him to Kentucky.

INDEPENDENCE

Lee's Resolution. The first year of conflict, 1775–1776, was one of armed protest against British tyranny. As time went on the protests took the form of demands for complete separation of the American colonies from the control of the mother country. These demands were voiced in the Second Continental Congress. On July 2, 1776, it adopted the famous resolution offered by Richard Henry Lee "that these colonies are, and of a right ought to be, free and independent states."

The Declaration of Independence. At the time that Lee's resolution was voted upon, Pennsylvania had seven members in the Continental Congress. Benjamin Franklin, James Wilson, and John Morton voted in favor of independence; Thomas Willing and Charles Humphreys opposed it. The other members, John Dickinson and Robert Morris, failed to vote upon the resolution. On July 4, 1776, the formal Declaration of Independence, written by Thomas Jefferson of Virginia with the aid of Benjamin Franklin of Pennsylvania and John Adams of Massachusetts, was presented to the members of Congress for their signatures. Not all members signed the Declaration on

111

July 4, however, and by the time all of the Pennsylvania signatures were affixed, new members had replaced most of those who had opposed Lee's resolution or failed to vote upon it. The nine signers from Pennsylvania were: George Clymer of Philadelphia who was a Justice of the Court of Common Pleas; Benjamin Franklin of Philadelphia who had helped to write the Declaration of Independence; Robert Morris of Philadelphia, a prosperous merchant memorable as the financier of the Revolutionary War; John Morton who had served in the Provincial Assembly for many years; George Ross of Lancaster, a lawyer and former member of the Provincial Assembly; Benjamin Rush of Philadelphia, the famous physician; James Smith of York County, a lawyer; George Taylor, an iron master and one of the earliest members of the Pennsylvania Committee of Correspondence; and James Wilson of Reading and Carlisle, a lawyer.

Greeting the News. After the Declaration was printed, the sheriffs of all Pennsylvania counties were ordered to read the Declaration of Independence at public gatherings. In most counties this ceremony took place at the county courthouses, and the courthouse bells were rung to herald the great event. Most of the old counties have their own liberty bell. But the greatest celebration was held in Philadelphia, when, on July 8, the momentous document was read in the State House yard, and the huge bell which bore the Biblical quotation "Proclaim Liberty throughout the land unto all the inhabitants thereof," was pealed. The bell was cast in London in 1751, by order of the Pennsylvania Assembly, which had selected the inscription twenty-five years before it rang out the message of independence. The bell, the most cherished relic in all American history, is known as the Liberty Bell.

PENNSYLVANIA IN THE WAR FOR INDEPENDENCE

Protecting Philadelphia. At the time of the Declaration of Independence there were no British troops in or near Pennsylvania. Most of the fighting during the early stages of the conflict had taken place in New England. When the hostilities took on the grim aspect of a war which might last for many years, Pennsylvania undertook to defend herself against invasion, as well as to send men and supplies to the Continental Army fighting under General Washington in New England and

112

New York. Because the city of Philadelphia was an important port, an effort was made to block the Delaware River by stretching a chain of logs from shore to shore, and pilots were assigned to guide friendly ships through the network. Several forts were built along the Delaware, and a Pennsylvania navy was hurriedly constructed.

The Pennsylvania Navy. It may come as a surprise to many to learn that Pennsylvania had its own navy before the Congress of the United States organized any naval forces. In July, 1775, the first boat, named the *Experiment*, was launched from the shipyards of John Wharton in Philadelphia. One week later the *Bull Dog* was completed in Kensington. Congress did not act to form a navy until October, 1775. By that time the Pennsylvania fleet consisted of fourteen ships. These ships were propelled by rowers, and each boat carried two heavy guns and smaller swivel guns which could be rotated horizontally, besides muskets and small arms. These vessels helped to protect the city of Philadelphia from attack by British warships which otherwise might have sailed up the Delaware River. In 1775 the United States Marine Corps was organized in Philadelphia.

Preparations. Inland from Philadelphia local committees of safety were continuing to organize military units for home defense. Continental Congress ordered that three special units for the Continental Army, to be known as the Flying Camp, be organized. Two of these units were recruited in Pennsylvania and one in Maryland. The Flying Camp served as a home guard, checking the activities of the Loyalists (also called Tories) and responding to the call of General Washington whenever British armies threatened the capital at Philadelphia. One unit of the Flying Camp, recruited largely in Berks and Northampton counties, rendered outstanding service during the battles fought in New Jersey. Pennsylvania's chief contribution to the main army of the young nation was known as the Pennsylvania Line, commanded by General Anthony Wayne.

Invasion Dangers. After the British troops had left Boston, General Washington moved his army to Long Island. He was forced to retreat, however, when he was attacked by General Howe who had come from Halifax with a strong army. The first approach of enemy forces to Pennsylvania came when Hessian

113

soldiers under Colonel Rahl occupied Trenton, New Jersey, and General Washington was forced to take his army to the Pennsylvania side of the Delaware in order to put the river between his forces and the powerful foe. Excitement ran high in eastern Pennsylvania as men prepared to resist the invaders. Militiamen, Associators, and other units of Bucks and Northampton counties rallied to swell the ranks of Washington's army.

Washington Crosses the Delaware. Then Washington decided upon a bold stroke. Instead of waiting for the enemy to attack him at his headquarters at Newtown, in Bucks County, he decided to attack the foe at Trenton. This daring venture was undertaken on Christmas night, 1776. It meant crossing the Delaware River in boats which had to dodge between cakes of floating ice; it meant that every move had to be secret in order that the enemy might be taken by surprise. Three separate units of the army were ordered to cross the river at different points, but only the one commanded by General Washington succeeded in making the crossing.

The Hessian Prisoners. The Hessians were taken by surprise, and Washington's men succeeded in capturing 1000 prisoners. After an encounter with some other units of the British Army at Princeton, the American Army returned to Pennsylvania, bringing the Hessian prisoners with them. These captured soldiers were paraded through the streets of Philadelphia to hearten the people of the city by the impressive victory that had been gained. Later these prisoners were sent to inland cities in Pennsylvania where they were confined to barracks. Congress made use of many of these men by hiring them out to ironmasters in Pennsylvania to assist in manufacturing cannons and other vital war materials.

Campaigns of 1777. The year 1777 was the most important year of the Revolutionary War (1776 to 1783). For Pennsylvania it was a very trying year because it brought the war to Pennsylvania soil. In order to understand how the war came to eastern Pennsylvania, we must reconstruct the military picture at that time and understand the British plans to conquer the colonies in one ambitious campaign. The main British army under General Howe was in New York City as the year opened, and Washington established headquarters at Morristown, New Jersey, after his victory at Trenton. Washington had selected this position in order that he might protect Philadelphia in case the British decided to march against the capital of the colonies by cutting across New Jersey.

During the summer of 1777 a second British army, commanded by General John Burgoyne, arrived in Canada and soon was fighting its way toward the northern reaches of the Hudson River in New York State. The British plan was to separate the American colonies, cutting off New England from her southern neighbors by driving a wedge from Canada to the Atlantic, through the valley of the Hudson River.

General Howe was to take his army northward along the Hudson to meet Burgoyne's forces moving southward. It was hoped that the junction of the two armies would split the colonies into two sections. If this strategy had succeeded a serious blow would have been dealt to the American cause. It failed because General Howe never read the instructions he received directing him to move northward.

Meanwhile Washington's army waited at Morristown, not knowing what Howe's next move would be. Late in the summer of 1777 scouts informed Washington that the British were loading ships in New York harbor. This might mean several things, of course, but when the British vessels sailed out into the ocean instead of up the Hudson River it looked like an attempt to attack Philadelphia by sailing around to the mouth of the Delaware Bay and then up the river. Accordingly, Washington moved his army back into Pennsylvania to guard the capital city. But General Howe had different plans.

Howe Sails to Baltimore. The chain of logs across the Delaware, the forts, and the Pennsylvania navy would have given the British a great deal to worry about. Instead of risking being turned back by these naval defenses, Howe sailed to the Chesapeake, landed at Baltimore, and then began to march northeast to Philadelphia. Washington's next move was to place his army as a barrier between Baltimore and Philadelphia. Taking stations at Chadd's Ford, on the Brandywine Creek in Chester County, Washington and his men tried to repel the oncoming British troops even though the patriots were outnumbered two to one.

Brandywine. The battle of Brandywine resulted in a severe defeat for the American forces. Washington had received

115

**YORK COURTHOUSE IN WHICH CONTINENTAL CONGRESS MET
FROM SEPTEMBER, 1777, TO JUNE, 1778**

incorrect information which led the American Commander to make poor decisions. After one day of fighting, Washington and his men were forced to retreat to the town of Chester. The young Frenchman, Marquis de Lafayette, who had come to help the American cause, was wounded in this battle. Many of the wounded Americans were taken to Ephrata in Lancaster County where they were cared for by the sisters of the Ephrata Cloisters. Others were taken to Bethlehem in Northampton County where the Moravians nursed many of them back to health. The Americans had lost this battle. The next move of the British was to try to capture the city of Philadelphia.

Meanwhile preparations were being made to continue the struggle, even if the chief American city were to fall into British hands. Congress moved from one Pennsylvania city to another, establishing itself for a time in Lancaster, and later in York, in order that it could continue to function. The precious Liberty Bell was taken to Allentown where it was hidden in the Zion Reformed Church of that city. The important papers of the state and of the new nation were taken to Easton for

116

safekeeping. Philadelphians destroyed bridges which crossed the Schuylkill, and all boats were tied on the eastern bank of that stream. Everything was done to slow Howe's advance.

Paoli Massacre. After the defeat at Brandywine, September 8, 1777, the American Army retreated to Chester, but on the next day they marched to Philadelphia. The British were advancing from the west, intent upon entering the city. Leading his forces westward, Washington's army met some units of the British at Paoli, but again misfortune befell the patriots, and they were forced to retreat, leaving fifteen hundred men of the Pennsylvania Line to protect the route. The muskets of the American soldiers were rendered useless by a

—Historical Society of Pennsylvania

NIGHT ATTACK AT PAOLI

THE BATTLE OF GERMANTOWN, AT CHEW MANSION

heavy shower. The British attacked this small American force on September 20, killing many of General Wayne's men. This encounter is known as the "Paoli Massacre."

The main American Army was maneuvering through Chester and present-day Montgomery County, trying to block the British advance, but, in spite of all that Washington and his men could do, the British crossed the Schuylkill on September 22 and entered Germantown, sending a portion of the army under Lord Cornwallis to occupy Philadelphia.

Battle of Germantown. Even then Washington did not give up the struggle. After reorganizing his troops while they were encamped at Whitemarsh, northwest of Philadelphia, he planned an attack in an attempt to dislodge the British in Germantown. Washington's plan of battle was excellent, but again the Americans were the victims of misfortune. Here a heavy fog concealed the movements of the troops, and to their dismay the Americans found that they had been firing at each other. The battle of Germantown, October 3, must be counted as another defeat for the American forces. The Continental Army returned to Whitemarsh, and the British held Philadelphia.

118

The Defeat of Burgoyne. This gloomy picture was soon brightened, however, when stirring news from the north brought the story of the surrender of the British Army under General Burgoyne at Saratoga, New York, on October 17, 1777. Thousands of prisoners had been taken, and all of New England and most of New York was cleared of the enemy. The terms of the surrender of Burgoyne called for sending the prisoners back to England, but the Continental Congress refused to agree to these terms, insisting that the Hessian prisoners taken at Saratoga be kept here until the end of the war. Accordingly, these captives were marched southward through Pennsylvania into the Shenandoah Valley in Virginia.

Valley Forge. The winter of 1777–1778 was approaching when Washington encamped at Whitemarsh. Hoping for better winter quarters, the Commander in Chief took the advice of his Pennsylvania General, Anthony Wayne, and moved his army to the hills towering above the village of Valley Forge on the Schuylkill. There his men built rude huts and threw up battlements. At Valley Forge there was very little shelter

WASHINGTON'S MEN GATHERING SUPPLIES AROUND VALLEY FORGE DURING THE WINTER OF 1776 TO 1777

119

against snow and bitter cold on the windswept ridges where the Continental soldiers shivered from December, 1777 until the spring of 1778. Food was difficult to obtain, medical supplies were lacking, and many other hardships beset the patriots in their exposed encampments. The heroism of the men who suffered there has made Valley Forge one of the nation's greatest shrines.

Not all of the days at Valley Forge were dreary, however. One day in February, 1778, there came glorious news. Benjamin Franklin, the American agent in France, had succeeded in forming an alliance with that powerful country. This event was honored by a special parade of the troops at Valley Forge. The men marched in columns thirteen abreast, symbolizing the unity of the thirteen colonies. Their new flag of thirteen stripes and thirteen stars cheered them on. Betsy Ross of Philadelphia had made that flag in the previous year. It had been unfurled in battle for the first time at Brandywine.

In spite of the bitter winter, the spring of 1778 found the American Army in a better condition than it had ever been before. The arrival of an able drillmaster, Baron von Steuben, had served to bring order and discipline to the troops. Von Steuben had been a member of the Prussian Guards, the favorite troops of Frederick the Great of Prussia.

The British in Philadelphia. In contrast with the miseries of the patriots on the snowy hills of Valley Forge is the picture of the gay life which the British enjoyed in Philadelphia throughout the same winter, 1777–1778. There, officers and men were warmed by glowing fireplaces in brick-walled houses; ships brought good food and choice liquors to the harbor; there was dancing and banqueting in the public buildings; theatrical performances were staged by a dashing young officer, Major Andre, who later was hanged by the Americans when he was captured and convicted as a spy. The greatest spectacle was known as the *Mischianza*, an elaborate pageant staged on the banks of the Schuylkill in honor of Howe and his soldiers.

The winter moved into spring. April and May of 1778 passed and the British made no effort to attack Washington's men at Valley Forge. Partly as a result of this dilatory policy, Howe was removed from his command in the spring of 1778 and was replaced by Sir Henry Clinton.

BETSY ROSS AND THE FIRST AMERICAN FLAG

The British Leave Philadelphia. General Clinton was ordered to evacuate Philadelphia in preparation for a campaign elsewhere. He set out in June, 1778, overland to New York. As soon as the British troops had abandoned Philadelphia, the Continental Congress returned to the city. After 1778 the chief battles of the Revolutionary War were fought in New York and in the South, particularly in South Carolina and Virginia, the final battle taking place at Yorktown in 1781. However, the removal of the threat of invasion did not bring back peacetime pursuits to Pennsylvania. The state was called upon to furnish war materials needed by the armies, and the Susquehanna Valley was the scene of bitter Indian warfare in 1778 and 1779.

Indian Massacres. The British had a number of Indian friends. These savages and some white traders allied with the Indians organized raids against the remote settlements of New York and Pennsylvania. In June, 1778, a terrible blow was struck by these savages near present-day Williamsport. Settlers were massacred, and property throughout the valley of the Susquehanna was destroyed. Soon afterwards, another force of

121

Indians and Loyalists entered the Wyoming Valley. A force of recruits led by Colonel Zebulon Butler offered resistance, but the patriots were cut to pieces. The marauding Indians conti ued to massacre and scalp their victims, receiving a bounty from the British for every white scalp they took. The feeble resources of local authorities were unequal to the task of fighting off the raiders.

The Sullivan Expedition. In 1779 Congress decided to put an end to the atrocities along the Susquehanna. General Sullivan, one of the chief officers of the Continental Army, was ordered to march his men into the Indian country and destroy their villages. Setting out from Easton, he led his forces into the Wyoming Valley, then northward into New York State, burning and destroying the Indian villages along the route. His army met a large force of Indians and Tories at Newtown in New York. In the battle which followed, the American armies won a decisive victory. Sullivan pushed on, into the heart of the Indian country, punishing the Six Nations and rendering them so weak that they ceased to be a threat to the frontier settlements.

PRISONERS FROM THE WYOMING VALLEY

The military service of Pennsylvanians during the struggle for independence was outstanding, but there was another field in which this state made notable contributions toward the success of the war effort. Wars cannot be fought without weapons and food. Armies must be equipped and transported, and money must be raised. In these fields of service Pennsylvania was the chief support of the Continental Congress. Her natural resources of iron, sulphur, charcoal, and saltpeter supplied materials for weapons and munitions; her fertile farms and industrious farmers provided grain, meat, and vegetables to feed the Continental Army; her skilled craftsmen built sturdy wagons for transport and rifled guns for the troops; and her thrifty merchants raised large sums of money for the American war fund. The iron industries were converted to the manufacture of rifles, cannons and cannon balls, shovels, picks, axes, blades, and wagon wheel rims.

The sturdy wagons built along the Conestoga Creek in Lancaster County served to transport the food grown on Pennsylvania farms and the munitions manufactured in Pennsylvania to the armies in the field. From 1778 until the battle of Yorktown (1781), Washington's main army was stationed in northern New Jersey. Pennsylvania wagons rolled across Coryell's Ferry, Bucks County, carrying the materials necessary for war.

In Philadelphia Robert Morris and Haym Salomon never wearied in negotiating loans to carry on the war.

Loyalists. Pennsylvanians played a noble part in the struggle for independence, and the vast majority of her people rallied to the patriot's cause. But there were some groups that opposed the war and others that actively aided the British. The Quakers and the Plain Sects were conscientious objectors, and although some of their members forgot their scruples and shouldered arms with their fellow Pennsylvanians, the majority of them did not take part in the actual fighting. Some Mennonites emigrated from Pennsylvania to southern Canada and settled in the Province of Ontario, but others joined in raising money and food and caring for the wounded. The Scotch-Irish, Germans, Irish, and continental Europeans generally, were whole-heartedly on the side of the patriots. When independence was finally achieved, all groups became Americans, sharing equally in the blessings of the liberty that had been won.

1. What were the causes of the Revolutionary War? How was Pennsylvania affected by the Proclamation of 1763? by the Stamp Act? the tea tax? the Boston Port Bill?

2. Why did the colonists object to paying taxes levied by the British Parliament?

3. Pennsylvania now uses the slogan "The Nation's Birth State." Explain the meaning of the slogan.

4. Explain the phrase in the Declaration of Independence "That to secure these rights, Governments are instituted among Men, deriving their just powers from the consent of the governed."

5. Why did George Washington call for riflemen to report to Cambridge, Massachusetts?

6. Why was the defence of Philadelphia of such vital importance during the war? What protective measures were taken?

7. Why is Valley Forge endeared to the hearts of Americans today? Independence Hall? the Liberty Bell?

8. Why was Sullivan's expedition against the Indians necessary?

9. Why did the united colonies rely so heavily upon Pennsylvania for war material? Show the importance of Pennsylvania agriculture and industry in providing for the national safety today.

Chapter VII

THE COMMONWEALTH OF PENNSYLVANIA

Lee's Resolution, adopted by the Second Continental Congress on July 2, 1776, declared that "these united colonies are, and of a right ought to be, free and independent states." With this declaration Pennsylvania ceased being a province and became an independent state. The transition from the old form of government to a new one was not easy. During the war there were problems of organizing a new government for the Province, disposing of the large estates still owned by the Penns, satisfying the demands of the many diverse elements among the people, and aiding in the War for Independence.

FORMING A STATE CONSTITUTION

Pennsylvania's Constitutional Convention. On May 10, 1776, more than two months before the Declaration of Independence was signed, the Continental Congress asked all of the colonies to form new governments. The Congress believed that the provincial governments would be inclined to take the side of the King and of Great Britain in the struggle between the colonies and the mother country. Then, too, Congress may have foreseen the day when independence would require the colonies to establish governments of their own. At this request of Congress, therefore, Pennsylvania set about the task of writing a constitution to replace the Charter of Privileges which had been in force for seventy-five years. The experience gained in conducting the affairs of the Province proved useful in forming a state government.

A new constitution might have been drawn up by the existing Provincial Assembly. This body had responded fairly well in the past to the demands of the people for strong measures of protest against the acts of the British Ministry and Parliament. Nevertheless, when it came to actual rebellion, the people of Pennsylvania ignored the Assembly and elected a convention for the purpose of forming a new constitution.

The main objection to the Provincial Assembly was that it was not truly representative of all sections of the Province. In February, 1776, the apportionment of representatives in the Provincial Assembly had been revised to give additional seats to the newer counties. This revision was still unsatisfactory to the new counties, however, since the old counties of Philadelphia, Chester, and Bucks had thirty votes, while the five new counties were given only twenty-eight votes altogether. In electing members to the constitutional convention of 1776 each county was allowed eight votes. The city of Philadelphia was separated from Philadelphia County and each given eight votes.

Ninety-six delegates attended the convention which met for the first time in July, 1776. The meetings were held in Independence Hall, Philadelphia—some of the sessions coinciding with the meetings of the Continental Congress which were held in an adjoining room. Benjamin Franklin became the president of the Pennsylvania convention. Franklin's popularity was so great that he was elected to serve in both the Continental Congress and the Pennsylvania convention at the same time, moving from room to room in the State House while debates were being held in both chambers. George Ross became the vice-president of the state constitutional convention and Jacob Garrigues served as secretary.

Disregarding the old Provincial Assembly completely, the convention immediately took over the task of running the affairs of Pennsylvania. The old Provincial Assembly continued to meet for a time, but it was unable to enforce its authority since the people believed in the convention. On September 26, 1776, the Assembly passed a resolution denouncing the constitutional convention and then adjourned, never to meet again.

The First Constitution. The constitutional convention of Pennsylvania remained in session from July 11, 1776, to September 28 of the same year. Much of this time the convention was dealing with urgent problems caused by the war. The actual drafting of a constitution was not begun until the final days of the session and then it was done hurriedly.

The full title of the new constitution was the Bill of Rights and Constitution of the Commonwealth of Pennsylvania. The word, commonwealth, means a government organized by the whole body of the people, or a state in which the people rule.

126

The use of the word commonwealth in the title of Pennsylvania's first constitution explains the official designation used today—the Commonwealth of Pennsylvania.

The new constitution represented the first attempt by the people to set up a government of their own. It provided for a unicameral legislature (that is, a law-making body of only one house) to be known as the Assembly. It was to be elected annually. Representation in the Assembly was based upon the number of persons paying taxes in each county and in the separate district of Philadelphia. In 1776 the County of Philadelphia still included the area which today forms Montgomery County, which was not organized until 1784.

The right to vote was given to all free men over twenty-one years of age who paid taxes on property and had lived in the state for a period of at least one year.

The executive branch of the government was to consist of a Supreme Executive Council of twelve members—one member from each of the eleven counties and one from the city of Philadelphia. Members of the Council were to serve for three years. The President of the Council was to be the head of the government. He was also to be chosen for a term of three years from one of the twelve members of the Supreme Executive Council by a joint vote of the Council and the Assembly.

A unique feature of the constitution was the provision calling for a Council of Censors. This was a body consisting of two men from each county and the city of Philadelphia whose duty it was to meet every seven years to pass judgment upon how the affairs of the Commonwealth had been administered. Amendments to the constitution could be made only if two-thirds of the Council of Censors voted to call a convention.

The new constitution was not submitted to the people for ratification. By the proclamation of the convention it was declared to be the law of the Commonwealth. The Commonwealth government was inaugurated when the newly-elected members of the Assembly met in Philadelphia on November 28, 1776. The first President of Pennsylvania was Thomas Wharton, Jr., of Philadelphia.

Not all of the people in Pennsylvania were agreed on the question of adopting the new constitution. In the convention itself there had been two groups representing opposing points of view. While all of the delegates were in favor of forming a new government, there were differences over the kind of government best suited to the new state. Benjamin Franklin, Joseph Reed, and George Bryan, who were the leaders of the radical group, wished the new government to be as democratic in form as possible. With the spirit of revolution in the air, these men triumphed. Men like Robert Morris and John Dickinson were more conservative in their point of view. These members of the convention objected to the new constitution on the grounds that it had been drawn up too hastily and had too many weak points. Political parties formed along the lines of those who favored the new government, who were known as Constitutionalists, and those who opposed it, who were called the Anti-Constitutionalists. Most of the opposition came from the eastern counties of the state. One reason for their opposition was the fact that they suffered in the reshuffle of representation which gave more votes in the Assembly to the newer counties.

PROBLEMS OF THE NEW GOVERNMENT

Carrying on the War. Governments organized during wartime are confronted with many perplexing problems which must take first place over the administration of civil affairs. The officers of the young Commonwealth of Pennsylvania were busy meeting the demands of the Continental Congress for men and supplies for the army. Laws were passed confiscating the property of Loyalists, and several prominent residents of Philadelphia were arrested on suspicion of acts of treason.

The finances of the state were a source of grave concern. Paper money was printed and issued with nothing for security except the promise of the Commonwealth to pay in gold or silver at some future time. Thus, the currency was good only so long as people believed the state's promises to pay. As time went on, more and more money was printed. The colonies still were not winning the war and people began to doubt whether the state could ever make good its promises. The paper money became almost worthless even though the Assembly attempted to maintain the credit of the state by levying a fine upon those who refused to accept the new issues of money at their face value.

The Penn Estates. In 1759 Benjamin Franklin estimated the value of the Penn estates in Pennsylvania at approximately

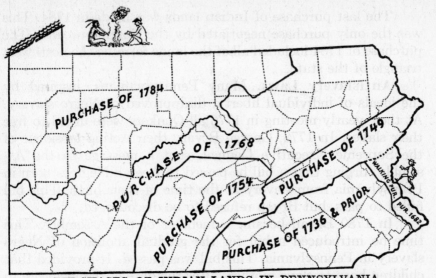

PURCHASES OF INDIAN LANDS IN PENNSYLVANIA

A certain portion of the lands gained by the Walking Purchase is shown by a dash line, as the actual line has never been clearly determined.

10,000,000 English pounds, or $50,000,000. When Pennsylvania became independent, the new state government wished to gain control of the vast land estates still owned by the Penn family. Their first action was to suspend the Penn rights until some plan could be worked out to pay the Penns for their lands.

By the terms of the Divesting Act, passed by the Assembly on November 27, 1779, the Penns were permitted to keep their private estates and all lands which had been surveyed for them before July 4, 1776. But there were great tracts of land included in the original grant to William Penn which had never been surveyed. These lands were to become the property of the Commonwealth. The Penn heirs were paid 130,000 English pounds (more than one-half million dollars) for these lands.

The End of the Indian Problem. We have seen how General Sullivan led an expedition against the Indian villages in the Wyoming Valley in 1779, ridding eastern Pennsylvania of all danger from further Indian raids. But those who had migrated to the western portions of Pennsylvania had been forced to protect themselves against Indian raids throughout the Revolutionary War. General William Irvine, commanding local militiamen, had held the western frontiers secure against Indian raids during this time.

129

The last purchase of Indian lands was made in 1784. This was the only purchase negotiated by the Commonwealth. The purchase of 1784 included all of the lands forming the northwest triangle of the state.

Antislavery Laws. Many Pennsylvanians, inspired by the ideals of individual liberty, disapproved of Negro slavery. At their yearly meeting in 1776 all Quakers were urged to free their slaves. In 1778, George Bryan, then Acting-president of the Supreme Executive Council, sent a message to the Assembly, urging that a bill be passed to free all Negroes born in Pennsylvania from slavery at the time of their birth. This bill failed to pass, but Bryan refused to be discouraged.

In 1780 Bryan became a member of the Assembly. This time he introduced a bill for the gradual abolition of Negro slavery in Pennsylvania. This bill was passed. It provided that children born to slave mothers after the date of the law were to be set free when they reached the age of twenty-eight. All living slaves were to be registered by their owners before November 1, 1780, and all Negroes born after that date would become free at the age of twenty-eight. The twenty-eight year period of service meant that no slaves were really freed by this act before

—*Ewing Galloway*
SIGNING OF THE CONSTITUTION OF THE UNITED STATES IN PHILADELPHIA, 1787

the year 1808, and slaves already living at the time the act was passed would never be free during their lifetime. Slavery continued to exist in Pennsylvania as late as 1840. Sixty-four slaves were listed in the census of that year.

THE FEDERAL CONSTITUTION

The Constitutional Convention of 1787. The lessons learned by the lawmakers during the early years of independence revealed certain weaknesses in both the state and federal governments. The period of experiment was passing and a new and permanent federal constitution was drawn up in Philadelphia in 1787. Philadelphia had been host to the Continental Congress throughout the Revolutionary War and the city continued to be the capital of the colonies during the period of the Confederation. When the states were asked to send delegates to a convention to draft a new constitution to replace the Articles of Confederation under which the young republic had been governed, Philadelphia was again chosen as the meeting place. Delegates from all of the states assembled in May, 1787, and continued to meet throughout the summer. The new constitution was completed on September 17, 1787. Among the distinguished members of the convention who represented other states were Alexander Hamilton of New York, James Madison of Virginia, and John Dickinson, who had moved from Pennsylvania and now represented Delaware. George Washington, representing Virginia, served as President of the convention. The Pennsylvania delegation included Benjamin Franklin, Thomas Mifflin, Robert Morris, George Clymer, Thomas Fitzsimmons, Jared Ingersoll, James Wilson, and Gouverneur Morris—all Philadelphians. The aged Franklin did not participate in the debates on the floor of the convention. His chief role was that of advisor to the younger men who took the lead in drafting the constitution. Often he was able to suggest ways to compromise differences of opinion that arose among the members of the convention, thus enabling the group to continue its work when a deadlock threatened.

Ratifying the Federal Constitution. The new constitution of the United States was to go into effect when it had been ratified by the people of nine of the thirteen states. Delaware was the first to ratify and Pennsylvania was second. The speedy

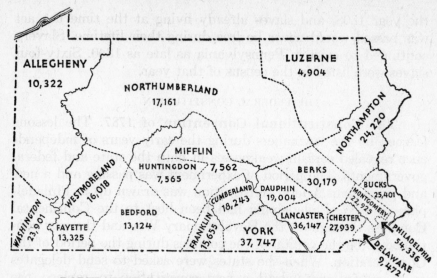

POPULATION DISTRIBUTION BY COUNTIES IN 1790

action on the part of Pennsylvania did not mean, however, that the people of the state were unanimously in favor of the new constitution. On the contrary, a spirited campaign was carried on in an attempt to defeat its ratification. Most of the opposition came from frontier counties (Westmoreland, Washington, Fayette, and Franklin) where the spirit of democratic independence was strongest. The pioneers were inclined to look suspiciously on all authority, and they feared that the new constitution with its provisions for a strong national government was a threat to their newly-won independence. In the older regions around Philadelphia, businessmen had come to see the need for a strong government which would protect their business interests and would enable the new nation to develop economically.

The election of delegates to the ratifying convention was held in November, 1787. Many of the contests were decided by close margins, but when the votes were counted the supporters of the new federal constitution had won the day. On November 21, 1787, the delegates met in Philadelphia. For three weeks they debated the issue, but when the final vote of the convention was taken it was overwhelmingly in favor of ratification.

The National Capital. The State House in Philadelphia, commonly known as Independence Hall, served as the Capitol for both the state and federal governments during the Revolutionary War. In 1789 the national capital was moved to New York. There, George Washington was inaugurated as President of the United States. The following year, however, Congress decided to accept the offer by Virginia and Maryland of a tract of land on the Potomac River for a permanent national capital. In the same bill which established the District of Columbia, it was stated that the capital would return to Philadelphia for a period of ten years, allowing time for the construction of government buildings in the new city of Washington.

First Political Parties. During the early years of our national history the first national political parties were organized. The people of the United States were divided in their opinions of how much power had been given to Congress and the federal government by the new federal constitution. One group, under the leadership of Alexander Hamilton, believed in a strong national government and insisted that Congress hold not only the powers specifically granted to it by the constitution but other powers which could be implied. The opposing group, led by Thomas Jefferson, believed that the Congress had only the powers stated by the constitution. All other authority, according to this view, remained with the individual state. While this was the large issue over which the two groups were divided, there were other differences. The followers of Hamilton, who were called Federalists, were of aristocratic background and they honestly doubted the ability of the common people to govern themselves. Jefferson and his friends, who were known as Democratic-Republicans, had more faith in the good sense of the common people. They wished to have strong state governments which were more directly responsible to the wishes of the people and a national government which would not be strong enough to become tyrannical or oppressive.

The two great political parties formed during Washington's administration over these national issues. However, the views which their members held on national issues often influenced the way they felt toward state issues. Thus the original parties in Pennsylvania—the Constitutionalists and the Anti-Constitutionalists—disappeared in time as state and national questions became so intertwined that only national party organizations were maintained.

The Whisky Rebellion. An excise is a tax levied upon goods manufactured and sold within a country. Americans pay excises on tobacco, liquor, and other articles manufactured in this country. The federal constitution of 1787 gave Congress the power to levy excises provided that such taxes be uniform throughout all states. In 1791, upon the insistence of Alexander Hamilton, then Secretary of the Treasury, an excise law was enacted by Congress fixing a tax of eight cents a gallon upon whisky—the money to be collected from the distillers by agents of the federal government. This law met with opposition in the western counties of Pennsylvania, where angry farmers and distillers refused to pay the tax in open defiance of the government of the United States. The uprising is known as the Whisky Rebellion.

Because the farmers of western Pennsylvania lived a great distance from the eastern markets, they found it difficult to sell their wheat, rye, and corn. The cost of hauling the grain over the Allegheny Mountains to Philadelphia was so high that they could not sell at a profit. If the grain were converted into whisky, however, the greater value of a smaller quantity made it possible to transport the liquor and make a profit. One horse could carry only four bushels of rye on his back, but if rye were transformed into whisky, one horse could carry the equivalent of twenty-four bushels of rye. For this reason the farmers of western Pennsylvania converted their produce into whisky, and its sale was their chief source of income. Because money was scarce in the newly settled areas west of the Alleghenies, the farmers maintained that they did not have the cash with which to pay the tax. Whisky, itself, was frequently used as a means of exchange in place of money when the western settlers transacted business among themselves. A tax on whisky, they believed, would ruin their business.

Trouble began when federal agents first entered the western counties to collect the taxes. The agents were roughly treated by bands of settlers bent upon preventing them from making collections. After a few months of disorder, however, there was comparative quiet in the region. A number of distillers paid their taxes, and there was a prospect of a peaceful settlement of the issue.

134

—Reprinted from The Story of America
in Pictures by Alan C. Collins,
Doubleday, Doran, and Company

THE WHISKY REBELLION
Tarring and feathering federal officer who tried to collect the tax on whisky.

In 1794 trouble broke out anew when the federal government began to arrest the distillers who had continued to refuse to pay the tax. The offenders were served with warrants ordering them to Philadelphia for trial. This action, forcing them to travel three hundred miles to Philadelphia, further enraged the farmers. With some justification they maintained that courts should be established west of the mountains in order that they might be tried nearer their homes.

At first the rebellious farmers prepared to organize themselves for open war against the federal authorities. Many of them had had plenty of military experience in the Revolutionary War and were ready to shoulder arms again if they were to be subjected to what they considered oppression. In July, 1794, a group organized as militiamen marched to the home of General John Neville near Pittsburgh to demand that he surrender his commission as a government inspector and turn over the official papers containing the evidence against the offenders. When General Neville refused, a fight took place and blood was shed.

During the rest of the summer the farmers continued to prepare for actual resistance. On August 7, President Washington issued a proclamation warning the offenders that the laws must be obeyed and expressed his "earnest wish to avoid a resort to coercion." This was the first challenge to the authority of the new government of the United States and could not be ignored.

The militia of eastern Pennsylvania and New Jersey, Maryland, and Virginia were called by the President to march against the rebels in the western counties of Pennsylvania and also against a section in western Virginia which was also protesting against the whisky tax with violence.

At the same time a commission of five men was appointed to investigate the troubles in western Pennsylvania. This was a joint commission of the state and federal governments acting together. The commission set up its headquarters at Pittsburgh.

The insurgents met at Parkinson's Ferry, now Monongahela, in Washington County, on August 14, 1794. There they decided to send delegates to the commissioners to discuss a way of settling the dispute. The commission held that before any discussion of issues could take place, the people of the region must pledge themselves to submit to the law peaceably. The commissioners therefore requested that the rebellious farmers sign statements promising to recognize the federal authority. When the statements were collected, the commission declared that they were unsatisfactory and sent James Ross to Philadelphia to report to the state and federal governments. As a result the armies that had been organized were ordered to cross the mountains and prepare to restore order by force. General Lee of Virginia was placed in command of the combined armies. Meanwhile, Washington, Hamilton, and several other officials traveled to Carlisle in order to be closer to the scene of events.

Awed by the powerful forces being organized against them, the rebellious farmers held another meeting at Parkinson's Ferry on October 2. This time they agreed to submit to federal authority, and delegates were sent to Carlisle to assure President Washington that order would be restored. Another group met with General Lee at Uniontown and gave similar assurances. Early in November the main forces of the army were withdrawn. No further violence followed. The government of the United States had shown that it could enforce its laws.

The Fries Rebellion. A second test of federal authority developed in eastern Pennsylvania a few years later. In 1798 Congress levied a tax upon land, houses, and Negro slaves. There were few slaves in Pennsylvania, but the tax fell heavily on the owners of houses and farms. The Germans living in

Northampton, Bucks, Berks, Lehigh, and Montgomery counties, particularly, did not understand the new tax. When the federal assessors came to evaluate their property, they resisted with violence. John Fries, an auctioneer living in Bucks County, became the leader of the resistance. When some of the farmers were arrested and taken to Bethlehem for trial, Fries collected a band of followers, marched them to Bethlehem, and forced the government officials to release the prisoners.

President John Adams issued a proclamation declaring that the acts of Fries and his followers were treason against the United States government. Governor Mifflin declared that the President was determined to call for military force to quell the disorders because "the essential interest of the United States demands it." A force of militiamen commanded by Brigadier General William MacPherson entered eastern Pennsylvania and began to arrest the rioters. John Fries was captured while hiding in a swamp. This display of force soon quieted the disturbances. None of the farmers was prepared to challenge the United States Army. Again the federal government had proved that it was strong enough to enforce its laws.

Fries and fourteen others were tried for treason, and several others were charged with minor offenses. Fries was found guilty of treason and sentenced to be hanged, but in 1800 President Adams pardoned him and all of the others who had been involved.

PENNSYLVANIA UNDER THE FEDERAL CONSTITUTION

The Constitutional Convention of 1790. The first constitution of the Commonwealth had been written during the war emergency. Because of the haste with which it had been drawn up, there were several impractical and unpopular features in it. In the meantime, years of experience in government, both state and national, had shown how some of the laws could be improved. Between 1776 and 1787 when the new federal constitution was framed there had been a number of demands by the citizens of Pennsylvania for a new state constitution. But these demands had always been blocked by the refusal of the Council of Censors to issue a call for a state constitutional convention. In 1789 the Assembly acted upon its own initiative and instructed the counties to elect delegates for a convention

137

to meet in Philadelphia. The convention met for several months, completing a new constitution in February, 1790. The constitution was put into effect in September of the same year and it remained in force for forty-eight years—until 1838.

The New Constitution. The Supreme Executive Council of the constitution of 1776 was unwieldy. When twelve men were charged with the duty to carry out the laws, it was difficult to fix responsibility on any one of them. The addition of new counties would logically have called for the addition of new members to the Supreme Executive Council. When we consider that there are sixty-seven counties in Pennsylvania today, we can see how impractical it would be to have sixty-seven persons equally responsible for the executive branch of the government. The provision of the federal constitution centering executive power in the hands of one man, the President of the United States, served as an example to the framers of the second state constitution. This constitution provided for a governor to be elected for a term of three years. The Governor could succeed himself in office, but no one was to serve for more than nine out of twelve consecutive years.

Another unpopular feature of the first constitution was the unicameral legislature. Many persons felt that a single legislative body could be swayed by the whims of the people without giving due consideration to laws that were passed. Here again, as in the case of the executive branch, the delegates adopted the plan of the federal constitution and organized the state legislature into two houses, a House of Representatives and a Senate. The Senators were to be elected for a four-year term, and members of the lower house for a one-year term. No provision was made for a Council of Censors. The second constitution remained in force down to 1838.

The first Governor to be elected under the new constitution was Thomas Mifflin. At the time of his election he was not closely associated with any political party. During his first term as Governor, however, he came to sympathize with the views of Thomas Jefferson and his followers. When he was a candidate for re-election in 1793, therefore, it was as a member of the Democratic-Republican party. Thus Mifflin became the first of a long line of Democratic-Republican governors to control the executive department of the state.

138

A New State Capital. The most important issue in state politics during Mifflin's administrations was the location of the state capital. As settlers began to fill up the western and northern lands, pressure on the government increased to move the capital nearer the geographic center of the state.

The demands of the western settlers received additional support when in 1793 an epidemic of yellow fever struck the city of Philadelphia. The disease had been brought to the city by ships from West Indian ports. More than four thousand deaths occurred as a result of the plague and more than one-half of the population of the city fled during the summer months. Officials of both the federal and state governments moved to Germantown during this period. For the next three years the city was visited annually by an outbreak of the disease and, although never again was the epidemic of such serious proportions, it furnished a strong argument for moving the seat of the government.

In 1795 a movement began to select Carlisle as the new capital. A bill passed the state House of Representatives but failed in the Senate. The following year the House tried again. Reading and Carlisle were voted upon, but both failed, and Lancaster was selected by a majority of two votes. Again the Senate failed to approve any change. In 1798 a third effort was made to change the capital, this time to Wrightsville in York County. The Senate by now was willing to agree to a change of the capital but favored Harrisburg for the site. The House refused to accept Harrisburg, however. Finally in 1799 both houses of the Assembly agreed to move the seat of government to Lancaster. The first session of the Assembly to be held in Lancaster opened in December, 1799. Here the capital remained until 1812 when the offices of the state government were moved to Harrisburg. Sessions of the state Assembly were held in the courthouse in Harrisburg until 1821, when the newly constructed capitol was ready for occupancy.

The removal of both the state and national capitals within one year was a blow to the prestige of Philadelphia. But the United States Mint remained there; the National Bank of the United States continued to be the center of financial activity; and the harbor of Philadelphia was to be the chief port of entry for many more years. Philadelphia continued to be the largest city in the United States until she was surpassed by New York in 1830.

Looking Back. After the victory over France in 1763, England wished to strengthen the bonds which held her empire together. No one, either in England or America, foresaw that the attempt would result in independence for the American colonies. The British government felt that the colonists should bear part of the cost of defending their country, but the Americans were impatient with any restrictions imposed upon them by the mother country. Efforts to tax the colonists not only failed completely, but increased their determination to resist. When resistance took the form of war, the Continental Congress assumed the task of governing the colonies. At first, most of the colonists believed that they were fighting for redress of their grievances against Britain. Soon complete independence became the goal. In the war, Pennsylvania had an important role which the state played nobly. At the time, the American colonists could not know that their gallant struggle for independence would have far-reaching effects, inspiring oppressed peoples in many parts of the world to fight for their freedom.

The winning of independence from Great Britain brought new problems in government to the newly-created states of North America. The change from provincial governments under royal and proprietary authority to self-governing states under a democratic federal constitution called for patience and wisdom while experiments were being tried. It would have been an empty victory, indeed, if, after securing independence from Great Britain, the states had fallen to warring among themselves, or if the blessings of liberty so bravely won had not been made secure. Fortunately for us today, these blessings are ours to be enjoyed under a strong and united nation.

We have seen how Pennsylvania played an important part in establishing the new government. It was here that the federal constitution was formed, appropriately in the same building where the Declaration of Independence had been signed. Philadelphia was the capital of the United States during most of the critical years. Two severe tests of the authority of the new federal government took place on Pennsylvania soil— the Whisky Rebellion in the western counties, and the Fries

Rebellion in the east. Both were settled in ways which showed that the United States government was strong enough to enforce its laws.

QUESTIONS FOR STUDY AND REVIEW

1. Why was it necessary to form a new government for Pennsylvania in 1776? What difficulties confronted the framers of the first state constitution?

2. How were the members of the Penn family treated by the independent government of Pennsylvania? Do you think the Penns received fair treatment?

3. Outline the various steps taken by Pennsylvania to abolish Negro slavery. Were all slaves freed immediately? What reasons can you suggest for Pennsylvania's leadership in the antislavery movement in America?

4. From the preamble of the United States constitution find the purposes which the constitutional convention of 1787 set for itself.

5. In what respects was the second state constitution an improvement over its predecessor?

6. Why was the Whisky Rebellion in western Pennsylvania of national importance? the Fries Rebellion?

7. What arguments were there in favor of moving the state capital?

8. Review the life and services of Benjamin Franklin to the state and the nation. Where would you rank him among the American statesmen of his time? of all times?

PROBLEMS AND ACTIVITIES

1. Show the difference between the colonists theory of "actual" representation and the British theory of "virtual" representation. (See *The History of the United States*, by W. B. Guitteau, pp. 111–112.)

2. In a textbook on American history find the meaning of the following terms: The Declaratory Act; Writs of Assistance; Quartering Act; Quebec Act; the Parson's Cause. Show how they aided in bringing on the Revolutionary War.

3. Conduct a meeting protesting against the Stamp Act. Prepare arguments opposing the act and in its favor.

4. Read one of John Dickinson's *Letters* to the class. (See *Pennsylvania History Told by Contemporaries*, by Martin and Shenk, pp. 93–98.)

5. Have a student introduce Lee's Resolution before the class which has been organized as the Continental Congress. Then hold a debate on the question of independence for the American colonies.

6. Memorize a portion of Henry Armitt Brown's "Oration at Valley Forge." Select a passage which describes the hardships of the soldiers stationed there.

7. How was the money raised to conduct the Revolutionary War? (See *Historic Currents in Changing America*, by Carman, Kimmel, and Walker, pp. 115–116; also, *The American States During and After the Revolution*, by Allan Nevins, pp. 470–543.)

8. Organize a Committee of Congress which will interview a group of Hessian prisoners and contract for their services in a war industry in colonial Pennsylvania.

9. Prepare a summary of Pennsylvania's contributions to the Revolutionary War. (See *The History of Pennsylvania*, by W. F. Dunaway, pp. 171–199.)

10. Prepare a book report on one of the following novels: *Hugh Wynne: Free Quaker*, by S. Weir Mitchell; *The Free Man*, by Conrad Richter; *Rifles for Washington*, by Elsie Singmaster; *One Red Rose Forever*, by Mildred Jordan; or any of the other novels listed at the end of this unit.

11. Prepare a report on the Indian wars in Pennsylvania from 1783 to 1795. Show how these wars affected the settlement of western Pennsylvania. (See *The Indian Wars of Pennsylvania*, by C. Hale Sipe, pp. 686–719.)

12. By consulting a textbook on American history, prepare a brief report on: The Articles of Confederation; Shay's Rebellion; The Annapolis Conference of 1786. When you have finished, write an essay on why a new federal constitution was needed in 1787.

13. Hold a meeting of the class organized as the Pennsylvania House of Representatives of 1798 at which the relocation of the state capital is being discussed. Various members of the class can debate in behalf of the different cities being considered. Include your own city or county seat. If your home is in Philadelphia, you will want to keep the state capital there.

14. Show how the second state constitution adopted ideas which were first included in the federal constitution of 1787.

15. Organize the class as a constitutional convention and draw up a constitution for some school organization. You will probably find that first you will need to divide the class into committees to prepare the different sections of the constitution. Once the sections are written, then the convention as a whole can consider them and debate on their advisability.

16. Conduct a trial for John Fries and his followers; or, organize the class into a session of President John Adams' cabinet discussing the pardon of Fries.

SUGGESTIONS FOR FURTHER READING

Revolutionary War

Charles H. Lincoln, *The Revolutionary Movement in Pennsylvania*, Philadelphia: University of Pennsylvania Press; Asa Earl Martin and Hiram H. Shenk, *Pennsylvania History Told by Contemporaries*, New York: Macmillan; Allan Nevins, *The American States During and After the Revolution*, New York: Macmillan; W. T. Root, *The Relations of Pennsylvania with the British Government from 1696 to 1765*, Philadelphia: University of Pennsylvania Press; C. H. Van Tyne, *The American Revolution, 1776-1783* (American Nation Series, vol. 9) New York: Harpers; Harry Emerson Wildes, *Valley Forge*, New York: Macmillan.

The Constitutional Period

Leland D. Baldwin, *Whiskey Rebels: The Story of a Frontier Uprising*, Pittsburgh: University of Pittsburgh Press; R. L. Brunhouse, *Counter-Revolution in Pennsylvania, 1776-1790*, Harrisburg: Pennsylvania Historical Commission; John Paul Selsam, *The Pennsylvania Constitution of 1776*, Philadelphia: University of Pennsylvania Press.

Biographies

Gertrude B. Biddle and Sarah D. Lowrie, *Notable Women of Pennsylvania*, Philadelphia: University of Pennsylvania Press; William Bell Clark, *Gallant John Barry*, New York: Macmillan; James E. Gibson, *Dr. Bodo Otto and the Medical Background of the American Revolution*, Springfield, Ill.: Thomas; Burton Alva Konkle, *Benjamin Chew, 1722-1810: Head of the Pennsylvania Judiciary System under Colony and Commonwealth*, Philadelphia: University of Pennsylvania Press; Burton Alva Konkle, *Thomas Willing and the First American Financial System*, Philadelphia: University of Pennsylvania Press; Burton Alva Konkle, *George Bryan and the Constitution of Pennsylvania, 1731-1791*, Philadelphia: Campbell; J. M. Palmer, *General von Steuben*, New Haven: Yale University Press; E. S. Parry, *Betsy Ross, Quaker Rebel*, Philadelphia: John C. Winston Co.; Sarah Wister, *Sally Wister's Journal*, Philadelphia: Ferris and Leach.

Fiction

J. A. Altsheler, *The Riflemen of the Ohio*, New York: Appleton; Amelia E. Barr, *The Maid of Maiden Lane*, New York: Dodd, Mead; John E. Barrett, *Red Shadow: A Romance of the Wyoming Valley in Revolutionary Days*, Scranton: The Colonial Press; Thomas Boyd, *Mad Anthony Wayne*, New York: Putnam's; Charles Brockden Brown, *Arthur Mervyn: or Memoirs of the Year 1793*, Philadelphia: David McKay; Charles C. Coffin, *The Boys of '76*, New York: Harpers; Mari-

143

belle Cormack and William P. Alexander, *Land for My Sons: A Frontier Tale of the American Revolution*, New York: Appleton-Century; Gertrude Crownfield, *Freedom's Daughter*, New York: Dutton; Howard Fast, *Conceived in Liberty*, New York: Simon and Shuster; Paul L. Ford, *Janice Meredith*, New York: Dodd, Mead; H. R. Gordon, *Red Jacket, Last of the Senecas*, New York: Dutton; R. S. Holland, *Steadfast at Valley Forge*, Philadelphia: Macrae-Smith; Bruce Lancaster, *Guns of Burgoyne*, New York: Stokes; Henry McCook, *The Latimers: A Tale of the Western Insurrection of 1794*, Harrisburg: Pennsylvania Book Service; John T. McIntyre, *Drums in the Dawn*, New York: Doubleday; John T. McIntyre, *With Fighting Jack Barry*, Philadelphia: Lippincott; B. G. Marshall, *Old Hickory's Prisoner*, New York: Appleton; F. W. Mason, *Three Harbours*, Philadelphia: Lippincott; S. Weir Mitchell, *Hugh Wynne: Free Quaker*, New York: Appleton; Helen Orton, *Hoofbeats for Freedom*, New York: Stokes; Lucy F. Perkins, *American Twins in the Revolution*, New York: Houghton Mifflin; Elsie Singmaster, *Rifles for Washington*, New York: Houghton Mifflin; Neil Swanson, *The First Rebel*, New York: Grosset and Dunlap; Agnes Turnbull, *The Day Must Dawn*, New York: Macmillan.

144

UNIT IV
DEMOCRACY MOVES FORWARD

In the preamble to our federal constitution the aims of the founders of the United States of America were set down: "To form a more perfect union, establish justice, insure domestic tranquillity, provide for the common defense, promote the general welfare, and secure the blessings of liberty" for the citizens of the republic now and in the future.

Pennsylvania caught the spirit of these noble ideals, and as the years passed tried to put them into practice. Democracy is more than a theory; it is a way of life. In a democracy people can have the good things of life provided they are willing to strive hard enough to get them, and provided the masses of voters understand how to act intelligently and loyally in a common purpose.

During the first half of the nineteenth century the Commonwealth of Pennsylvania was concerned with promoting the general welfare and securing the blessings of liberty for its citizens. Roads, canals, and railroads made possible the settlement of the remote interior regions of the state and brought them into closer association with the prosperous seaboard cities. Free public schools were established. A new and more democratic state constitution was adopted in 1838. Reform movements of all types worked for the spiritual and intellectual development of the men and women of Pennsylvania.

The industrial revolution came to America in the middle of the nineteenth century. Nowhere in the United States were its effects more far-reaching than in Pennsylvania. Industries grew by leaps and bounds as men learned to use machines to do work formerly done by hand. These growing industries and the promise they offered of unlimited economic opportunity now led Old World immigrants to the state as, in an earlier day, the guarantee of religious freedom and the fertile soil to be found here had brought settlers to colonial Pennsylvania.

145

Chapter VIII

SECURING THE BLESSINGS OF LIBERTY

Although political independence had been won and a new government formed, it remained to be seen how the young republic and the states which made up the nation would use their freedom and apply the democratic principles upon which the constitution was founded. In one sense, it may be said that William Penn's Holy Experiment was to be tried on a national scale. Could free people govern themselves? How could the masses of people make their wishes known to those in authority? Could the common people be trusted to use their ballots wisely? Or would there be uprisings after elections in which the friends of defeated candidates would try to win with bullets what they could not win with ballots? How could all of the people be educated so that they might become responsible citizens? Just how would this democracy work? We shall see in this chapter the experiment in government working out.

WESTERN PENNSYLVANIA

In Colonial Times. The early history of Pennsylvania centers around Philadelphia and the eastern counties. Most of the western part of the state was still dense forest at the time of the Revolutionary War. West of Cumberland County there were only a few small settlements clustered around the forts which had been built along the Forbes Road. West of the Allegheny Mountains the cities of Pittsburgh and Uniontown were just starting to grow when American independence was won. It is estimated that western Pennsylvania had but 50,000 settlers in the years preceding the Revolutionary War.

There were several reasons why the western part of the state remained largely unsettled. Before the Indians had been subdued, the territory was too dangerous to risk taking women and children into a region so far removed from the eastern cities. The Indian danger diminished after the victory over the French and Indians at Fort Duquesne and after Chief Pontiac's braves

146

had been put to rout. But the Proclamation Line of 1763 still prevented white settlers from taking lands west of the highest ridges of the Allegheny Mountains. Another reason for the slow growth of the region was the boundary dispute between Pennsylvania and Virginia over the southwestern limits of Pennsylvania. Settlers hesitated to buy lands there until they could be sure that the deeds to these lands would be valid.

After Independence. After the colonies declared independence from Great Britain, settlers were no longer obliged to consider the Proclamation Line. Even during the war years, brave men and women began to move out into the valleys of western Pennsylvania. Life was still dangerous on the frontier, however, because the Indians were being incited by the British to attack white settlers. There were other white men who helped the Indians spread terror throughout the sparsely settled regions. One of the most notorious of these was Simon Girty, whose name today is associated with crimes which made life on the frontiers of western Pennsylvania hard and dangerous.

The first census shows that western Pennsylvania had a population of 75,000 in 1790. In the next few years settlement was rapid. The location of the boundary assured settlers of their land titles. Danger of Indian attacks vanished after General Anthony Wayne administered a crushing defeat to the Indians at the Battle of Fallen Timbers in Ohio in 1794. After that victory the red men moved farther west and were no longer a threat to Pennsylvania.

Between 1790 and 1800 the population of the western districts of the state grew rapidly. Ten new counties were formed in 1800, all in the west and northwestern area. There was no great wave of settlers moving westward. Instead, there was a fairly constant movement of people from the east where land prices were high to the cheaper lands in western Pennsylvania. Later, when canals and railroads spanned the state from east to west, movement into the west and northwest was hastened. In one sense it may be said that it was a colonizing period all over again.

Democratic Ideals. The settlers carried with them the strong devotion to liberty and democracy which had led their parents and grandparents to America. Perhaps they were even more devoted to these ideals than were those who remained in

147

the eastern cities and villages. In roadside taverns and in country stores they discussed state and national problems. Because they were meeting new problems daily in their struggle to earn a living on the frontier, they were more ready to advocate or accept new ideas in government. As early as 1808 their votes elected a western Pennsylvanian, Simon Snyder, as Governor of the state. Snyder was the first governor who did not come from Philadelphia. For seventy-five years thereafter all governors of the state were from outside of Philadelphia. This does not mean that there was any ill feeling toward the great port city in the east, but it does show how political life in the state was influenced by the development of the state west of Philadelphia. The shift of political strength from the colonial center in Philadelphia westward was a natural result of democratic development.

Pittsburgh, the Giant of Western Pennsylvania. Soon after the British captured Fort Duquesne in 1758 and renamed it Fort Pitt, houses began to be built along the banks of the river near the fort. The growth of the community was comparatively slow during the first thirty years. The land upon

—Western Pennsylvania Historical Society

FORT PITT (PITTSBURGH)

The population of Pittsburgh in 1758 consisted of a garrison of 200 men and a settlement of 250 people, including men, women, and children. Note the junction of the rivers and compare this picture with the one on page 149.

AERIAL VIEW OF PITTSBURGH TODAY

The "Golden Triangle" is in as strategic a position at the present time as any time during its military history. What has become of the small islands in the rivers?

which the present city of Pittsburgh is built was surveyed for the Penn heirs in 1769. Because the Divesting Act permitted the Penns to retain possession of land surveyed before July 4, 1776, the Pittsburgh area was still the property of the Penns at the end of the Revolutionary War. In 1784, Tench Francis, a Philadelphia merchant acting as the agent for the Penns, had land laid out in building lots. These building lots were soon sold. In 1794 Pittsburgh was a town of two hundred houses. As early as 1786 the town had a newspaper, the *Pittsburg Gazette*, founded by John Scull, and in the same year Hugh Henry Brackenridge, one of the leaders in western Pennsylvania, predicted that Pittsburgh "would one day be a town of note." During its early years the chief business of the town was the fur trade with the western Indians. In 1797 James O'Hara and Isaac Craig arranged for the building of a glass factory, the beginning of an important industry. Late in the eighteenth century the construction of river boats was begun. On May 19, 1798, an ocean-going vessel named the *John Adams* was launched at Pittsburgh. Soon others were built. These vessels sailed down the Ohio and the Mississippi rivers to the Gulf of Mexico.

In 1812 the United States government became involved in a second war with Great Britain. The conflict grew out of British interference with American ships and sailors on the seas, and the belief held by many Americans that England was inciting the Indians in the northwestern portion of the United States to attack outlying American settlements. When war was declared on June 18, 1812, Pennsylvania's Governor, Simon Snyder, issued a call for volunteers to fill the state's quota of 14,000 men for the armed forces. So great was the enthusiasm and patriotism of Pennsylvanians that 40,000 men offered their services within a short time.

Repelling Threats of Invasion. Pennsylvania was not invaded during the thirty-one months of the war, but attempts were made by the enemy against the city of Erie on Lake Erie and Philadelphia on the Delaware River. Soon after the war began, a band of Indians in the employ of Britain was reported to be gathering for an attack on Erie. Arms and munitions were rushed to supply the militia stationed there. Prompt action by the state militia prevented the enemy from risking an attack.

The second threat to the state came in March, 1813, when a British fleet blockaded the Delaware River, cutting off most of

PERRY AT THE BATTLE OF LAKE ERIE

Philadelphia's sea-going commerce. However, the British were not able to do more than block the passage of ships through Delaware Bay. Every effort to make a landing along the coast was repulsed by the Pennsylvania militia.

The presence of a British fleet in Lake Erie was a constant threat to the American settlements along the southern coasts of the Great Lakes. In order to protect these towns, the national government decided to build a fleet of four warships at Erie, Pennsylvania. Daniel Dobbins of that town began the building of these ships, using lumber from nearby forests. Other materials were brought to Erie by a long, tedious route overland from the seacoast cities. The warships were launched during the summer of 1813, and Commodore Oliver H. Perry was placed in command of the new fleet. On September 10, Perry attacked the British fleet in Lake Erie, capturing all of the enemy vessels. In reporting his success, Perry sent his famous message to General William Henry Harrison: "We have met the enemy and they are ours."

Distinguished Leaders. There were many distinguished Pennsylvanians in the armed forces during the War of 1812. General Jacob Brown, commander in chief of the armies operating against Canada and in command of the American Army at the battle of Lundy's Lane near Niagara Falls, was a Pennsylvanian, as was Commodore Stephen Decatur, who gained fame in the naval battles of the war. Perhaps Decatur is best remembered for his toast: "My country, in her intercourse with foreign nations, may she ever be right; but, right or wrong, my country!"

Financing the War. Three Pennsylvanians figured prominently in financing the war. Albert Gallatin of Fayette County was one of the nation's most famous secretaries of the treasury. He held that position from 1801 to 1814, when he resigned to go to Europe as one of the men chosen to make the treaty of peace which ended the war. He was succeeded in office by another Pennsylvanian, Alexander J. Dallas, an expert financier.

In 1814 the federal government wished to sell five million dollars' worth of war bonds in order to finance the war. At first only a small fraction of this sum was subscribed by the citizens. Then Stephen Girard of Philadelphia came forward and purchased all of the unsold bonds. Stephen Girard had made a fortune in New Orleans before he moved to Philadelphia. Although earlier his funds had largely been invested in European countries, his keen knowledge of international affairs had led him to have those funds transferred to the United States before the war actually began. Thus, he was able to purchase such a large number of government bonds.

The War Ends. The war ended in 1815 when the news of the peace treaty reached the United States. Although the military and naval battles, except for the victory of General Andrew Jackson at New Orleans, were indecisive, the prestige of the United States was greatly increased in the eyes of the world. There could no longer be any doubt that the young nation was strong enough to have her point of view in world affairs recognized.

POLITICAL PARTIES

How Parties Developed. Political parties were not provided for either in the state or the federal constitution. From the beginning of our national history, however, we have had political parties. They came into existence because the voters needed some kind of organization through which they could carry their wishes into effect. Through the party platform, the party supporters can express their desires and unite behind a candidate pledged to carry them out. Of course, only one party can win on election day, but that does not mean that the losing party has no effect on the policies of those elected. If the winners of an election are not true to their pledges, the opposing party may succeed in winning enough votes to overthrow them in the next election. Once elected, an officeholder must act as the servant of all of the people, regardless of party loyalty.

Party organizations are constantly changing as new questions arise. In this period we shall see a number of parties formed. Many did not last very long, but they showed that people were learning to use the democratic machinery of government.

Political Parties in Pennsylvania. We have seen that there were parties in Pennsylvania during colonial times. At that time the lines were between the Governor's Men, who favored the colonial governor, and those who upheld the Provincial Assembly. Soon after the national constitution was put into effect, parties developed along national lines. It will be remembered that these parties, known as Federalists and Democratic-Republicans, differed on the interpretation of the national constitution. The Federalists wished to give the federal government great power, while their opponents wanted to limit the power of the national government, thereby giving more authority to the states. Before 1800 the Federalist party was in control of the national government, but in that year the Democratic-Republicans won the national elections.

The Democratic Party. For sixty years after 1800 Pennsylvania supported candidates of the Democratic-Republican party, or the Democratic party as it came to be known in the time of Andrew Jackson. There were two reasons for this long-continued loyalty to one party. First, the westward expansion of Pennsylvania gave more and more voting strength to the inland settlements, most of whom favored the principles of Thomas Jefferson and his successors. Later it was Andrew Jackson who came to represent the rights and views of the common man. He won the support of the farmers who felt that the old Federalist party had favored the wealthy business interests of the seacoast. Second, in some of the eastern counties of the state, particularly in Berks, Lehigh, and Northampton, the old Federalist party was never forgiven for certain undemocratic laws which the Federalists had put into effect during the administration of John Adams. One of these laws, known as the Sedition Law, tried to punish newspaper editors who printed articles criticizing the government. Such laws were contrary to the spirit of democracy in the eyes of these people. From then on, voters of some of the older counties joined with western Pennsylvania in supporting the Democratic party.

The Whig Party. For a long time after the defeat of the Federalists in 1800 the Democratic-Republican party was the only one well organized in national or state politics. Temporary party organizations would spring up at election time in support of a candidate or of a political issue, but once the election was over the organization would disappear, to give rise to a new one before the next election. Toward the close of Andrew Jackson's administration, however, the opponents of President Jackson's policies united to form a fairly large party. This group came to be known as the Whig party.

Throughout the 1840's the Whigs opposed the Democrats in all national elections. The Whigs never had a real platform of political objectives but relied upon opposition to Democratic policies to attract voters. The party was not strong in Pennsylvania, and eventually its lack of any real program brought about the break-up of the party. By 1854 it had disappeared from the national scene.

Although Pennsylvania always voted for candidates of the Democratic party in national elections, factions developed within the party when it came to state affairs. The old Federalists and later the Whigs were in such a small minority that the only influence they could exert was by joining the divisions within the Democratic party. These divisions were not constant, however, and new factions were found in almost every state election.

The Anti-Masonic Party. One of the bitterest political fights in Pennsylvania was led by a small organization known as the Anti-Masonic party. It had started in New York State and from there spread to Pennsylvania. Its chief principle was opposition to all kinds of secret organizations or societies such as lodges or fraternal orders. The fraternity of Free Masons was the most important secret organization at that time and therefore the object of most criticism. This explains the name, the Anti-Masonic party. In 1835 the Anti-Masons succeeded in getting Joseph A. Ritner elected as governor of Pennsylvania. Ritner's election was the result of a split in the Democratic party which had led to the nomination of two Democratic candidates. Ritner, the candidate of the new party, won the largest number of votes, although the combined votes of his two Democratic opponents would have defeated him.

The Buckshot War of 1838. Ritner's administration was marked by disputes and squabbles with the Legislature. The bitterness of party strife during his term in office came to a crisis in what is called the "Buckshot War." In the elections of 1838, the Anti-Masons won a sufficient number of seats in the state Senate to control it, but they lost the governorship, and it appeared that they had failed to win control of the state House of Representatives. Eight seats in the lower house were contested in the election districts of Philadelphia. Both parties—Democrats and Anti-Masons—claimed to have won them. An election commission composed of partisan Anti-Masons

WILLIAMSPORT IN 1854

The foreground shows haying in the early morning—the nine o'clock lunch ready in the basket.

decided in favor of the eight candidates of the Anti-Masonic party. The Democrats refused to accept the decision of the commission. When the time came for the Legislature to meet, a mob of citizens who favored seating the men elected by the Democrats gathered at Harrisburg. The Anti-Masons, fearing that there might be violence, appealed to Ritner, who was still Governor, to protect the Legislature.

Ritner called on the state militia to come to Harrisburg. When the militia arrived, the soldiers were issued buckshot cartridges, a kind of bullet used to shoot large game. However, the commander of the militia refused to use the troops against the protesting citizens. Another militia unit was called, and the second commander took the same attitude. An effort to use a third militia unit against the unarmed citizens met with the same refusal.

The refusal of the militia to use armed force against unarmed citizens in a political dispute is a striking example of how democracy differs from dictatorship, which relies upon military force to impose its will upon the people. Such tactics do not work in America. The Pennsylvania militia gave convincing proof of this in the Buckshot War.

The problem of who should have the contested seats was finally settled when several Whig members of the House of Representatives decided to vote with their Democratic colleagues to assure the seating of the eight Democratic legislators from Philadelphia. The citizens were satisfied, and the Anti-Masonic party was forced to accept the turn of events. The Buckshot War ended the power of the Anti-Masons in state affairs.

The Know-nothings. In the 1840's another loosely constructed political organization founded on prejudice rather than reason appeared on the national scene. It was called the Know-nothing party because its members were told to reply "I know nothing" if they were questioned about the aims or organization of the party. The deep secrecy of its meetings and ceremonies and the use of a password made the Know-nothings seem more like a lodge than a political organization. Officially it was called the American party, a more dignified name to place on the ballot than Know-nothing. It tried to stir up feeling against Irish immigrants who were at this time flooding the country with cheap labor and against the Roman Catholic Church of which the Irish were members. The Know-nothings urged that immigration be restricted and that only native-born Americans be allowed to hold offices. Today such a party would be branded as fascist. But to the young, ignorant country, the appeal of "America for Americans" was considerable. In 1844 the Know-nothings polled a sizeable vote in Pennsylvania, and in 1855 they were strong enough to swing the state election —not to a candidate of their own, but to the Whig nominee for governor. Thus, they accomplished their purpose, which was to defeat the Democratic candidate, Governor William Bigler, who was a Catholic. Governor Bigler was a candidate for re-election in 1855.

Fortunately, the majority of the American people were too sincerely devoted to democratic principles for the Know-nothing party ever to assemble a large following. The principles on which the party was founded have no place in a democracy, since no democratic government is worthy of the name that denies the rights of citizenship to any group within the nation.

Need for a New Constitution. In the state election of 1835 the voters were asked to mark ballots for or against calling a constitutional convention. The group favoring a convention won by 13,000 votes. These voters believed that the constitution of 1790 was out of date, that it did not provide for expanding business, and that it was not democratic enough in form. The third state constitution was drawn up by a convention which began its work in May, 1837, and ended the following February.

Changes Made by the New Constitution. The new constitution limited the power of the governor by making elective many offices which had been filled formerly by executive appointment. The governor's term of office was to be three years, but not more than two terms could be served by the same person within a period of nine years. The term of state Senators was reduced from four to three years, and judges were given fixed terms of service instead of life tenure as the previous constitutions had provided. State Supreme Court judges were to serve for fifteen years, other judges for ten. All were eligible for re-election.

All of these revisions were steps toward a more democratic government. The restrictions upon the length of terms for officeholders meant more frequent elections. Efforts to extend the vote to Negroes at this time failed, but the right to vote was given to all white men without the property qualification of previous constitutions. Another step forward was made when the voters were permitted to vote for adoption of the third constitution. This was the first time that a state constitution was ratified by popular vote in Pennsylvania.

THE ESTABLISHMENT OF PUBLIC SCHOOLS

Democracy is based upon the right and ability of the people to govern themselves. They do this by voting for persons to represent them in making and enforcing the laws. If such a system is to work properly, then every voter should be educated. Equal opportunity to learn is regarded today as an absolute necessity for all young persons. It is one of the blessings of liberty that has come to all of us. Public education came into being as democracy moved forward.

Early State Legislation. The first act of the Pennsylvania Legislature to provide for universal education of all children came in 1802. In this year a bill was passed requiring that county officials, known as the Overseers of the Poor, were to see that children whose parents were too poor to pay tuition be sent to the schools of their neighborhoods. The costs were to be paid from public funds. Two years later, another law required that teachers accept all children recommended by the Overseers. In 1824 it was provided that superintendents be elected to supervise the education of the poor, and local districts were permitted to organize their own free public schools. In 1831 a law was passed setting aside state funds for the support of public schools in various parts of the Commonwealth.

The Free School Act of 1834. In 1834 the Legislature passed the Free School Act which stated that schools were to be financed by local taxation, supplemented by appropriations from state funds. Local school directors were to be elected to administer the schools, which were to be open to all who applied for admission. The Free School Act marks the real beginning of public education in Pennsylvania.

Strong opposition to free schools developed in the counties inhabited largely by descendants of the early German settlers. Their opposition was not based on hostility toward education, for they honestly believed that their own system of church schools, conducted largely in the German language, would better serve the needs of their children. They feared that English schools would confuse their children, who spoke German at home.

The opposition to the Free School Act grew so strong that the state Senate voted in 1835 to repeal the law. When the issue came before the House of Representatives, the law was saved from repeal largely through the brilliant oratory of Thaddeus Stevens. The House of Representatives refused to concur with the Senate, and the public school law was saved.

The Free School Act did not force local communities to establish public schools. It merely provided state funds for those districts which accepted the provisions of the law. Approximately one half of the state's school districts accepted the appropriations as soon as they were available.

A new law was passed in 1836 requiring that elections be held every three years in the school districts that had rejected

—*Pennsylvania State Education Association*

FIRST SCHOOL IN CLEARFIELD COUNTY, PENNSYLVANIA

the Free School Act of 1834. These elections would determine, from time to time, whether the voters still wished to refuse the state funds to help them organize public schools. As time went on, more and more districts complied with the Free School Act, but it was not until 1868 that all of the one thousand districts in the state had established public schools. At the beginning of that year there were still twenty-three districts without public schools. The state Legislature then passed a law granting payment of all appropriations which those districts would have received if they had accepted the law in 1860. This inducement brought the twenty-three hesitating districts into line.

The District School. The early public schools of Pennsylvania did not offer as many opportunities to young people as do our schools of today. The buildings were small, usually containing only one room which was heated by a large coal- or wood-burning stove tended by the teacher or older pupils. In country schools the shelves lined the walls on which children placed their lunch boxes when they arrived in the morning. Lunch was eaten during the noon recess. Coats and hats were hung on hooks and pegs along the schoolroom wall. The teacher's desk stood on a raised platform at the front of the room, while the students sat on benches facing the teacher.

159

Very few women were employed to teach in the early public schools. There were several reasons for this. First, there were few schools where women could secure the advanced education needed to qualify them as instructors, and, second, teaching was then regarded as man's work. Discipline was maintained by whipping with a rod. Only a man would have sufficient strength to handle the older boys. Moreover, the teacher was janitor as well as instructor, and this involved hard physical labor.

The rural district school offered only elementary subjects, extending through the eighth grade. In the towns an effort was made to divide the students into separate rooms according to grades. The grammar school, corresponding to our seventh and eighth grades, was still the highest grade taught in most communities.

In spite of its shortcomings as measured by our schools today, the district public school was a great step forward in providing opportunities for the young people of the state. The education received in these schools helped to train future citizens to meet the problems which they were to face as the years passed.

—Hildreth Collection and Index of Historic Prints

THE SCHOOL EXAMINATION
The visiting school board examines the students.

William Penn had referred to his undertaking in the New World as a Holy Experiment. For a century and a half after Penn's death, Pennsylvania continued to be a proving ground for social ideas.

The broad promises of freedom made during the early days of the settlement of Pennsylvania continued to attract groups of people who were trying to work out new ways of life for themselves. During the colonial period, the brothers and sisters at Ephrata had organized a communal life. After the formation of the United States, other groups sought the shelter of Pennsylvania hills as a haven from Old World troubles. Two of these groups we shall describe.

The French Asylum. Early in 1793 a group of refugees from France came to Philadelphia to escape the horrors of the French Revolution. They were royalists who had escaped from France and the French colonies. As the number of these refugees increased, it was decided to establish a separate colony in the northern counties of Pennsylvania. A group of prominent refugees, aided by Philadelphia citizens, raised a sum of money for the purchase of lands in present-day Bradford County, south of the town of Towanda. Assisted by Robert Morris of Philadelphia and Mathias Hollenback of Wilkes-Barre, the leaders of the refugees organized the Asylum Company and secured titles to lands in the north central part of the state. They intended to sell these holdings to their followers.

There followed a great deal of land speculation, both by Americans and foreigners, most of whom never intended to live at the Asylum. A number of those who actually did move into the region found the life unsuited to their taste. Many of the refugees had been wealthy people in France, accustomed to luxuries which they could not hope for deep in the Pennsylvania woods. News from home was scarce and long-delayed. Many suffered from anxiety over relatives and friends left behind in France and from homesickness. In spite of their hardships, they managed to build a small settlement of fifty homes and several business establishments. For ten years they continued to cultivate the fields, growing wheat for market in Wilkes-Barre and flax for their clothes. Maple trees were tapped for sugar and tar was made from pine trees.

161

The leaders of the colony were the Viscount de Noailles, a brother-in-law of Lafayette, and Antoine Omer Talon, who had held important offices under the deposed French King, Louis XVI. When the settlement was founded, it was hoped that Marie Antoinette, the Queen of France, and her two children might escape and be brought to the Asylum. This hope was destroyed, however, when the unfortunate Queen was executed by the French Revolutionists in October, 1793.

Early in the nineteenth century the French exiles in Pennsylvania learned that Napoleon, who had gained control of affairs in France, was permitting certain royalists to return home and was restoring their property. The settlers of the Asylum received this news joyfully, and many of them abandoned the American venture, some to return to France or to French colonies in the West Indies, a few to move to New Orleans, Charlestown, Savannah, or Philadelphia. After 1805 the colony was largely deserted. The French settlers left a number of permanent traces in Pennsylvania, however, in the names of communities such as Laporte, Homet's Ferry, and Dushore.

—*Tioga Point Museum*

QUEEN'S HOUSE OR "LA GRANDE MAISON"
This house, no longer standing, was built for Queen Marie Antoinette.

THE SETTLEMENT AT NEW HARMONY
Why was it named *New* Harmony?

The Harmony Society. George Rapp, the son of a farmer in Wurttemberg, Germany, preached a doctrine of Christian living which opposed the teaching of the established churches of his homeland. He believed that men should live together without selfish purposes, each person working for the common welfare. When the churches of Germany denounced Rapp as a troublemaker, he sold his belongings and left his followers in charge of his assistant with instructions to follow him one year later. George Rapp came to America in 1803, landing at Baltimore. His followers, three hundred in number, arrived in Philadelphia on July 4, 1804. Meanwhile Rapp had purchased five thousand acres of land in Butler County, twenty miles northeast of Pittsburgh. There he established his society, which he named Harmony. One small group of Rappists founded a smaller settlement in Lycoming County, but most of them joined the Harmony Society.

The community at Harmony was a success because all of the members were inspired by the same ideals. Most of them were hard-working farmers and skilled craftsmen, and their willingness to work for the common welfare brought early prosperity to the new settlement. In 1809 nearly 20,000 bushels of grain were raised; the next year a woolen mill was established. By 1814 the settlement had grown too large to be cared for on the original tract. The Rappists then sold all of their land in Pennsylvania and moved to Indiana, where they founded a new colony which they called New Harmony. Again they prospered. Ten years later they sold their Indiana property to Robert Owen, an English philanthropist who wished to experiment with a socialist community.

In 1825 the Rappists returned to Pennsylvania and established a new settlement at Economy, now included in the borough of Ambridge in Beaver County. Rapid progress marked the beginning of the new venture. The Economy settlement engaged in numerous manufacturing enterprises. The chief industry was the making of textiles—cotton, wool, and silk. A cutlery shop was established which employed hired laborers including many Chinese. As time went on, new members joined the society. It continued to prosper through the middle of the nineteenth century. The funds of the society were invested in a bank which the Rappists founded and in shares in coal mines, sawmills, and oil wells. Because of the regulation which forbade the marriage of members, the society was not self-perpetuating, but by adding new members it continued to exist down to the early years of the present century. The buildings at Economy are now owned by the Commonwealth of Pennsylvania.

We have mentioned only two of the experimental societies which were established in Pennsylvania. There were a number of others which flourished for short periods of time and then dissolved. Either their ideals of economic and social change were unsound or their leaders were ineffective. It must be pointed out, however, that the Commonwealth of Pennsylvania permitted these people to try out new ways of life which seemed to them to offer a promise of better living. Only a democracy which recognizes the right of free men to seek a better life can permit such experiments to take place within its borders and can profit by the lessons learned from these experiments.

Social Changes. The years between 1830 to 1860 were marked by demands for social reforms. One important change which resulted was in the status of women in society. Colleges for women were established in many states. Women's magazines made their appearance for the first time. One of the first was *Godey's Lady Book* published in Philadelphia by Louis A. Godey and featuring the latest women's styles. Women began to emerge from the subordinate position in public life which they had previously occupied to take a place alongside the men in the world of affairs. They too found the blessings of liberty under democracy.

Religious revivals stirred the souls of great masses of citizens. Movements by temperance societies were begun to abolish the evil features of the drinking of intoxicants.

In the Eastern Penitentiary at Philadelphia a great step forward was made in prison reform when criminals were placed in separate cells. Reform schools were established in Philadelphia to separate young offenders from old and hardened criminals.

In a later chapter we shall see how the efforts to abolish Negro slavery gained momentum as the spirit of reform surged through the nation.

QUESTIONS FOR STUDY AND REVIEW

1. The War of 1812 is sometimes called the second war for independence. Can you explain why?

2. What is the function of political parties in a democratic government? What do our political parties stand for today?

3. How was the constitution of 1838 more democratic than the preceding constitution?

4. Why is education for all citizens necessary in a democracy? Should education be compulsory? Do you think the state should provide free college education for all who can meet the requirements?

5. Why did the experimental societies cease to exist in Pennsylvania? Can you mention some social experiments now being tried?

6. Why did the western portion of the state develop slowly before 1800? Why did it grow so rapidly afterwards?

Chapter IX

PROMOTING THE GENERAL WELFARE

During the first half of the nineteenth century many great changes took place that affected everyone, from the richest to the poorest. These changes made a great difference in the individual's way of living, his methods of working, and his general outlook on life. The kind of world in which we live today is very different from the world as it was before these changes took place. Before 1800 the world had made comparatively slow progress. The speediest method of traveling that George Washington knew was by horseback—a mode of travel used from very ancient times. Look about in your classroom and note the many objects which would have to be explained to an early Pennsylvania settler if it were possible for him to visit your school. He would be mystified by electric lights, radiators, fountain pens, blotters, drinking fountains, and many other things we now take for granted. Or, if he were to look out of your classroom window, imagine his surprise at beholding automobiles, networks of wire strung on telephone poles, or airplanes overhead. All of these things and many more are a part of our everyday life.

MANUFACTURING

The Industrial Revolution. One of the greatest changes that took place in this period was the invention of machines to do much of the work that had formerly been done by hand. The shift from hand manufacturing in the home to machine manufacturing in a factory is known as the Industrial Revolution. In many ways the Industrial Revolution touched the individual's life more directly than did most political revolutions because it changed and is still changing so many things which enter into our everyday lives, such as food, clothing, shelter, health, and amusement. This great industrial change began in England late in the eighteenth century when inventors began to devise machines to aid human labor. These machines were used

166

first in the textile industries in the spinning and weaving of cloth from flax, wool, or cotton fibers. Later, machinery was introduced into other industries, and the process is still going on today as machines are invented to do more and more of our work. Goods manufactured by machine cost much less than handmade articles and can be made in far greater quantities. Their form and quality can be standardized.

Industries in the United States were not able to adopt the new methods of manufacturing at first because the machines were made in England. British manufacturers would not permit them to be sent out of the country, nor would they allow plans for building the machines to come into American hands. We were England's best customer and it seemed to her that it would be folly to help America become a competitor instead of a customer. But there was no way to prevent intelligent American workmen from going to England and learning how to operate the machines. Some of these shrewd workmen were able to learn the details of the machines at which they worked. When they returned to this country, they could show machinists how to build them. Once the United States had a start at machine manufacture, our economic independence was certain, for we had raw materials in abundance. Soon American genius took the lead in devising new ways to use machines in industry.

Pennsylvania played and continues to play an important part in the industrial life of the nation. That area which was once known merely as Penn's Woods became one of the greatest sources of raw materials used in the great industrial expansion which took place in America during the nineteenth century. Deep in the earth was coal to provide fuel and iron ore which could be forged into tools and machinery; on the surface of the earth stood vast forests to provide timber for factories and houses in the growing cities. The cleared fields were fertile; the rivers provided waterpower; and highly skilled workmen were ready to make use of the wealth of natural resources. We shall see how the gifts of nature combined with man's intelligence and skill made Pennsylvania the great industrial state it is today.

Coal. Coal is the most important mineral resource of Pennsylvania. The value of the annual production of our coal mines today is greater than the value of all the gold and silver mined in the United States. Bituminous, or soft coal, is found in several states east of the Mississippi, notably in West Virginia and Alabama, but Pennsylvania is doubly favored by nature in that both bituminous coal and anthracite, or hard coal, are to be found in abundance within her borders. Of the sixty-seven counties in the state, more than half produce coal, ten producing anthracite and twenty-five, bituminous coal. Consult the map on page 280.

Anthracite. Hard coal was not known to the European settlers before they came to America. At first they called it "stone coal" because, while it resembled the coal they had known in Europe, they did not know how to make it burn and thought it was as useless for fuel as an ordinary stone. Eventually, blacksmiths in the interior counties of Pennsylvania learned how to use it under the forced draft of their forges, but attempts to burn it in stoves with natural drafts were still unsuccessful. In 1812 Colonel George Shoemaker of Pottsville brought nine loads of hard coal to Philadelphia. He sold two loads and then was forced to leave the city because the purchasers claimed he had cheated them by selling them stones. After many experiments it was discovered that the secret of getting the black stones to burn in grates was to be patient and not shake the grates or stoke the embers.

Gradually the public learned to use hard coal for domestic purposes. In 1820 the Lehigh Coal Company began the shipment of coal to Philadelphia by way of the Lehigh and Delaware rivers. When transportation methods were improved by the building of canals and later railroads, the hard coal industry grew rapidly. In 1820 only 365 tons were shipped, but by 1846 this had grown to 7,000,000 tons, and just before the War Between the States began, 8,500,000 tons of anthracite were being shipped annually.

Bituminous Coal. Soft coal was found by white settlers in western Pennsylvania as early as 1759. It is known that British soldiers stationed at Fort Pitt used coal to heat their buildings during the winter months of that year. The use of bituminous coal for fuel was known to Englishmen, as it was similar to the coal mined in England. For this reason, soft coal was in common use in western Pennsylvania long before easterners had learned how to burn anthracite in their stoves and furnaces. Because of

168

**WEIGHING OF COAL CARGO IN THE WEIGH LOCK OF A
PENNSYLVANIA CANAL**

poor transportation facilities, however, such a bulky commodity as coal could not be brought to the seaboard until canals and railroads were constructed. The earliest shipments of bituminous coal were westward and southward from Pittsburgh, down the Ohio River in flatboats.

In 1804 the first boatload of bituminous coal to reach the eastern part of Pennsylvania was sent from Clearfield County, down the Susquehanna, to Columbia in Lancaster County. The first boatload of soft coal reached Philadelphia in 1828, but many years were to pass before this type of fuel came into general use east of the Alleghenies. It was not until 1860 that any large quantities reached Philadelphia. By that time bituminous coal mines in western Pennsylvania were yielding 2,500,000 tons of coal a year.

Coke. Coke is to coal what charcoal is to wood; it is produced in much the same way—by a process of charring or baking away all substances except the carbon texture of the coal. It is used in blast furnaces instead of raw coal because it is more efficient, giving off a more intense heat. In the process of converting coal to coke, many valuable by-products are secured.

169

The coke industry had its origin in America in 1817, in Fayette County. Pennsylvania still ranks first in the nation in the production of this commodity. At first coke was burned in pits much as charcoal was burned, but the Connellsville ovens, which were established in 1841, introduced the method of manufacturing coke in ovens shaped like beehives. Later the use of beehive ovens was discontinued because the valuable gases were wasted. The Connellsville ovens in Fayette County became the most productive coke district anywhere in the world. The first products of the Connellsville ovens were shipped to Cincinnati in 1842. At first coke was used only in forges because iron manufacturers did not believe it could be used in blast furnaces. It was not until 1850 that coke was tried successfully in the manufacture of pig iron. After that date, however, it came into general use in the iron industry. In a few years coke was used more extensively than charcoal. By 1875 its use in blast furnaces was greater than the use of anthracite.

Iron Industries. We have already noted that an iron industry had developed in Pennsylvania even before the Revolutionary War. All of the colonial furnaces and forges were in the eastern part of the state, largely in the valley of the Schuylkill. After the war, enterprising settlers developed the industry in the interior counties of the state, and as time went on iron manufacture spread westward to Pittsburgh.

TIMBER

The early German settlers knew the value of trees on their farms. The fields had to be cleared, in order to plow and cultivate them, but at the crest of every hill a little copse of trees was left standing. These farmers knew that the roots of trees drank in the water at the time of heavy rainfall, holding it there to be released gradually. In this way they prevented erosion of their fields and made sure that their creeks and springs would not run dry. The trees helped to prevent floods in the valleys at the same time. Then too, there would always be an ample supply of timber for building fences, logs for houses and barns, firewood to do the cooking, and fuel to keep the homes warm. The indulgent care given to the trees on the farms of eastern Pennsylvania helps to account for the remarkable fertility of the soil in such counties as York, Lancaster, Berks, and Lehigh.

170

A flourishing lumber industry developed along the north and west branches of the Susquehanna, but the felling of the trees did not reach the tree-butchering stage which later characterized this industry in the western parts of the United States. Timber was cut to provide building materials, to furnish props for the mines, ties for the railroad tracks, poles for the telegraph wires, and materials for furniture, wagon bodies, canal boats, ships, and many other useful products. But the great expanse of Pennsylvania's timberland remains to this day its noblest natural resource, providing scenic beauty which few parts of the world can equal, and at the same time assuring us that the topsoil will not be blown away by windstorms, that the rivers will always be filled with water to turn the wheels of industry and generate electric power, and that game animals and bird life will find sanctuary.

AGRICULTURE

Great strides were made in agriculture between 1800 and 1860. New inventions and new methods of farming served to lighten the labor on the farm and to increase the fertility of the fields. The yield of the farms of southeastern Pennsylvania increased greatly. There was hardly a farm that did not produce a surplus of farm products which were hauled or shipped to distant places. The development of industry in Pennsylvania did not draw great numbers of farm boys and girls to the cities or to the mines during the prosperous years between 1840 and 1860. Farming was a profitable enterprise, and the ownership of land was looked upon as the surest form of investment. Therefore, people stayed on the farms.

New Implements. The crude, homemade implements which farmers used during the colonial period were replaced by machine-made tools built of iron and steel once the Industrial Revolution had made itself felt in America. Wooden plows were replaced after 1820 by plows with metal shares and moldboards. Cultivators came into use about 1840. Soon mechanical cornplanters took the place of the tedious planting by hand and hoe. The mowing machine saved the farmer back-breaking hours of wielding a scythe. The reaper replaced the cradle and sickle; the threshing machine saved hours of swinging flails; the seed drill sowed the grain in regular rows, replacing the uncertain system of seeding by throwing handfuls of seed broadcast. These and other devices revolutionized the labor on farms before 1860.

Crops. In 1840 Pennsylvania ranked first in the nation in the production of rye and buckwheat; second in wheat; third in potatoes. Her rank in the production of corn and tobacco was far from the top, but the yield per acre planted was high. Many new varieties of fruits were developed, especially new varieties of apples. No farm was complete in the period before 1860 unless it had a vineyard, filled with grapevines and berry bushes, an orchard with several kinds of apple trees, pear trees, cherry trees, peach trees, quince trees and mulberry trees. Chestnut and walnut trees were spared when the land was cleared in order that nuts could be harvested in abundance.

The nineteenth century Pennsylvania farm was a self-sufficient community. There was a smokehouse in which to cure and store meats; a springhouse in which to chill the milk, cream, and homemade butter; an outdoor baking oven; a summer kitchen; a granary, a woodshed, wagonshed, pigpen,

—The Bettmann Archive

THRESHING IN THE BARN
What work is being performed by the horses?

EARLY REAPER, CONESTOGA WAGON, TRAIN, AND STEAMSHIP

chickenhouse, corncrib, and occasionally a mill or a blacksmith shop. Under such an economy the farmer needed very little money, since he could supply most of his family's needs with produce grown at home. To get cash he sold his surplus products to local dealers, who transported them to the distant markets.

TRANSPORTATION

Coal, coke, iron, timber, farm produce, and the articles manufactured from these raw materials had to be moved from the rural areas where they were produced to the thickly-settled areas where consumers lived. City and country people demanded better roads, more canals, and eventually railroads. Improvement in transportation was necessary to promote the general welfare. Citizens believed they had a right to ask the government to assist in the construction of internal improvements because roads, canals, and railroads were for the benefit of all. In a democracy it is possible for the people to promote their own welfare through governmental action.

Canals. In 1790 the state Assembly appointed a committee to study ways of improving transportation in Pennsylvania. The committee suggested that a canal be built connecting the Schuylkill and Susquehanna rivers. It was pointed out that such an inland waterway would serve to bring the produce

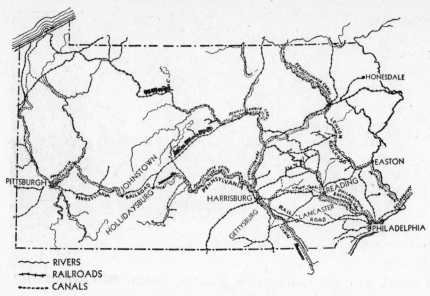

CANALS AND RAILROADS IN PENNSYLVANIA, 1861
Can you suggest reasons for locating railroads and canals along the routes
indicated?

from the western farms to the port of Philadelphia. The Assembly did not appropriate any funds for this project, but it did grant a charter to a private company which was quickly organized. The company offered one thousand shares for sale. As there were more applicants for shares than could be accommodated, lots were drawn to determine who should have a chance to buy them.

Many prominent citizens were interested in the canal. In 1793 President Washington, in company with a group of distinguished men, including Robert Morris and David Rittenhouse, visited the Lebanon Valley where the Tulpehocken Creek joins the Schuylkill River at Reading. These men were shareholders in the newly-formed canal company. Rittenhouse surveyed the territory for the canal which came to be known as the Union Canal.

Before 1826 the General Assembly encouraged the building of canals by private companies, by granting charters to these companies and by purchasing shares in them or extending loans. Between 1826 and 1829 the state made direct appropriations for internal improvements such as roads, bridges, and canals.

174

More than six million dollars were appropriated during the three-year period. The money was raised by selling bonds.

The Pennsylvania canal-building program was responsible for the building of a network of inland waterways connecting various parts of the state. The Schuylkill Canal tapped the anthracite mining region north of Reading; a spur line of the Union Canal extended to Pinegrove in Schuylkill County and provided another outlet for the hard coal mines. The Delaware Canal connected with the Raritan in New Jersey and provided a waterway to New York City.

By 1829 Pennsylvania faced a serious financial crisis. The canal-building program was proving more and more expensive each year, and the Commonwealth was finding itself deeper and deeper in debt. The credit of the state could be saved by stopping the building program, but the canals were only partially completed and of little real use. The other course was to complete the program and hope to collect enough money eventually in the form of tolls to pay the debt. The latter plan was adopted.

The Pennsylvania Canal. The most ambitious venture in canal-building was the Pennsylvania Canal. The plan called for a waterway along the Juniata River westward to Pittsburgh, with numerous smaller canals branching from the main one. The canal could not be dug through the Allegheny Mountains,

—Pennsylvania Historical Society

**THE OLD PORTAGE RAILROAD ACROSS THE ALLEGHENIES
ABOUT 1840**

so the boats were to be pulled up one side of the mountain by railroad locomotives and allowed to slide down the other side. These over-mountain hauls were called railroad portages. The largest portage was built at Hollidaysburg. The Pennsylvania Canal, including all of its branches, was to be 907 miles in length, 790 miles of which would be waterways and 117 miles railroad. In 1834 the main line of the canal from Philadelphia to Pittsburgh was opened to traffic. Some of the branch lines were built later, but the project was never completed as originally planned. The state verged nearer and nearer to bankruptcy as the building of canals proved increasingly costly.

End of the Canal-building Era. Before the canal program was finished, railroads were built along routes which paralleled the canals. Barges moving at two miles an hour could not compete with the railroads which could travel twenty miles an hour. When winter came, the canals were frozen over with ice; the spring thaws filled the channels with mud; muskrats bored holes in the canal walls and let the water escape; after heavy rains high water covered the towpaths; and during droughts the water fell too low for traffic. In the face of these disadvantages the canals were doomed in competition with the puffing locomotives running on steel rails in all kinds of weather and during all seasons.

In 1857 the state sold the main line of the Pennsylvania Canal to the Pennsylvania Railroad Company for $7,500,000. The railroad bought the canal primarily to remove the small element of competition it still offered. Soon afterward it was abandoned. The Union Canal continued to do a little business until 1884, and some sections of the Schuylkill Canal were still in operation as late as 1905. Bulk goods such as coal, bricks, lumber, and lime could still be transported by canal for about one third of the rate charged by the railroads.

The canal-building program was a financial failure for the Commonwealth. The tolls which had been counted upon to pay for their construction were never collected. The canals were the victims of the rapidly changing times, but they answered their purpose until a more satisfactory means of transportation was invented.

Early Railroads. When we think of railroads today we usually envision parallel bands of steel rails over which steam locomotives pull a string of cars. But the first railroads were built of wooden tracks and the cars were pulled by horses. The first railroad in Pennsylvania was only one mile in length. It was built in Delaware County in 1809 to haul stone from a quarry. The second was built in Armstrong County in 1818 and was also a very short line designed to carry materials to a blast furnace. The Mauch Chunk Railroad built in Carbon County in 1827 connected two coal mines nine miles apart. All of these roads had wooden rails. In 1829 a wooden railed road was built between Carbondale in Lackawanna County and Honesdale in Wayne County. The first railroad for passenger traffic connected Philadelphia, Germantown and Norristown. It was constructed in 1832.

Locomotives. The first locomotive in the state to use steam was invented in 1804 by a Philadelphian, Oliver Evans. He called his curious vehicle the Oruktor Amphibolis, meaning a machine which could travel on land or in water. It was a steam engine mounted on a boat-shaped body with wheels. Evans demonstrated his invention to the people of Philadelphia, who were amazed to see it puff its way along the streets of the city and then dip itself into the Schuylkill River and continue on its merry way. Evans failed to secure a patent for his machine because people refused to believe that it could do anything useful.

The first steam locomotive to run on American tracks was brought from England. It had been made in Stourbridge, England, and had the head of a lion painted on the front of the boiler; hence it was known as the Stourbridge Lion. The engine had a trial run on the wooden rails of the Honesdale to Carbondale road during the summer of 1828. It wobbled its way for three miles beyond Honesdale where it was halted by faulty tracks. A second run was made later over reinforced tracks, but this was no better. Steam locomotion had to wait for steel rails and firm roadbeds.

Railroad Systems. After 1832 the building of steel-tracked railroads developed rapidly. By 1836 there were 314 miles of railroads with steel rails in Pennsylvania, and by 1860 there were nearly 2600 miles.

A charter was granted the Philadelphia and Reading Railroad Company in 1833 to build a road between those two cities.

The road opened for business in December of 1839. Later the road was extended to include branch lines which connected with railroad centers north, east, and west of Reading.

In 1846 the Pennsylvania Railroad Company was chartered to build a road from Harrisburg to Pittsburgh. The original plans did not provide for a railroad extending from Philadelphia to the growing city in western Pennsylvania. The connection was made, however, a few years later, when the Pennsylvania Railroad Company acquired several other systems in the eastern section of the state. One line, running from Philadelphia to the Susquehanna River at Columbia, Lancaster County, had been operating for several years before the Pennsylvania Railroad was chartered. Another road connecting Harrisburg and Lancaster began operation in 1838. By incorporating these lines into one great system, the Pennsylvania Railroad Company established an unbroken line from Philadelphia through Lancaster and Harrisburg to Pittsburgh. This is commonly known as the Main Line. As time went on the Pennsylvania Railroad secured control of many smaller lines branching north and south of the Main Line until it became the greatest artery for commerce through the state.

THE STOURBRIDGE LION, THE FIRST LOCOMOTIVE IN AMERICA
The first locomotive to turn a wheel on an American railway was given its trial trip on August 8, 1828, at Honesdale, in northeastern Pennsylvania.

EARLY TRAIN CROSSING, NORTH QUEEN STREET IN LANCASTER

The third railroad system to be chartered was the Lehigh Valley Railroad Company, also in 1846. Originally it was known as the Delaware, Lehigh, Schuylkill, and Susquehanna Railroad Company. Its present name was assumed in 1853 when the company was reorganized.

The Steamboat. We have mentioned Oliver Evans, the inventor of the Oruktor Amphibolis, which was both a steamboat and locomotive. Even earlier, in 1787, John Fitch, the real inventor of the steamboat, had demonstrated a steam-propelled boat on the Delaware River. Fitch, like Evans, was unable to convince people that his invention had any useful purpose. It was another Pennsylvanian who was to gain world renown as the inventor of the steamboat. Robert Fulton, born and reared near Pequea Creek in Lancaster County, finally convinced the world that steam navigation was practical when his boat, the *Clermont*, chugged up the Hudson River in New York in 1809. Fulton's invention used steam to turn a paddle wheel which propelled the boat.

The steamboat revolutionized world commerce. At first the advantages of steamships were, chiefly, the regular schedules they could keep, since they were not at the mercy of the winds, and the larger cargoes they could carry. Eventually steam vessels became even faster than the famous sailing clipper ships. Thus, perishable products like bananas could be brought from distant places because less time was spent in transit.

179

AT DOCK STREET WHARF IN PHILADELPHIA
The train and the steamship making inroads on the horse and sailboat
as transportation.

FINANCING PROGRESS

Promoting the general welfare brought new tax burdens to the people of Pennsylvania, but for the most part these burdens were cheerfully borne. We have seen how the canal-building program plunged the state heavily into debt. Public schools, the building of roads and bridges, the formation of police forces in the cities, prison reform, medical aid for the poor, and other social services did not come without cost. The expenses of many of these improvements in living were offset in part by the increase in taxable wealth of the Commonwealth as new industries were developed, the western parts of the state settled, and farms grew increasingly prosperous.

In the early years of the state, most of the money collected for taxes went to pay the cost of government—for the salaries of officeholders and for routine costs of administration. As the years passed, more and more of the public funds were used for the welfare of the people. How far we have come along this line can be best illustrated by analyzing the way in which tax money was spent recently. In the two-year period between 1941 and 1943 only six per cent of the state revenue was spent for the administration of the government. Forty per cent of the state income was spent for relief of needy citizens; thirty-three per cent for schools; fourteen per cent for public health and welfare; and about seven per cent for the protection of persons and property. Ninety-four per cent of all state revenue was used to promote the general welfare. The developments of the early half of the nineteenth century which we have just studied have continued down to the present. We owe to those early citizens the ideals of social progress that we cherish today.

Some Problems Were Solved. In this unit we have seen how democratic theories were put into actual practice. After our second war with Great Britain the United States began to grapple with problems growing out of industrial and territorial expansion. The problems were solved in the democratic way.

Pennsylvania sought to promote the general welfare of its citizens by encouraging the building of roads, canals, and railroads. Her natural resources made possible the establishment of great industries which provided employment for her people and enriched the nation with the products of her mines, factories, forests, and farms. The blessings of liberty were made secure by providing for the education of all young people. Progress was made in granting more rights to women, in humanitarian legislation, in prison reform, and in securing cultural independence. One great problem still confronted the nation, however, for no nation can call itself entirely free if any of its people are held in slavery. Before America could honestly call herself a democracy that problem had to be solved.

QUESTIONS FOR STUDY AND REVIEW

1. Name some kinds of employment which now exist but which were unknown before the Industrial Revolution. What comforts that you now enjoy were made possible by the inventions and discoveries of the Industrial Revolution?

2. How was Pennsylvania's economic importance increased by the Industrial Revolution?

3. Why are forests an important natural resource? What is being done in your community to protect our forests? to plant new ones?

4. What farm improvements were developed during the first half of the nineteenth century?

5. What were the advantages of water transportation? Why were canals built instead of roads? Are there any canal locks still to be seen in your locality?

6. Show how the railroads answered the problem of transportation better than the canals did. What railroad systems serve your community? Why were they built where they are? What industries attracted them? What population centers do they serve?

PROBLEMS AND ACTIVITIES

1. Selecting your material from an American history textbook prepare a report on the important battles of the War of 1812 which occurred outside of Pennsylvania.

2. What is meant by the following terms: impressment of seamen; freedom of the seas; "third party"; minority governor; Buckshot War; Know-nothing party.

3. Assume that you live in a sparsely-settled community in western Pennsylvania and that a railroad is being built through your valley. Write to a friend in Philadelphia expressing the hopes which the people of your community have for the future of that section of the state.

4. Show how public education serves to train citizens in a democracy. Show how citizenship lessons can be learned in science; English; physical education; modern languages; shopwork; mathematics; commerce; and other subjects.

5. Where does the money come from to support public schools? Where are the teachers trained? Are educational opportunities equal for all children in the state? in the nation? in the world?

6. What is meant by the term Utopia? Report on Utopian societies other than those we have discussed (see *Pennsylvania Cavalcade*, pp. 271–316).

7. From a textbook in European or world history prepare a report on the inventions in the textile industry in England during the last quarter of the eighteenth century.

8. Describe the early efforts to use anthracite coal (see Martin and Shenk, *Pennsylvania History Told by Contemporaries*, pp. 450–451).

9. Explain how the Industrial Revolution greatly increased the demand for coal, both hard and soft.

10. Explain the factors which led to the growth of Pittsburgh as a manufacturing center.

11. Perhaps some student will make a model of a canal lock, showing how it operated to raise and lower boats to different levels of water.

12. What trees would furnish the best timber for the following:

Furniture	Fence posts
Railroad ties	Porches
Mine props	Baseball bats
Telephone poles	Spokes in a wagon wheel
Packing crates	Boardwalk at the seashore

13. Is it the duty of the state to give financial aid to enterprises such as the canals? Should the government—city, state, or nation—assist in the building of airlines?

14. On a map of Pennsylvania show what railroads connect important cities, tap the coal fields, haul iron ore from the Great Lakes.

15. Write an article in which you support or deny this statement: Of all the states in the Union, Pennsylvania could be the most nearly self-supporting. Explain your position.

16. What are some of the proposals to promote the general welfare now being discussed by citizens of the state? of your town or community?

SUGGESTIONS FOR FURTHER READING

War of 1812

K. C. Babcock, *Rise of American Nationality* (American Nation Series, vol. 13) New York: Harper; William W. Dobbins, *Battle of Lake Erie*, Erie: Ashby Printing Co.; *Erie: A Guide to the City and County*, compiled by the Work Projects Administration of the State of Pennsylvania, Harrisburg.

Western Pennsylvania

Leland D. Baldwin, *Pittsburgh: the Story of a City*, Pittsburgh: University of Pittsburgh Press; Leland D. Baldwin, *The Keelboat Age on Western Waters*, Pittsburgh: University of Pittsburgh Press; Solon J. and Elizabeth H. Buck, *The Planting of Civilization in Western Pennsylvania*, Pittsburgh: University of Pittsburgh Press; Russell J. Ferguson, *Early Western Pennsylvania Politics*, Pittsburgh: University of Pittsburgh Press; *Guide Book to Historic Places in Western Pennsylvania*, compiled by the Western Pennsylvania Historical Survey, Pittsburgh: University of Pittsburgh Press; Elizabeth Moorhead, *Whirling Spindle: The Story of a Pittsburgh Family*, Pittsburgh: University of Pittsburgh Press; S. K. Stevens and D. H. Kent, *Wilderness Chronicles of Northwestern Pennsylvania*, Harrisburg: Pennsylvania Historical Commission.

Political Parties

Sister Theophane Geary, *History of Third Parties in Pennsylvania, 1840–1860*, Washington, D. C.: Catholic University Press;

Philip S. Klein, *Pennsylvania Politics, 1817–1832: A Game Without Rules*, Philadelphia: Historical Society of Pennsylvania; H. R. Mueller, *The Whig Party in Pennsylvania*, Harrisburg: Pennsylvania Book Service.

Establishment of Public Schools

J. J. McCadden, *Education in Pennsylvania, 1801–1835, and Its Debt to Robert Vaux*, Philadelphia: University of Pennsylvania Press; James Mulhern, *History of Secondary Education in Pennsylvania*, Harrisburg: Pennsylvania Book Service; *One Hundred Years of Free Public Schools*, Harrisburg: Department of Public Instruction; L. G. and M. J. Walsh, *History and Organization of Education in Pennsylvania*, Indiana, Pa.: Walsh and Walsh; T. F. Woodley, *The Great Leveller: The Life of Thaddeus Stevens*, Harrisburg: Pennsylvania Book Service.

Experimental Societies

Frances S. Childs, *French Refugee Life in the United States, 1790–1800*, Baltimore, Md.: Johns Hopkins Press; John S. Duss, *The Harmonists: A Personal History*, Harrisburg: Pennsylvania Book Service; Elsie Murray, *Azilum, The Story of a French Royal Colony of 1793*, Athens: Tioga Point Museum; *Pennsylvania Cavalcade*, Writers Program of Pennsylvania, Philadelphia: University of Pennsylvania Press.

Economic Changes

H. I. Bogen, *The Anthracite Railroads, A Study in American Railroad Enterprise*, New York: Ronald Press; *Industrial Directory of the Commonwealth of Pennsylvania*, Harrisburg: Department of Internal Affairs; C. L. Jones, *The Economic History of the Anthracite Tidewater Canals*, Philadelphia: University of Pennsylvania Press. *Pennsylvania Cavalcade*, Writers Program of Pennsylvania, Philadelphia: University of Pennsylvania Press; James M. Swank, *Progressive Pennsylvania*, Philadelphia: Lippincott.

Fiction

Leland D. Baldwin, *The Delectable Country*, New York: Lee Furman; Margaret Bloom, *Down the Ohio*, Chicago: Albert Whitman; Thomas Boyd, *Poor John Fitch*, New York: Putnam's; Thomas Boyd, *Simon Girty: The White Savage*, New York: Putnam's; Frank Cowan, *American Story-Book: Short Stories from Studies of Life in Southwestern Pennsylvania*, Greensburg: the Author; Phyllis Crawford, *Hello, the Boat*, New York: Henry Holt; Sister M. Fides Glass, *The Prince Who Gave His Gold Away: A Story of the Russian Prince Demetrius Gallitzin*, St. Louis: B. Herder Co.; Samuel H. Glassmire, *Olea: A Story of the Norsemen in Pennsylvania*, New York: Knickerbocker Press.

UNIT V

PENNSYLVANIA HELPS TO SAVE THE UNION

The strength of an arch depends upon the center stone which is called the keystone. If the keystone is weak, the arch will crumble and the whole structure supported by the arch will fall. Early in the history of the Commonwealth, Pennsylvania came to be called the Keystone state. At first the term was used to describe Pennsylvania's central geographic position among the thirteen original states, but as time went on the name came to signify the economic and political position of Pennsylvania in the Union.

The Union was in grave danger of being broken apart during the middle of the nineteenth century as a result of the bitter struggle between the northern and southern sections of the United States. That struggle was basically over the question of slavery, but, as we shall discover, it was complicated by other differences between the two sections. Many times in the years preceding the outbreak of war with the Confederacy, Pennsylvania lived up to its reputation as the Keystone state. The Underground Railroad, which helped slaves to flee from their southern masters and find freedom in the north or in Canada, had its origin in the state. It was proved beyond doubt that the Fugitive Slave Law of 1850 could not be effectively enforced in the face of northern public opinion after the Christiana Riot took place in Lancaster County in Pennsylvania.

Once war was joined, Pennsylvania's geographic position, her industrial might, her natural resources, her rich farms, her man-power—all of these—meant that the state was destined to become the bulwark of the North in the War for the Union. In this unit we shall study the part played by Pennsylvania in the severest test the nation had yet faced.

185

Chapter X

THE GATHERING STORM

During the first half of the nineteenth century, America was a young nation throbbing with the growing pains of national development. Below the surface, however, forces were at work driving the nation toward civil war. Let us see briefly in what ways the North and South differed, so that we may better understand what these forces were and how they affected Pennsylvania.

The Northern States. The North teemed with prosperity. Farming was the principal occupation, although manufacturing was developing rapidly and railroads were spinning out their networks, knitting the ports closer to the interior. Cities increased in size as European immigrants streamed into the North attracted by the cheapness of land and the almost unlimited opportunities to prosper that the growing nation offered.

The Southern States. The South presented a far different picture. Slavery rather than free enterprise was the system upon which it based its economic foundation. There was no manufacturing of importance and few railroads when compared with the North. Europeans immigrating to America did not come to the South, for here was no thriving country, but rather one that was dying under the weight of its "peculiar institution," as slavery was called. Free laborers could not get jobs on plantations worked by unpaid slaves. Reformers were unwelcome in the South where people would not tolerate attacks on the institution of slavery.

SECTIONAL ISSUES

Keeping in mind how different the two sections were, let us now look briefly at the actual issues at stake in the quarrel which developed between them.

Economic Differences. Each section possessed a different economic system. The difference was so great that neither side could even begin to see the other's point of view. The North,

186

STRENGTH OF NORTH AND SOUTH
AT OUTBREAK OF CIVIL WAR – 1861

POPULATION: Each symbol represents 2,000,000 people
Black symbols=Negro Population

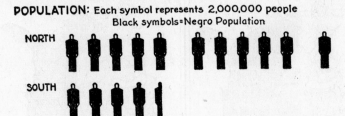

SOLDIERS: Each symbol represents 500,000 soldiers

RAILROADS: Each symbol 🚃 represents 10,000 miles of railroad

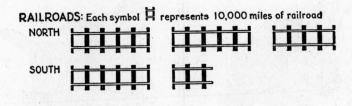

BUSINESS: Each symbol ● represents 100,000,000 dollars

—*From "Our Constitution" issue, Building America*

without slavery, prospered; the South held more closely to slavery as its prosperity lessened. The growing of cotton had offered large profits since the cotton gin, a machine for the quick cleaning of cotton, had come into use. As a result the whole South had turned more and more to the raising of cotton to the neglect of other industries, and even to the neglect of most other agricultural products. The raising of cotton, sugar

187

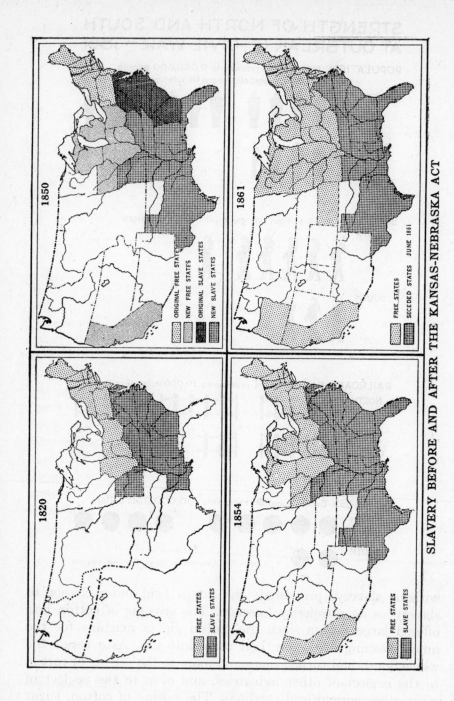

SLAVERY BEFORE AND AFTER THE KANSAS-NEBRASKA ACT

188

cane, rice, and tobacco became the chief occupations in the South, with cotton far in the lead. All of these articles required large numbers of laborers to do the work in the fields, and Southerners felt that without slave labor their chief means of earning a living would cease to be profitable.

Political Differences. Of course, two such different economic systems meant that northern and southern interests clashed at every turn. The President and Congress had to make frequent compromises which satisfied neither section and increased the ill-feeling on both sides. For example, some northern interests demanded a high tariff on certain manufactured articles brought from Europe. This was particularly true in Pennsylvania, where a high tariff was needed if goods made by industries which were just starting were to compete successfully with similar products which could be brought in from abroad. The South, on the other hand, preferred a low tariff since it could then import needed manufactured articles at a lower price.

The question as to which section should have its way became increasingly important as each strove to gain control of national affairs. The greater population of the North gave this section a majority in the House of Representatives. But in the Senate each section was represented equally. As long as there were as many slave as free states in the Union, the South could prevent any legislation it believed unfavorable to its interests.

The Western Territories. Thus the problem of what was to be done about the vast western territories opened up to settlement by the War of 1812 and the Mexican War became the issue between the North and South that troubled American politics from 1820 to 1860. Should the balance of free and slave states be kept, and how? Could a balance be maintained in those territories which lay in the border region between slave states and free states when these territories were brought into the Union, as they inevitably must be? If not, which system should prevail? In answering this last question, time was on the side of the North. Its growing population overflowed into the western lands and established the system of free enterprise without waiting for the decisions of the lawmakers.

The Theory of States Rights. As sectional bitterness widened the rift between the North and the South, more and more Southerners came to the conclusion that disagreement lay too deep to be solved except by the most drastic means. Secession, or separation from the Union, seemed to them to be the only answer.

Dissatisfied minorities had seriously considered secession before. It had been threatened by the Federalist party which was in control of the New England states during the War of 1812. In 1832 South Carolina threatened to leave the Union, on the grounds that the high tariff on manufactured goods was favoring the North at the expense of South Carolina. President Andrew Jackson took a firm stand for the Union in that crisis and at the same time he used his influence to lower the tariff. But already sectional bitterness was mounting.

There were good arguments legally and historically for secession. It could be shown that the Union had been formed as a voluntary agreement between the states. Why, then, should not a state be allowed to withdraw from the Union when it was no longer desirable to abide by that compact? There were a number of ways to answer the arguments of the South, but Northerners were not interested in any theories of the right of secession. They saw their beloved Union threatened. To them the Union was one and indivisible, and it must continue to be so if the country was to fulfill its destiny of becoming a great nation. The North felt that arguments and theories about how the Union had come into existence should not be allowed to interfere with the free development of democracy—a system based upon the principle of majority rule. The interests of minorities like the South should receive due consideration and their rights should be guaranteed, but Northerners would never admit that such minorities might break up the Union whenever they felt that they had been treated unjustly.

The Slavery Question. In another way, too, time was on the side of the North. Slavery as an institution was disappearing all over the civilized world. Even in Russia, then a backward country, it was abolished in 1861 by the Czar's decree. International conferences had been held, dedicated to the overthrow of slavery everywhere. At an early date in the northern states there were many reformers who looked upon slavery as a moral wrong that needed to be stamped out. These reformers organized antislavery clubs or societies, and the members of the societies were known as Abolitionists. Their number was small, but by the wounds they inflicted upon southern sensibilities in their speeches and in their writings they were a mighty force in the cause of freedom. The Abolitionists were impatient and violent in their criticisms, not only of slaveholders, but of all who did not work openly to abolish the system. In the North these Abolitionists were regarded by the more moderate citizens as troublemakers. Southerners at first thought of them as fanatics, but as resentment between the sections mounted, they became convinced that the Abolitionists represented the views of the North as a whole. This small group of reformers fanned the flames of sectional bitterness, stirred to wakefulness the sleeping conscience of the world to the moral wrong of slavery, and lashed the South into a fury of resentment and anger.

Slavery as an issue had first thrust itself into the political forefront in 1820. At that time Missouri was insisting upon admission to the Union as a slave state. It was sectional pride more than the moral issue of slavery that led the North to object. This time it was settled by admitting Maine as a free and Missouri as a slave state, thus maintaining the balance between slave and free states. The latitude of 36° 30′ was set as the northern boundary of territory that in the future would be slave. Missouri, which lay north of this line, was to be the only exception. This was known as the Missouri Compromise. This time the ugly problem of slavery had been put aside easily, but the far-sighted Thomas Jefferson, living in retirement at Monticello, wrote prophetically: "This momentous question, like a fire bell in the night awakened me and filled me with terror. I considered it at once the knell of the Union."

Texas and the War with Mexico. As Jefferson watched the developments of the years following the Missouri Compromise, his alarm must have increased. In the early 1820's Southerners were moving westward faster than were the national boundaries. In the search for new cotton land they moved into the then Mexican state of Texas.

By 1836 Texas was American in population, but it still belonged to Mexico. Frightened by the continuing immigration which the Mexicans had encouraged, the government of Mexico now placed one restriction after another upon the settlers from the United States. Slavery was abolished. Although few

Texas settlers were Catholics, they were ordered to contribute to the state-supported Roman Catholic Church of Mexico. In the face of these hostile acts on the part of the Mexican government, the settlers of Texas revolted and proclaimed their independence. When Mexico sent an army against them, they made good their claim by force of arms. After winning their independence in 1836, Texans hoped for annexation to the United States, but it was not until 1845 that their hopes were realized. In the nine years intervening, Texas was an important factor in the rising hostility between the North and South. To the South, it seemed only natural that Texas should be admitted to the Union, but the North regarded the revolution in Texas with cold suspicion. Was this not evidence of a plot by Southerners to strengthen the slave system?

In 1845 Texas was quickly annexed when it appeared that Great Britain had become interested in the fate of the little republic and was ready to recognize its independence. There was no real reason why the admission of Texas into the Union should have led to war with Mexico, even though the proud Mexicans were deeply offended by this act. But President Polk had his eye on other lands owned by the Mexican government—in particular, California. He hoped to get these lands by purchase. Therefore, he began a diplomatic chess game in which he attempted to put pressure on the Mexican government by claiming for the United States all of Texas to the Rio Grande. This set the boundary far to the south of the territory that Texas had tried to control during its nine years of independence. The Mexicans chose to fight rather than to negotiate with President Polk's representatives, and in 1846 clashes occurred on the disputed border. Soon California and Santa Fe, in New Mexico, were seized. During the next two years American armies under General Zachary Taylor and General Winfield Scott fought their way into Mexico City. This victory made possible the purchase from Mexico of the territory which later became the states of New Mexico, Arizona, and California.

Pennsylvania in the War with Mexico. The actual fighting took place far from the borders of Pennsylvania, but a large number of Pennsylvanians responded to President Polk's call for volunteers. Two regiments were mustered into military service and served throughout the war. One of these units, from

Cambria County, was known as the American Highlanders. It was commanded by John W. Geary, who later became Governor of the Commonwealth. Other Pennsylvanians, notably George B. McClellan and Winfield S. Hancock, who were at that time serving with the regular army, found on the battlefields of the Mexican War valuable experience which they turned to good account fifteen years later in behalf of the Union.

The Wilmot Proviso. It was the war with Mexico that furnished the occasion for again flaunting the problem of slavery before the American people. In 1846 it was David Wilmot, a Congressman from Pennsylvania and until this time of little national fame, who aired the touchy question. On the floor of the House of Representatives he demanded that a proviso accompany the appropriation which the President was asking of Congress for the purpose of buying Mexican territory. Wilmot's proviso demanded that slavery be prohibited in any land purchased from Mexico. The proviso did not pass, but it released the dammed up flood of sectional ill feeling. The question of the extension of slavery, so long smouldering under the surface, suddenly became a raging issue.

ANTISLAVERY MOVEMENT IN PENNSYLVANIA

With this background of national events in mind, let us turn back and see what was happening in Pennsylvania during the years of dissension over the issue of slavery. In an earlier chapter we described how slavery came to be abolished within the state.

The Pennsylvania Society. The first organization in America devoted to the abolition of Negro slavery was formed in Philadelphia in 1775. Its full title was the Pennsylvania Society for Promoting the Abolition of Slavery and the Relief of the Negroes Unlawfully Held in Bondage, but it was usually known just as the Pennsylvania Society. After the Revolutionary War similar organizations were formed in other northern states. Benjamin Franklin served as president of the Pennsylvania Society from 1787 until his death in 1790. During its early years, the society devoted itself chiefly to sending petitions to Congress advocating the abolition of slavery and the protection of free Negroes from being kidnapped and carried south to be sold as slaves. The Society continued in existence until the War for the Union had freed the slaves and rendered its purpose no longer necessary.

Kidnapping Negroes. Because the southern boundary of Pennsylvania bordered on slave territory, the kidnapping of free Negroes often took place within the borders of the state. Runaway slaves from Virginia and Maryland headed northward seeking shelter in free Pennsylvania. In 1795 Congress had passed a law which permitted slaveowners to follow their escaped slaves into any free state and recapture them. There was a provision in the law, however, that once the owners had recaptured their slaves, they must go before the courts of the state in which the slaves were taken and secure permission to take the slaves back to the state from which they had fled. This provision was designed for the protection of free Negroes living in the North.

In spite of the provision, however, an evil practice developed. Unscrupulous white men in the North made a business of kidnapping free Negroes, chaining them together with recaptured slaves, and selling the entire group to southern plantation owners who were anxious to get additional slaves and who asked no questions about where they had come from. The situation was particularly bad in the southwestern corner of Pennsylvania. Governor Findley pointed out this shameful abuse of the law in a message to the state Assembly in 1817 and again in 1818, but very little could be done to stop it since the region had not been completely settled, and the courts, which were charged with seeing that the law was properly enforced, were not firmly established.

Antislavery Society. In 1833, the citizens of Philadelphia and nearby communities formed the Pennsylvania Antislavery Society. This society was a part of the national movement for the abolition of slavery. Among the leaders in Philadelphia were Lucretia Mott, the great reformer who had gained national fame in the cause of women's rights; her husband, John Mott; and Reverend Dr. William H. Furness, a Unitarian clergyman. John Greenleaf Whittier, the Quaker poet, edited an antislavery magazine published in Philadelphia by J. Miller McKim. The Pennsylvania Antislavery Society was energetic in the cause of freedom for Negroes. Most Philadelphians were not in sympathy with the extreme views of these Abolitionists, and, on several occasions, the differences of opinion led to riots between white men and Negroes living in Philadelphia.

FUGITIVE SLAVES

Runaway slaves faced many dangers in their efforts to escape from their masters. Many of those who tried to escape were recaptured before they reached the free states. Severe punishment awaited those who were unsuccessful in their attempts to gain freedom. There was no real safety for them, even if they did succeed in crossing the Mason and Dixon Line, because all states were required to permit the masters to come after their runaways. Only by reaching Canada, far to the north, could the Negroes be certain of freedom.

The Underground Railroad. Most of the fugitives had no idea of where Canada was or how far they would have to travel. Had it not been for the help given them by northern sympathizers, they would have been recaptured or would have

RUNAWAY SLAVES ARRIVING AT A STATION ON THE UNDERGROUND RAILROAD

perished for want of food and shelter. The Northerners who aided them organized a system of stations at farmhouses about one night's journey apart. The fugitive traveled at night, reaching some friendly household before dawn the next day. There the runaway slave was given food and a place to sleep and hide during the day. At night he would be sent northward again to the next station on the route to Canada. This system of helping slaves to freedom was known as the "Underground Railroad." Most of those who conducted stations were lawabiding men and women in other respects, but were willing to risk fines or imprisonment for the sake of human liberty.

The first underground station in the country was at Columbia, Pennsylvania, in Lancaster County on the Susquehanna River. There, in 1804, Samuel Wright hit upon the scheme of dispatching Negro fugitives to stations north of the town. Soon many other routes were established, not only in Pennsylvania, but in Ohio, Indiana, and Illinois as well.

It is impossible to know how many slaves escaped from the South by way of the Underground Railroad. The operations were carried on secretly and few records were kept. It has been estimated that during the years just before the war the number of travelers on the Underground Railroad averaged a thousand a year.

Effects of the New Fugitive Slave Law in Pennsylvania. While there had always been penalties for aiding slaves to escape, a new law was passed as part of the Compromise of 1850, known as the Fugitive Slave Law, which made these penalties far more severe. Yet so far as the North was concerned, it had almost the opposite effect than was intended. Northerners who were willing to work actively in the cause of freedom refused to be frightened by threats. But the Southerners resolved to take full advantage of the law. Thus, this Fugitive Slave Law actually increased the hostility between the two sections. Two incidents which took place in Pennsylvania illustrate the northern reaction to the law.

The first event in Pennsylvania which stirred public opinion against the law took place in Columbia. William Smith, a Negro who had escaped from slavery long before the Fugitive Slave Law of 1850 had been enacted, lived in Columbia and had won a respected place for himself as a useful member of the community. One day while he was at work he saw a band of slave catchers approaching him. Frightened at the prospect of being returned to his former master, Smith began to run. The brutal slave hunters shot and killed him while they were pursuing him.

The Christiana Riot. A second incident occurred in the same year, 1851, also in Lancaster County. William Parker, a former slave who had escaped from the South, lived near the village of Christiana. Parker used his home as an Underground Railroad station, assisting other Negroes who came to him for help. In September of 1851, one Edward Gorsuch of Baltimore came to Parker's home and demanded that he surrender two escaped slaves that Parker was accused of sheltering. With Gorsuch was a posse of armed men under the command of a United States Deputy Marshal. When Parker refused to surrender the fugitives, these armed men surrounded his house. The Negroes living in the neighborhood had arranged a signal by which they could summon help if it was needed. Parker's wife gave the signal from a bedroom window by blowing a horn which could be heard throughout the countryside. The armed men fired at the bedroom window, but Mrs. Parker was not hurt. William Parker's neighbors, all of them Negroes, came to his rescue.

William Parker came out of his house to talk to the Deputy Marshal and Gorsuch, the leader of the slave catchers. During the discussion, Gorsuch's son fired a shot at Parker which passed through his hat. A fight followed in which Gorsuch was killed and a number of his party wounded. The Deputy Marshal and his band left the scene, unwilling to become involved in bloodshed. Soon the slave catchers were forced to flee, hotly pursued by the victorious Negroes.

A detachment of forty-five United States marines and nearly one hundred Philadelphia policemen were rushed to Christiana to restore order. Thirty-five Negroes were arrested and taken to Philadelphia. Two white men who had refused to aid the Deputy Marshal, and Joseph Scarlett, a Quaker who had come upon the scene during the fighting, were also taken into custody. All of the prisoners were charged with treason for refusing to help in enforcing the Fugitive Slave Law. The indictment accused them of levying war against the United States.

197

The charges were obviously unfair, as was pointed out by the judge at the trial.

When the trial was held in the Federal Court at Philadelphia, the authorities had difficulty in finding a jury to sit on the case. Citizens called for jury duty claimed they were deaf. It was one week before enough jurors could be found who would accept duty. The lawyer for the defense was Thaddeus Stevens, an ardent Abolitionist and a famous Pennsylvania politician. When the case was submitted to the jury for its decision, only a few minutes were required to reach a verdict of not guilty. The entire nation had watched the trial. The North was pleased with the verdict, but to Southerners it was more evidence of northern hostility toward the South. Both sections realized that it was proof that the Fugitive Slave Law could not be enforced. The compromise which had promised so much was falling apart.

A DECADE OF STRIFE

The 1850's were a decade in which sectional friction rubbed raw the feelings of both sides. Incidents multiplied, driving steadily deeper the wedge of disunion. In 1854 the Kansas-Nebraska Act was passed by Congress. This Act repealed the agreement reached under the Missouri Compromise that slavery would not be permitted in any territory north of 36° 30′ and substituted the principle known as "popular sovereignty" by which the majority of the inhabitants should determine which system—slave or free—should be adopted. The Kansas-Nebraska Act led to armed clashes in Kansas as Abolitionists and Southerners financed immigrants to enter the region, each side determined to capture the territory for itself. Elections became pitched battles as Kansas developed into a small battleground which warned of the approach of civil strife on a national scale.

The old parties, Democratic and Whig, had begun to break up in the 1840's. Factions appeared in each and tension inside the parties tightened as issues arose which cut across party lines. Various antislavery parties had appeared, all of minor importance at first. But as the slow-burning conviction spread throughout the North that the extension of slavery into the new territories must be stopped, many voters began to turn away from the old parties. Northerners were tired of indecision

—*Harper's Weekly*

PRESIDENT BUCHANAN AND HIS CABINET
President Buchanan is seated at the head of the table.

and compromises and looked for action to new political organization which would not refuse, like the older parties, to face and settle the matter of the extension of slavery.

It was such men who founded the Republican Party in 1854. Their first presidential candidate lost the election of 1856 to James Buchanan. It was significant, however, that Buchanan carried only three northern states, one of which was his home state of Pennsylvania.

James Buchanan. The only President of the United States to be elected from Pennsylvania was James Buchanan of Lancaster. Elected to the highest office in the nation in 1856, Buchanan was faced with the difficult problems growing out of the struggle for Kansas and the many incidents which were leading the two parts of the nation closer and closer to war.

In 1853 Buchanan became United States Minister to Great Britain. Thus, he was not in the United States during the bitter struggle over Kansas and had not been forced to take sides on the slavery issue. He had made no powerful enemies, either in the North or the South. It was this fact which contributed to his nomination for President by the Democratic party in 1856. The newly formed Republican party was seen as a great threat to the Democrats in the North. Buchanan's nomination, however, would assure the party of the electoral votes of Pennsylvania, and this could mean winning the election.

John Brown's Raid. In the last year of the 1850's a final bombshell was tossed into the explosive issue of slavery by John Brown's raid into Virginia. A stern old Abolitionist, Brown hoped to seize the United States arsenal at Harper's Ferry, Virginia, and distribute the weapons stored there to the slaves who would then organize and fight for their own freedom. Brown had fought for his beliefs earlier in Kansas. In 1859 he moved quietly to Chambersburg, Pennsylvania, with a small band of followers including several of his sons. There he made the preparations for his raid.

The raid never had a chance of success. The slaves were far more terrified of the fierce old Brown than of their masters. John Brown and his men were trapped after capturing the arsenal. Some were killed, a few escaped, and Brown, himself, was captured, tried, and hung. His undoubted sincerity stirred the North to sympathy and sent a shudder through the South. For it appeared after this to Southerners that their entire economic and social system was threatened with violent overthrow.

QUESTIONS FOR STUDY AND REVIEW

1. Contrast the economic life of the North with that of the South. How did labor conditions differ? business activities? agricultural pursuits? Why did immigrants from Europe settle only in the North?

2. Why was the South determined to extend the system of slavery to the newly-formed states? Give the political and economic reasons for its attitude.

3. What is meant by "states rights"? Can you name some rights which states exercise today without interference from the federal government? Do states today have the right to withdraw or secede from the Union?

4. Why was slavery allowed to exist in the southern states even after it was abolished in other parts of the civilized world? Why were Northern reformers active in agitating against it?

5. Why were the Northerners opposed to the Fugitive Slave Law of 1850? What events taking place in Pennsylvania proved that it could not be enforced?

Chapter XI

THE WAR FOR THE UNION

Resentment had reached the point in 1860 where all realized the critical aspects of the presidential election. During the 1850's, presidents Pierce and Buchanan had failed to take a stand on the issues besetting the nation. Both were northern Democrats who recognized the southern point of view, and only such a compromise had thus far kept the South in the Union. In 1860, however, Abraham Lincoln was elected on a platform that uncompromisingly opposed any further extension of slavery. When the election was over, southern leaders immediately began to organize the Confederacy, at the same time announcing the secession of their states. In vain Lincoln pleaded for them to reconsider. In vain he promised not to interfere with the South's "peculiar institution" where it was already established. To the South, Lincoln was a Black Republican, more dangerous than John Brown and a man not to be trusted.

Historians have found fault with Buchanan's administration of the office of President, especially during the last four months. It is pointed out that often his policies were weak and inconsistent at a time when a strong hand was most needed if the Union were to be preserved. Buchanan was personally opposed to slavery, but he was unwilling to do anything which would force the Southerners into more extreme action. It was his hope that in some way a compromise could be worked out which would enable the two sections to continue to live together peaceably, and he clung to this hope long after events seemed to have made such a settlement impossible. Thus, after the election of Abraham Lincoln as President, Buchanan did nothing to prevent the secession of the southern states or to preserve the Union. It is true, as has been said, that Buchanan may have felt that it was not his place to commit his successor to a policy which would have to be followed out once it was set in motion. On the other hand, as President he was under oath to preserve and defend the nation. Yet for four months he allowed the southern states to withdraw from the Union and organize a government unmolested.

THE BEGINNING OF THE WAR

By the time Lincoln was sworn into office in March, 1861, the South had formed its Confederacy and elected as its first president Jefferson Davis, former United States Secretary of War and Senator from the state of Mississippi. The Confederacy adopted a constitution very similar to that of the United States except that it guaranteed the undisturbed continuation of the slave system. When Lincoln took over the office of President he faced a nation divided. The following month, Confederate soldiers fired upon a United States fort in Charleston harbor named Fort Sumter. This was rebellion. It could not be ignored, and Lincoln issued a call for volunteers to create an army to preserve the Union.

Pennsylvania was in the midst of the War for the Union. It was to provide the decisive battleground of the war at Gettysburg. It was to provide, too, several of the most effective military leaders in the Union cause. But before taking up the events that touched the state, let us glance briefly at the war as a whole.

The Union Strategy. The plan of campaign adopted by the Union Army was, in brief, to cut off the southern states west of the Mississippi by driving down the great river to New Orleans, while at the same time attacking the capital of the Confederacy, Richmond. It was also intended to starve the South by blockading its seacoast. Both the blockade and the campaign in the West moved forward slowly but surely. In the eastern theater of war, however, each northern campaign met with costly defeat. Fortunately for the Union, each defeat, though stinging, was not totally disastrous, since the Confederacy was unable to follow up its successes by a counter-drive into northern territory. In Europe, diplomatic agents of the South worked feverishly to gain recognition and support from England and France. If they had succeeded, the blockade could have been broken and the South might have won its independence.

The Emancipation Proclamation. The possibility of European intervention in this American quarrel seemed quite

202

possible so long as the reason for fighting seemed to be limited to an interpretation of the federal constitution and completely divorced from the moral issue of slavery. Partly for this reason, and partly to satisfy opinion at home, Lincoln eagerly waited for a victory to make more telling his proclamation of emancipation of the slaves. The slaves had showed no signs of revolting against their owners, but instead were carrying on the work on the plantations and releasing their masters for military service. The Emancipation Proclamation, therefore, could be considered a war measure by the President, who hoped by issuing it to disrupt the enemy's home front. Lincoln wished to wait, however, until the North had won a decisive victory before issuing the proclamation, since if it were issued in the face of a long series of defeats, no one, either in the South or in Europe, would be likely to take it seriously.

It was not until the battle of Antietam in September of 1862 that the northern forces in the eastern theater of the war could claim a victory. In the late summer of 1862 General Lee had administered a crushing defeat to the Union Army and had driven it out of Virginia. Sensing his opportunity to carry the war into northern territory, Lee led his army across the Potomac River above Washington and into Maryland. General Lee hoped to win Maryland for the Confederacy, thus surrounding the federal capital with hostile territory, but he also had his eye on the railway bridge over the Susquehanna River at Harrisburg, Pennsylvania. If he could win possession of that bridge he could not only surround Washington, but also cut off a part of the Union so that their only line of communication with the West would be a roundabout route up the Atlantic coastline, then along the Hudson River and the Great Lakes. Such a telling blow at the Union would be almost certain to bring foreign intervention in behalf of the South. The battle between McClellan's forces and Lee's army took place at the crossing of Antietam Creek in Maryland not far from the Pennsylvania border. Casualties were heavy on both sides and neither won a clearcut victory, but the Confederate Army was forced to turn back into Virginia. On this basis Lincoln claimed the victory for the North and hastened to follow up with his Emancipation Proclamation, which declared that after January first, 1863, all slaves in the Confederate States were forever free.

The effect upon the slaves was slight at the time it was issued, but politically it was a wise move. England could not come to the aid of slavery, which the majority of Englishmen considered immoral.

With the retreat of the Confederate Army, Pennsylvanians heaved a great sigh of relief. Whether they were aware of Lee's objective at Harrisburg, or not, they knew that he had come entirely too close to their state for comfort. From the very beginning of the war, Pennsylvanians had realized that their position on the border of the Union placed special responsibilities upon them in aiding the war effort. They had been meeting these responsibilities nobly.

PENNSYLVANIA IN THE WAR FOR THE UNION

The First Defenders. From the first the Commonwealth of Pennsylvania responded patriotically to the President's call to arms. With the national capital separated from the Confederate state of Virginia only by the Potomac River, all nearby loyal states were called upon urgently once the war had begun to furnish troops for the defense of Washington. Pennsylvania units reached the capital first and earned for themselves the name of the "First Defenders." The units hastening to Washington included the Ringgold Light Artillery of Reading, the Logan Guards of Lewistown, an infantry and an artillery unit from Pottsville, and the Allen Rifles of Allentown.

Camp Curtin. In his first call for volunteers, President Lincoln asked for 75,000 men. The response in Pennsylvania was enthusiastic when Governor Andrew G. Curtin asked for the state's quota of fourteen regiments. Volunteers rushed to Harrisburg from all corners of the state. In order to provide training quarters for the recruits, a military camp was quickly constructed near Harrisburg which was named Camp Curtin in honor of the Governor. Here most of Pennsylvania's soldiers received their training throughout the four years of the war.

The Gettysburg Campaign. In June of 1863 General Lee resolved to make another attempt to carry the war into the North. His army lay in Virginia along the Rappahannock River. It had recently administered a defeat to the Union Army under General Hooker at Chancellorsville. Now, needing to replenish his supply of food in a less battle-scarred region, and hopeful

204

of a final military victory which might bring peace to the South, Lee decided to move north. Leaving one corps to protect Richmond, the Army of Northern Virginia moved northwest through Winchester, across the Maryland border to Hagerstown, and late in June crossed into Pennsylvania at Mercersburg. Lee established his headquarters at Chambersburg. He knew nothing of the movements of the Union Army under Hooker, for he was separated from his cavalry whose duty it was to keep him informed of the enemy's movements and strength. Jeb Stuart, dashing leader of the Confederate cavalry, had clashed with Union forces while on a raid. When he attempted to rejoin Lee, he found himself cut off and was unable to get back to the army until the battle at Gettysburg was nearly over. Thus Lee had to feel his way, whereas Hooker knew where his enemy was. Hooker followed Lee into Pennsylvania.

At Chambersburg, Lee impatiently awaited news from Stuart. At the same time he extended the left wing of his army as far north as Carlisle and to within three miles of Harrisburg. Governor Curtin sent frantic telegrams to Washington. Hooker suddenly resigned his command and was replaced by a Pennsylvanian, General George G. Meade.

Perplexed and in the dark as to the position of the Union Army, Lee stared at the map on June twenty-eighth. Placing his finger on the little town of Gettysburg, from which roads spread out like spokes of a wheel in all directions, he mused: "Hereabouts we shall probably meet the enemy and fight a great battle, and if God gives us the victory, the war will be over."

On the evening of June 30, a force of Confederates occupying Cashtown heard that shoes, always a prize of greatest value to the poorly-shod Confederate soldiers, were to be found in Gettysburg. Upon reaching the town, the Confederates encountered a small force of Union cavalry. The battle developed the next day as re-enforcements arrived from both sides. Ewell's southern troops moved south upon the town from Carlisle, and General Reynolds arrived with the first federal forces from the east. Informed of the accidental clash, Lee was puzzled. He did not know whether the entire Union Army was nearby or not. If it was, he preferred to wait for the arrival of a third of his army under General Longstreet before joining battle. On the other hand, it would be better to crush the Union forces in

Gettysburg at once before re-enforcements should arrive if this were possible. Actually, re-enforcements were some distance away, and General Lee decided to attack at once. General Ewell drove the Union troops through the town to a point just south, which afforded an excellent defensive position. This point was known as Cemetery Hill and just east of it was Culp's Hill, an even higher bastion. From these positions the Union troops held on grimly. They had lost five thousand prisoners and many casualties. It looked like another defeat for the Union Army.

Ewell did not press his attack further, however. As evening fell, a thin blue line occupied the strong defenses of Cemetery Ridge which faced the main Confederate approaches from the west. The battlefield was ready. With the fierce skirmishes of the first day over, the situation was this:

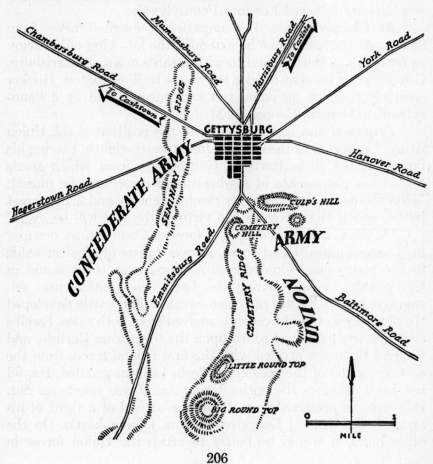

CAMP CURTIN, NEAR HARRISBURG, A MEETING PLACE OF THE
PENNSYLVANIA VOLUNTEERS

Governor Curtin had collected thousands of volunteers, and more were
flocking in daily—on horse and on foot.

Lee hoped to attack Cemetery Ridge early on the second
day if it had not been too heavily re-enforced during the night.
By that time, the fresh troops of Longstreet should be in position. At the same time, Ewell could renew his attack by trying
to seize Culp's Hill. Early on the morning of the second day
Lee scanned Cemetery Ridge eagerly through his field glasses.
No sizeable force of Union troops was there. But where was the
attacking force of Longstreet? The latter had disapproved of his
Commander's plan. But once the decision had been made, most
generals would have carried out their orders. Instead, Longstreet, in this decisive moment, sulked and sabotaged Lee's
plans. He failed to attack until late in the afternoon. By that
time a federal (northern) army corps under Sedgwick had poured
into the gap. Cemetery Ridge was as powerfully held as a
Gibraltar. Lee changed his plan and ordered an attack aimed at
outflanking the left of the federals. Round Top was briefly in
possession of the Confederates, but they were forced to withdraw. Again Longstreet's attitude contributed to the failure of
the assault on the federal left. Credit should also be given to
the Union Army which, under the direction of Meade and the
inspired leadership of Hancock, fought as it never had before,
with a heroism that refused to give ground more than temporarily.

Nevertheless, Lee still had hopes on the third day of July of delivering a crushing blow to Meade's army. After considerable discussion with his officers, it had been planned to advance against the center of the Union lines which lay along Cemetery Ridge. First, the Confederate artillery laid down its most concentrated barrage of the war. Then the still-disapproving Longstreet permitted one of his corps commanders, Pickett, to give the order to attack. The flower of the Confederate Army moved across the open country. While they were still nearly half a mile away, the blue-clad soldiers on Cemetery Ridge opened with a withering rifle and artillery fire. The Confederates, though dropping fast, kept gallantly moving ahead. A handful reached their objective but could not hold on. The last charge had failed, and Lee knew that his only course lay in returning to Virginia. Stuart, who at last had arrived, covered the retreat while the gray columns were set in motion moving south.

Gettysburg was one of the bitterest battles ever to be fought on this continent. Each side had suffered heavy casualties. Lee

GENERAL HANCOCK AND STAFF, AT THE BATTLE OF
GETTYSBURG

DEDICATION CEREMONY AT GETTYSBURG
The platform from which Lincoln spoke is in the square beyond the arch.

had lost 23,000 men, nearly a third of his army. Meade had lost about the same number, but he could better afford the loss. Most important of all, the last great attempt at invasion of the North had been turned back. On the same day, Vicksburg had surrendered, and the northern campaign to cut the Confederacy in two was realized as the Mississippi River was brought completely under the control of the Union. From this day forward, the North was never again threatened with invasion, although much hard fighting remained before the South submitted and victory was won.

Lincoln's Gettysburg Address. In November, 1863, the battlefield at Gettysburg was dedicated "as a final resting place for those who here gave their lives" that the United States might live. President Lincoln came to Gettysburg to deliver an address on the occasion. Before the President's turn came to speak, Edward Everett, a great orator, spoke for more than an hour. At the close of his speech the great audience thundered applause. Then President Lincoln began: "Four score and seven years ago our fathers brought forth on this continent a new nation, conceived in Liberty, and dedicated to the proposition that all men are created equal." As the President uttered his closing words, ". . . and that government of the people, by the people, for the people shall not perish from the earth," the crowd was hushed. There was no applause, but the silence was an even more eloquent tribute to the President's moving words.

Those words, spoken on the battlefield at Gettysburg, have continued to live in the hearts of free men.

In coming to Pennsylvania, Lincoln was visiting the state from which his ancestors had migrated. In Exeter Township, Berks County, stands the ancestral homestead of the Lincoln family. Here Abraham Lincoln's grandfather had tilled the soil. In a brief autobiography written before he became President, Abraham Lincoln wrote that his ancestors "who were Quakers, went to Virginia from Berks County, Pennsylvania." From Virginia they moved to Kentucky where Lincoln was born.

Raids on Chambersburg. Soon after the Gettysburg campaign, General Grant became commander of the northern armies in the east, and throughout 1864 he pressed his costly but unrelenting attack upon Richmond. Only once in this year did Southerners reach into Pennsylvania. In June a desperate raid was made by a southern detachment upon the town of Chambersburg. This town had been raided once before. In 1862, Jeb Stuart had led a band of cavalry into the town. His mission had been to cut communications, destroy military supplies, and capture horses and food for his men. The raid had been entirely successful, but Stuart had been careful that his

*—From an etching by A. J. Volck.
Library Company of Philadelphia*

**A CONFEDERATE RAIDING PARTY RETURNING FROM
PENNSYLVANIA**

210

men refrain from stealing and that they conduct themselves with the utmost courtesy. There had been no bloodshed, for the citizens of the town, entirely defenseless, had offered no resistance. Despite McClellan's promise to President Lincoln that Stuart would be cut off and not allowed to return to Virginia, the bold Southerner had accomplished his task and escaped across the Potomac, carrying his booty with him.

The raid of 1864 was far different. Stuart had been killed two months before and another Confederate commanded the raiders. This time the purpose was more grim, since the raid was made in revenge for a destructive raid made earlier by northern troops into Virginia. The citizens of Chambersburg found no mercy now. They were robbed and their town put to the torch.

The End of the War. In 1865 Grant's continual pressure on Richmond and Sherman's victories in the West finally showed the South that further resistance was useless. In April, at Appomattox Court House, Lee surrendered. Soon after, Sherman received a similar surrender from the other major Confederate army still in the field. The threat to the Union had ended and the system of slavery had been forever abolished.

More than to any other northern state, the war was brought home to Pennsylvania. Her frontier was crossed three times by the Confederates. True, twice it had been merely a raiding party, and the third time the great invasion of 1863 had soon been turned back. But throughout the war, citizens of the state had constantly to be on the alert. When the enemy came, the people of Pennsylvania were able to meet him with fortitude.

THE DRAFT

At first the Union Army was organized from volunteers and units of the state militia. As the war continued, however, and it became clear that it was not going to be won quickly or easily, it was decided that men for the army and navy should be drafted. Today we have come to accept the principle of the draft as the fairest way of determining who should serve with the armed forces, but until the War for the Union such a plan had never been tried in the United States.

From the very beginning there had not been united sentiment in the North in favor of the war. Some people honestly felt that it was better to let the southern states withdraw from

DRAWING DRAFT NUMBERS FOR THE ARMY IN CIVIL WAR DAYS

the Union in peace than to try to hold them by force. The long string of northern defeats in the early years of the war had made others feel that final victory might be impossible, or, if it could be won, would prove far too costly. Most of these people would have been content simply to have no part in a cause for which they felt no enthusiasm, but the draft made it impossible for them to stand aside.

Moreover, there was objection to the draft on another ground. The law provided that men who did not wish to serve in the army might be excused if they provided someone who was willing to go in their place. This meant that wealthy men might pay a substitute to serve for them. To the men who could not afford a substitute, this was unfair.

In 1862 Pennsylvania passed a draft act to meet Lincoln's call for troops. There was opposition to this measure, particularly in Schuylkill County, where an organization of miners known as the Molly Maguires opposed it. We will meet this band of terrorists, the Molly Maguires, again in a later chapter.

In 1863 a national draft law was put into effect. This led to anti-draft riots in several northern states. A secret society had spread throughout the country, known as the Knights of the Golden Circle, which was actively opposed to the war and frequently took the lead in creating these disturbances. A unit of this society was established in western Berks County in Pennsylvania under the leadership of John Huber. In the spring of 1863 some of its members led a march on Reading in an effort to rescue a draft dodger from the hands of the law. The spirits of the marchers were chilled, however, when Reading firemen turned their water hoses on them, causing them to break ranks and flee.

In 1864 there was organized resistance to the draft in Cambria and Columbia counties. A military force was sent into these districts to enforce the law. These instances of opposition to military service were comparatively rare, however, for the majority of Pennsylvanians were devoted to the Union cause.

PENNSYLVANIA'S CONTRIBUTIONS TO VICTORY

What had Pennsylvania given to the four years of struggle? She had given bountifully of her manpower, for 362,000 of her sons had served in the Union armies. Another 14,000 had served in the navy. Her patriotic workers on the home front had

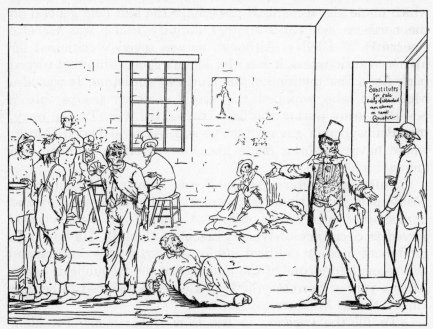

—From an etching by A. J. Volck.
Library Company of Philadelphia

A SOUTHERN CONCEPTION OF BUYING SUBSTITUTES IN THE NORTH

toiled in the mines to provide coal for her great war industries. And these in turn had provided in large part the munitions and supplies which had meant victory for the Union. On the farms had been produced the food needed by the army in the east.

Military Leaders. Some of the best military leadership the North could boast was furnished by the Keystone state. Meade, the victor at Gettysburg and one of the most reliable corps commanders in the colorful history of the Army of the Potomac, was one such leader. Indeed, it is a striking fact that in the test at Gettysburg Pennsylvania officers especially distinguished themselves. General John F. Reynolds arrived to take command on the first day of the battle in time to prevent complete disaster. He was killed while fearlessly directing his soldiers to take position while waiting for re-enforcements to arrive. The next day it was another Pennsylvanian, Winfield S. Hancock, who took command of the forces in the field by Meade's direction. Hancock's coolness and brilliant leadership rallied the federal army at the critical moment. Then as always throughout the war, Hancock showed that steadying influence which made him recognized as perhaps the best field general on the northern side. Still another military leader was General George B. McClellan. Although he was severely criticized for his over-cautiousness, it was McClellan's generalship that turned back Lee's first invasion of the North at Antietam. It was also McClellan who whipped the green northern troops into a powerful army during the first year of the war. To the navy, too, Pennsylvania gave a famous son, Admiral David Porter, whose naval victories made his state proud to number him among its heroes.

Political Leaders. Several Pennsylvanians held important positions in the national government during the war years and immediately afterwards. Simon Cameron of Pennsylvania served as Secretary of War in Lincoln's Cabinet. He had been prominent in state political life for a quarter of a century and was recognized as one of the founders of the Republican party. After a year as Secretary of War, Cameron resigned to become United States Minister to Russia.

To fill the vacancy in the War Department, President Lincoln appointed Edwin M. Stanton, born in Ohio but at that time and for many years a resident of Pittsburgh. Stanton had served as Attorney-general in Buchanan's administration. After the war began, Stanton, like many northern Democrats, shifted his allegiance to the Republican party. Edwin M. Stanton was a man of ability and intelligence, but unfortunately he was also ambitious and self-seeking. These qualities interfered with his statesmanship and he was not always loyal to President Lincoln in carrying out Lincoln's wishes.

Throughout the entire struggle over slavery, Thaddeus Stevens had been a sincere leader in the cause of freedom and equality for the Negro. It will be remembered that, in 1851, he successfully defended the persons tried for refusing to help enforce the Fugitive Slave Law at the time of the Christiana Riot. From 1858 until his death ten years later, he was a member of the United States Congress. In his bitterness against slavery, Stevens was determined to punish the southern states after the war had ended and believed the South should be treated like conquered territory. His narrow devotion to the principles he believed in left no room for generous feelings of sympathy for those Southerners who had suffered deeply in the war. Often, too, Stevens was blind to the best interests of the country. To gain his point, he was willing to keep alive the sectional hatred which had brought on the war. Wiser statesmen like President Lincoln believed that a policy of "malice toward none and charity for all" was necessary to permit the reunited nation to move ahead in peaceful progress.

"One Nation, Indivisible . . . with liberty and justice for all." The Union had survived the severe test of civil war. All of the stars and stripes remained in the flag that we salute so proudly. European nations watching the American struggle learned that here was a nation strong enough to remain united under the most trying stresses and strains; that Americans could settle their own affairs in this hemisphere and could make democracy work. Americans themselves learned that the constitution is the law of the land and that when some arise to attack it there are millions more who will spring to arms to defend it.

The surging spirit of democracy had broken down the barriers which denied Negro slaves the blessings of liberty.

In these struggles the enemies of the Union beat upon the bastions of Pennsylvania. Their might was hurled against one side of the keystone of the arch. But that keystone held its position, securely. The arch did not crumble and the Union did not fall.

QUESTIONS FOR STUDY AND REVIEW

1. Do you think President Buchanan did his duty? How would you have dealt with the problems that faced him between November, 1860, and March, 1861?

2. Why did President Lincoln delay the proclamation of emancipation of the Negroes? Had he promised to free the slaves prior to the outbreak of war?

3. What measures were taken to raise men for northern armies? What criticisms may be made against the system employed?

4. What military advantages did the Confederate armies hope to gain by invading Pennsylvania? To what extent did they succeed?

5. Why was the battle of Gettysburg one of the most important battles in American history? Name the Pennsylvania generals who distinguished themselves in that battle.

6. What issues were settled by the War for the Union?

PROBLEMS AND ACTIVITIES

1. Imagine that you were a merchant planning to open a store in 1850. You have your choice of location either in Easton, Pennsylvania or Birmingham, Alabama. Which city would you choose? Why?

2. Why would a state such as Pennsylvania favor heavy taxes on goods imported from foreign countries, and a state such as South Carolina oppose such tariffs? (Consult a textbook in American history. See especially the tariff laws of 1816, 1828, and 1832.)

3. Report to the class on the issue of states rights as shown by the Virginia and Kentucky resolutions; the Hartford Convention; South Carolina's Ordinance of Nullification; the Hayne-Webster debate.

4. Imagine that you are the owner of a big factory. You have your choice, whether to own 400 slaves or employ 400 freemen. Which will you choose? Give reasons. Does your answer help to explain why the North abolished slavery willingly?

5. Show how each of the following issues was part of the slavery question: the Missouri Compromise; the Dred Scott decision; the purchase of Mexican territory; the settlement of Kansas; the size of Texas; and the admission of California. (Consult an American history text for the provisions of the Compromise of 1850.)

6. Point out the various factors which served to place Pennsylvania definitely on the antislavery side of national issues. Begin very early in Pennsylvania history.

7. Why was the problem of runaway slaves so important in Pennsylvania? Can you find any evidence of the part your community played in the Underground Railroad or in John Brown's raid?

8. Prepare brief sketches on the following topics: James Buchanan; Lucretia Mott; the Lincoln homestead in Berks County; Thaddeus Stevens; Edwin M. Stanton.

9. Organize a meeting of the Pennsylvania Society in 1820 and have the members of the class prepare a petition to Congress urging the abolition of slavery.

10. Write a short story about a fugitive slave being passed along the Underground Railroad in your locality.

11. Prepare copy for an antislavery newspaper. Choose an editor who will construct the first page, selecting headlines from his classmates' contributions.

12. Dramatize a meeting between Abraham Lincoln and James Buchanan on March 4, 1861. What would they say to each other?

13. Memorize Lincoln's Gettysburg Address.

14. Prepare a list of Civil War monuments that you have seen.

15. Examine the constitution of the United States to find the provisions which gave freedom to the slave, made him a citizen, and gave him the right to vote.

16. Has all bitterness between the North and South vanished by now? Give examples supporting your answer.

17. Are all men created equal? Do they remain equal? Would you want to live in a society in which all persons remained equal? In what respects do you want to see equality established?

18. Show how the abolition of slavery was a long stride in the development of democratic government.

19. Show how our state's attitude on the questions which divided the nation was consistent with the principles upon which William Penn and his successors founded Pennsylvania.

SUGGESTIONS FOR FURTHER READING
War Between the States

The most easily available material for further study is a standard high school text on American history. Particularly valuable are the following: Carman, Kimmel, and Walker, *Historic Currents in Changing America*, Philadelphia: John C. Winston Co.; H. W. Elson, *History of the United States of America*, New York: Macmillan; William B. Guitteau, *History of the United States of America*, New York: Houghton Mifflin.

217

The following books dealing directly with the war and the background of the war are recommended: Herbert Aptheker, *The Negro in the Civil War*, New York: International Publishers; A. C. Cole, *Irrepressible Conflict* (History of American Life Series) New York: Macmillan; W. E. Dodd, *Cotton Kingdom* (Chronicles, vol. 27) New Haven: Yale University Press; E. D. Fite, *Social and Industrial Conditions in the North during the Civil War*, New York: Macmillan; Douglas Southall Freeman, *Robert E. Lee*, 4 vol., New York: Scribner's; J. G. Randall, *Civil War and Reconstruction*, Boston: Heath; James F. Rhodes, *History of the United States from the Compromise of 1850*, New York: Macmillan.

Pennsylvania in the War

Most of the publications dealing directly with Pennsylvania in the war have been printed in small editions and are not easily found. Veterans' organizations have published a number of memorial volumes, and local historical societies have printed articles in their journals. The following is a selected list of books: Samuel P. Bates, *History of the Pennsylvania Volunteers, 1861–1865*, Harrisburg: Telegraph Press; John Bigelow, *The Peach Orchard, Gettysburg, July 2, 1863*, Minneapolis: Kimbel Storer; C. B. Going, *David Wilmot*, New York: Appleton-Century; Samuel R. Kamm, *The Civil War Career of Thomas A. Scott*, Philadelphia: University of Pennsylvania Press; W. C. Storrick, *Gettysburg: The Place, the Battle, the Outcome*, available through Pennsylvania Book Service, Harrisburg; T. F. Woodley, *Great Leveller: The Life of Thaddeus Stevens*, Harrisburg: Pennsylvania Book Service.

Fiction

Hervey Allen, *Action at Aquilla*, New York: Farrar and Rinehart; J. A. Altsheler, *In Circling Camps*, New York: Appleton; Mary R. S. Andrews, *The Perfect Tribute*, New York: Scribner's; Stephen Vincent Benet, *John Brown's Body*, New York: Farrar and Rinehart; Charles W. Dahlinger, *Where the Red Volleys Poured*, New York: G. W. Dillingham; Mackinlay Kantor, *Long Remember*, New York: Coward-McCann; Laura Long, *Hannah Courageous*, Harrisburg: Pennsylvania Book Service; Joseph McCord, *Redhouse on the Hill*, Philadelphia: Macrea-Smith; S. Weir Mitchell, *Westways: A Village Chronicle*, New York: Century; Constance Noyes Robertson, *Salute to the Hero*, New York: Farrar and Rinehart; Elsie Singmaster, *The Loving Heart*, New York: Houghton Mifflin.

UNIT VI
POLITICAL AND INDUSTRIAL DEVELOPMENT

The War for the Union settled certain problems for the United States. Slavery was abolished. The question of whether a state or a section could withdraw from the Union if it chose to do so had been clearly answered. But the war created other problems no less critical and these had to be answered.

One change wrought by the war was the placing of the Republican party firmly in power in both the state and national government. This was to have important effects on the political developments of the era. The war stimulated business and industry to rapid expansion. Great corporations with enormous resources of capital were established. In Pennsylvania the growth of the Carnegie steel interests is a perfect example. Changes in the organization of industry led to serious changes in the status of the average industrial worker. The worker's efforts to protect himself from unfair treatment and to improve his working conditions often brought him into conflict with the leaders of industry. The industrial state of Pennsylvania was frequently the storm center of such conflicts.

In spite of industrial and political strife, many improvements in living were made possible by scientific inventions and the organization of business for mass production and distribution. The Centennial Exposition held in Philadelphia in 1876 showed the American people how far they had come in the past hundred years and gave them a fascinating glimpse into the future. Educational and recreational opportunities for all citizens of the state were extended and improved in this period.

Many of the issues and questions which challenged the best resources of the people of our grandparents generation remain unsolved today. By our study of this unit we shall see what events and circumstances called them into being; what earlier attempts to solve them accomplished; how the very problems themselves have changed with the passing of time and the pressure of new events.

Chapter XII

WORKING TOWARD POLITICAL REFORM

When the War for the Union ended, the people of Pennsylvania quickly returned to peaceful occupations. Although the war had been costly both in money and in lives, Pennsylvania had not suffered to a very great extent by the invasions of Confederate forces. The damage done in Cumberland, Adams, and York counties was serious for the people living in them, but the work of rebuilding was undertaken readily, and before long the only scars left were those etched into people's memories. Efforts were made to compensate property owners of the invaded areas for their losses, but these efforts were not wholly effective. Most of the unfortunate ones took their losses and began to rebuild without complaint.

PROSPERITY

The war had brought prosperity to Pennsylvania. The mines and factories produced great quantities of war equipment; the shipyards in Philadelphia produced battleships; and the farms furnished food and supplied horses, wagons, leather, and other articles needed by armies on the march. The railroads of Pennsylvania carried troops from New York and New England as well as the hundreds of thousands of Pennsylvanians who served in the armed forces. The newly-discovered oil field at Titusville provided almost all of the oil used by the Union armies.

The prosperity brought by the war had its effect on the finances of the state. The Commonwealth had been heavily in debt when the war began, as a result of the long program of financing internal improvements—roads, canals, and railroads. As the war industries expanded to supply material and equipment for the Union, the people began to earn more money and the state treasury received greater returns from taxes. Thus the debt of the state government was so rapidly reduced that there was actually a surplus in the state treasury when the war ended in 1865. In 1866 state taxes were reduced, and people looked forward to an unbroken era of prosperity and progress.

Social Progress. During the War for the Union many children lost their fathers on the battlefields. At first the churches in Pennsylvania tried to care for these unfortunate young people in homes built by funds contributed by their members. After the war the surplus in the treasury made it possible for the state government to aid the churches by appropriations from state funds.

The state also found it possible to increase the funds for the public schools. We have already seen how all school districts accepted the Free School Law in 1868 as a result of the attractive financial rewards offered by the state. After that time every child in the Commonwealth had the opportunity for an elementary school education.

There were many requests for funds for various causes, some of which were worthy, others merely selfish. Governor John W. Geary wisely vetoed a number of bills granting money which were passed by the Legislature. However, many hospitals, colleges, and charitable institutions were aided by state funds during the years of prosperity. Churches were excused from taxes on their property, as were other types of charitable and educational organizations which were chiefly engaged in serving the public rather than in making a profit.

During Governor Geary's administration, a Board of Public Charities was created to supervise the distribution of state funds for charitable purposes. In 1872 a Bureau of Labor Statistics was created to collect information that would help the rapidly growing industries in the state in planning new businesses and in building new factories.

THE FOURTH CONSTITUTION

In 1872 a new governor, John F. Hartranft, was elected. Like Geary, Hartranft had served as an officer in the Union Army during the war. He took office in 1873.

At the same election, the voters were asked to approve or reject a plan for calling a convention to revise the state constitution which had been drawn up in 1838. The plan for a convention was approved, and the 133 delegates who had been chosen met in Harrisburg late in November. At the first meetings the group organized for the work of drafting revisions. In January the convention met again, this time in Philadelphia, where it began the actual work of preparing a new state constitution. This constitution was adopted in 1874 by a majority of more than two to one.

Changes in the State Government. The constitution of 1873 is the fourth in the history of the state and is still in force. The members of the convention were interested in setting up safeguards against dishonesty in the state government. Severe penalties were imposed upon any state official found guilty of accepting a bribe. A lieutenant-governor was to be elected who would preside over the state Senate. He was to become governor if that office should become vacant before the close of the term. The office of state treasurer was made elective where previously it had been appointive. The governor's term was extended to four years instead of three. No limit was set as to the number of terms any one man might serve, but no governor may serve consecutive terms. Election dates were changed to take place at the same time as the national elections—on the first Tuesday after the first Monday in November.

A Board of Pardons was created to make recommendations to the governor on the pardoning of criminals who had been sentenced to terms in the state prisons. The governor issues the pardons, but he is not permitted to pardon anyone who has not been recommended by the Board. The latter is composed of the lieutenant-governor, as chairman, and three other members.

The state constitution also contains provisions for the regulation of business, the administration of city governments, the granting of charters to cities and corporations, and the regulation of the county governments.

The State Legislature. The number of representatives in the state Senate was increased to fifty, and in the lower house, first to two hundred and later to two hundred and eight. Senatorial districts were created on the basis of population. Sometimes several counties were combined to create a single district. For example, the counties of Clarion, Cameron, Clinton, Elk, and Forest form the Twenty-sixth District and elect one Senator. On the other hand, counties with large populations, such as Allegheny and Philadelphia, may contain several districts. Occasionally the districts cut across county lines, as in the case of the Seventeenth District which includes Lebanon and part of Lancaster County. The rest of Lancaster County forms the

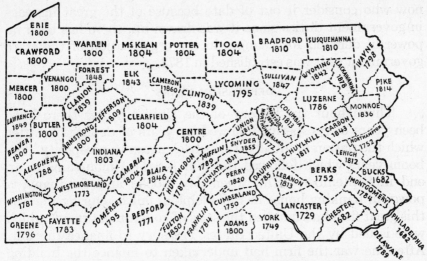

WHEN PENNSYLVANIA COUNTIES WERE FORMED

Twelfth District. In the House of Representatives every county has at least one representative, but the counties with large numbers of voters have more; Luzerne County has eight representatives; Allegheny, twenty-seven; Philadelphia, forty-one.

Who Might Vote. The right to vote was granted to every male citizen who has lived in the state for a year and in a voting district for two months immediately preceding the election. Negroes had been allowed to vote after the adoption of the fifteenth amendment to the federal constitution in 1870. This right was recognized by the new state constitution.

The State Constitution Today. The constitution may be amended by a majority vote of both houses of the Legislature, if their action is approved by a majority vote at the next general election. One provision which has been criticized in recent years prevents an amendment that has been rejected by the voters from being voted on again for five years. This period is considered by some critics as too long a wait for changes in an age when new problems may arise suddenly and require quick solution.

This state constitution was believed to be one of the best in force in any state at the time it was adopted and it has served very well down to the present day. Although there are people

223

now who consider it out of date because of the great increase in government duties since it was drawn up, there has been no powerful demand for changes in the organization of the state government as it was established in 1873.

Throughout the history of the United States there have been years of prosperity followed by years of depression, after which the nation gradually works back again to prosperity. The boom years which followed the War for the Union came to an end in September, 1873, when Jay Cooke and Company, a powerful banking house in Philadelphia, failed. During the war this great firm had handled the sales of government bonds which were issued by the United States Treasury to finance the war. After the war the firm had undertaken to finance the building of the Northern Pacific Railroad. But the people who had bought bonds and stocks as investments during the war were either unwilling or unable to buy stocks and bonds of private

—*From Harper's Weekly*

WATCHING THE TICKER-TAPE AT THE TIME OF THE PANIC OF 1873

companies to the same extent. As a result, Jay Cooke and Company were not able to sell enough Northern Pacific Railroad securities to meet their obligations, and the firm was forced into bankruptcy.

The failure of Jay Cooke and Company was followed by the failure of smaller banks throughout the country, and in turn this ruined business firms which depended upon the banks for loans and credit. A national depression was the result. Industries closed down; people lost their jobs; money was scarce; and hardship and poverty were felt by many who had formerly enjoyed a comfortable life. The depression which followed the financial panic of 1873 lasted until 1877, when business and industry became strong enough again to open new factories and build new railroads.

MACHINE POLITICS

The history of the last half of the nineteenth century is marred by the rise of a self-interested group of politicians who dominated the elections and the administration of state affairs for many years. Other states besides Pennsylvania have come under the domination of political machines from time to time. A party machine is an organization devoted to promoting the interests of a particular group, rather than to the welfare of the people. Political parties as such render valuable service in presenting issues to the voters and in focusing attention on problems of government which need to be solved. A party machine, however, has come to be regarded as something which works for the selfish interests of a few individuals. Such a machine tries to get and hold control over large numbers of votes by methods which are not in the interests of good citizenship.

One important factor in building a powerful political machine is money. Today, political parties are required to publish a financial statement showing the amount of money spent in a campaign and how it was spent. But for many years no such safeguard was in force. Funds were used freely to organize meetings, to prepare and distribute campaign literature, and for parades and concerts in honor of the candidate. Money was used, too, in less honest ways—to buy votes and to bribe election officials to see that the returns favored the party candidate. The funds were raised by contributions from officeholders who held their jobs as a result of the favor of the machine, and by pledges from large business firms or industries which hoped that the party, if it gained power, would work for their interests.

It is unquestionably the right of candidates for election to present their views to the public and to use party funds for rallies, speeches, and parades. Citizens also have every right to contribute funds for the use of the party of their choice. Some of the methods used by party machines in winning elections are no different, therefore, from those used by sincere political leaders who have the welfare of the people genuinely at heart. But in the buying of votes and bribing of election officials, the machine was making it impossible for the democratic process to work, since the people were prevented from honestly expressing their wishes about their government at elections.

Simon Cameron. With the election of Abraham Lincoln to the office of President, the Republican party swept into control of the national government. For a quarter of a century thereafter, its power was to remain unbroken. Pennsylvania, which had supported the Democratic party in nearly every national election up to 1860, in that year cast its vote for Abraham Lincoln. The leader of the Republican party in the state was Simon Cameron. He had been one of the founders of the party, and his influence in the national Republican organization helped him to build a party machine within the state. In 1860 Cameron worked hard for the election of Lincoln, and it was partly as a reward that Lincoln appointed him to the Cabinet as Secretary of War. After a short time, Cameron resigned to become United States Minister to Russia. In 1864 he returned to Pennsylvania and soon thereafter was elected to the United States Senate.

For some time Cameron had been organizing a group of followers dependent upon his favors and therefore loyal to him rather than to the party as a whole. His election to the United States Senate made it possible for him to increase this personal following. Before the civil service system was adopted for federal jobs, most vacancies were filled by appointment of the President. Since the time of Andrew Jackson, it had been customary for the President to ask the party leaders in Congress for recommendations in filling the federal offices in their respective states. There were many such positions, especially in the postal,

—*Harper's Weekly*

WAITING OUTSIDE SUCCESSFUL CANDIDATE'S OFFICE FOR JOBS

customs, and internal revenue services. Thus, Cameron was in a position to recommend his friends for important federal positions in Pennsylvania. These friends knew that only by working for Cameron's interests would they continue to hold their jobs.

Era of "Boss" Rule. Cameron's influence and power in the Republican party in Pennsylvania was so great that he was called the boss of the party. For more than half a century, the machine that he created controlled state politics, and for most of that time, the state government. When Cameron gave up his personal management of the machine, he handed it on to his son, J. Donald Cameron, who was also elected to his father's seat in the United States Senate. The younger Cameron was followed by Matthew Stanley Quay. We shall see how reformers made repeated attempts to break Quay's power. These attempts were unsuccessful, however, and Quay was followed in turn by Boies Penrose, who kept control of the state political machine until his death in 1921.

This unbroken line of bosses from 1865 to 1921 is a unique feature of Pennsylvania politics. In other states bosses have been able to construct powerful political machines, but usually the machines have broken apart when the boss died or lost an election as a result of a successful revolt by the voters.

227

With one of the Camerons or Quay always in control of the Republican party machine, the issues in state elections were often confused. It was to the advantage of the machine to secure the election of its candidates, and campaign promises came to mean little or nothing once an election was won. There were several attempts to revolt against the machine by Republicans who opposed the methods used to control the elections. On two occasions (in 1882 and 1890) the split within the Republican party resulted in the election of a Democratic governor. In both cases the man elected was Robert E. Pattison. After each election, however, Quay was able to win back his control. Unfortunately for the Democrats, Pattison could not succeed himself. He was their strongest vote getter.

THE JOHNSTOWN FLOOD

Twice during the years we have been studying, the citizens of Pennsylvania were forced to turn aside from their interest in political affairs and to deal with other kinds of problems. The first of these was the disaster at Johnstown in 1889. Situated in

THE GREAT CONEMAUGH VALLEY DISASTER
An artist's conception of the flood and fire at Johnstown in 1889.

a valley where the Little Conemaugh meets Stonycreek River, Johnstown had been visited by many floods during her early history. None of them caused great damage, until 1847 when a dam broke, covering one part of the city with water. In 1879 the dam was rebuilt and enlarged. Residents of Johnstown, knowing that the construction of the dam was faulty, urged that something be done to protect the people living in the valley in case of rising waters. These warnings were not heeded, however. Late in May, 1889, after a series of heavy rains, the dam broke, and four and one-half million gallons of water burst through the valley. Houses were crushed like eggshells; more than two thousand persons were drowned. Hundreds more were burned to death when a freight car carrying oil was derailed, spilling the oil on the rushing waters. The oil was ignited by the embers of overturned stoves, spreading flames to the tops of wooden structures on which people had sought shelter. Many thousands of families were left homeless. The neighboring cities, such as Somerset, Altoona, and Pittsburgh, sent food supplies immediately to help the sufferers. Clara Barton, the founder of the Red Cross, personally directed the work of relief, and Governor Beaver sent units of the National Guard to prevent looting and other disorders. Aid was soon sent from other parts of the state and nation.

Johnstown was rebuilt rapidly. In 1933 the city had a population of more than 100,000. In that year the city was flooded again, resulting in twenty-four deaths and the loss of $40,000,000 in property damage. Soon after this disaster the building of new dams was started under the supervision of the War Department of the United States government. It is hoped the construction of the new safeguards will end Johnstown's danger from serious floods.

THE SPANISH-AMERICAN WAR

In 1898 attention was again temporarily diverted from local political affairs by national events. For some time Americans had been in sympathy with the Cubans in their long struggle with Spain for independence. There had been demands on the federal government to aid the Cubans, even though it might mean war with Spain. In 1898 an American battleship, the *Maine*, was blown up in the harbor of Havana and 260 officers and men were killed. Just what happened to the *Maine* has never been discovered, but at the time the American people, already angry with Spain, believed that the Spanish government was somehow to blame. War fever ran high and President McKinley asked the Congress to declare war.

Most of the fighting took place in the islands southeast of the United States and in the distant islands of the Philippines. President McKinley's first call for troops fixed a quota for Pennsylvania of 10,600 men. This quota was quickly filled by volunteers and units of the National Guard. When President McKinley issued the second call, this time for 6,370 men, it was answered by more volunteers.

There were few casualities among Pennsylvanians who served in the war against Spain. Twelve died in action, thirty-three were wounded, and several hundred died of disease while in camp. Pennsylvania regiments saw service in the Philippines and in Puerto Rico until the end of war in 1898. Some soldiers were stationed in the Philippines for several years longer to protect American interests in the newly-acquired territory.

ATTEMPTED REFORM

By the turn of the century, boss rule in Pennsylvania was being challenged by many voters who felt that machine politics did not serve the best interests of the Commonwealth.

Quay Becomes a United States Senator. After 1899 Boss Quay was forced to exert himself to the utmost to hold on to the political power he had inherited from the Camerons. In that year, Quay was tried in the courts of Philadelphia for mishandling state funds and was found not guilty. Soon afterward he was appointed by Governor Stone to fill a vacancy in the United States Senate. The Senate has the power to refuse to admit new members by a majority vote within the Senate. Quay, because of his bad reputation, was refused his seat by a vote of thirty-three to thirty-one.

Prior to the seventeenth amendment to the federal constitution (adopted in 1913) Senators were elected by the state legislatures instead of by direct vote of the people. Thus, if Quay could control enough votes in the Legislature, he might still win the seat in the United States Senate that he was determined to have. In the campaign of 1900, Quay worked hard to secure the election of enough of his political friends to assure him a majority in the Pennsylvania Legislature. In this project he failed, but undiscouraged he went to work to form a temporary alliance between those of his supporters who had been elected and some of the Democratic members of the Legislature. By means of this political maneuvering he was finally elected United States Senator. This time the question of his admission to the Senate was not raised and Quay was permitted to enjoy his victory.

John Wanamaker. One of the chief opponents of Quay in these years was John Wanamaker, a Philadelphia merchant. The great merchant prince had entered public life in 1889 as Postmaster General in the Cabinet of President Benjamin Harrison. In 1896 Wanamaker had been a candidate for election to the United States Senate, but he was defeated by Quay's man, Boies Penrose of Philadelphia. Wanamaker then opposed William A. Stone, Quay's candidate for governor in the election of 1898. Again the Quay faction triumphed. Wanamaker again opposed Quay for the Senate seat which Quay finally won in 1900. All of these struggles took place within the Republican party with the machine supporters and reform elements striving to gain control.

Governor Samuel W. Pennypacker. With the approach of the election of 1902, Senator Quay realized that his machine could hope to maintain its control over the party only if the man nominated for governor was known to be honest. The choice fell upon Samuel W. Pennypacker, a judge in Philadelphia. Pennypacker was regarded as a man of high character. He had gained a widespread reputation as an historian, and his personal life was above reproach. The Democrats nominated their former candidate, Robert E. Pattison, who was eligible for a third term as governor because his previous terms had not been consecutive. Pennypacker was victorious by a majority of more than 50,000 votes.

Reforms under Governor Pennypacker. The new governor was not a mere figurehead or party tool. However, his first attempts at reform did not find favor with the citizens of the state. In 1906, Governor Pennypacker summoned a special session of the state Legislature to tackle the problem of providing for honest elections. One of the evils of the old voting system had been that it was possible for dishonest voters to vote several times on election day. Because election boards had incomplete lists of voters in their districts it was possible for these dishonest voters to go from one district to another, casting a vote each time they entered another polling place. To prevent this practice, the Assembly passed the Personal Registration Act which required voters to register before election day in the district in which they lived. On election day only those who had previously presented themselves for registration were allowed to cast a ballot. The Assembly also passed a Corrupt Practices Act fixing severe penalties for officials found guilty of dishonest conduct in elections.

During the Pennypacker administration steps were taken to unite the city of Allegheny and other boroughs in the metropolitan area of Pittsburgh into the municipality of Greater Pittsburgh. This union, begun in 1906, was completed in 1909. Other progressive acts of the Pennypacker regime were: the establishment of the Pennsylvania State Police, the formation of the Department of Health, and the establishment of a number of other bureaus for the more efficient management of the affairs of the Commonwealth. Finally, a beginning was made in the construction of a state highway system.

Stuart's Administration. Governor Pennypacker was ineligible for re-election in 1906. He was succeeded by Edwin S. Stuart, former mayor of Philadelphia. Courageously Stuart carried through his campaign pledges to see that dishonesty was eliminated from the departments of the state government. During his administration the various school laws were assembled into one body known as the School Code. This code went into effect in 1911, helping to establish uniform practices in all schools in the state. Other progressive acts of the Stuart administration included the organization of the Legislative Reference Bureau and the establishment of the State Museum in which the historical records of the Commonwealth are preserved. By careful administration of the finances, Stuart improved the condition of the state treasury. But most indicative of his firm stand for honest government is the manner in which he pressed the trial of officials involved in the capitol graft scandal.

The New Capitol. A fire had destroyed the state capitol at Harrisburg in 1897. This disaster had caused a great deal of

THE STATE CAPITOL AT HARRISBURG
How many government buildings can you identify?

inconvenience to the state officials until 1906 when a new capitol, built on the site of the old one, was finished. The state Legislature had met in the Grace Methodist Episcopal Church until 1899 when a temporary building was erected for its use. The executive departments had been housed in a government building which had not been destroyed by the fire.

In 1901 the state Legislature made an initial appropriation of $4,000,000 for a new capitol. Work was carried on during the administration of Governor Pennypacker. The new capitol is a magnificent building covering two acres. It is an imposing structure, one of the finest of its kind. There are 475 rooms, many of them beautifully furnished and decorated with fine paintings, murals, and statuary.

Unfortunately, charges of graft in handling the contracts for the building of the state capitol led to a scandal which involved several persons. When William H. Berry of Chester became state Treasurer in 1905 he brought the scandal to light. Berry was a Democrat, not responsible to the Republican party machine which had had control of the state government for many years. The election of Berry and the reforms growing out of the disclosure of graft in building the capitol illustrates one of the advantages of our two-party system of government. There

233

is always an opposition party to check upon the acts of those who are in power.

The graft scandal does not provide pleasant reading. It was shown that over $5,000,000 of the state funds had been spent dishonestly. The state was cheated on many articles purchased for furnishings. For example, a bootblack stand was said to have cost $500. The state was charged $15,500 for paneling an office when the actual cost was only $500. Gold paint was used in certain decorations instead of the gold leaf which the contract specified. These are but a few of the ways in which the taxpayers' money was wasted. State officials and building contractors who had been responsible for handling the funds and contracts were arrested and tried. Those who were tried were found guilty of misusing state funds and were sentenced to pay fines and to terms of imprisonment. The effect of the trials was to remind all officials that a public office is a public trust and that those who are elected to serve the people are responsible for performing their duties honestly.

Continued Progress under Tener. In the elections of 1910, John K. Tener of Charleroi was the successful candidate for Governor. The outstanding accomplishments of Tener's administration were: the passage of a road bill in 1911 providing for a survey of all state highways; the establishment of a Department of Labor and Industry; and the formation of the Pennsylvania Historical Commission.

Division in the Republican Ranks. The national election of 1912 was a further sign that the cause of political reform was gaining strength in the state. Pennsylvania's electoral vote went to Theodore Roosevelt, candidate for President on the Progressive party ticket. It was the first time since 1860 that the state had supported any one other than a regular Republican party candidate. By 1914, however, the Republicans in the state had reassembled their forces and were successful in electing as Governor, Martin G. Brumbaugh, former superintendent of the public schools of Philadelphia.

Governor Brumbaugh and Social Reform. The schoolmaster in the governor's chair had definite ideas about social reform. During his administration a number of laws were passed dealing with problems growing out of the changing relations between capital and labor. The Workmen's Compensation Law of 1914 provided that workers in factories and mines must be paid for injuries sustained in the performance of their duties, regardless of who was at fault. An injured workman was to receive money for his medical bills and some of the money lost by his inability to work. A Child Labor Law was passed prohibiting the employment of children in certain types of work. A state Commission of Agriculture was formed to assist the farmers; a Bureau of Vocational Education was established to supervise and encourage the training of youth for various trades. The state was well on the way toward solving the social and economic problems of the industrial age when the grim hand of war again checked progress temporarily and forced officials and citizens to turn their attention to winning the nation's battles.

QUESTIONS FOR STUDY AND REVIEW

1. Why was it possible for Pennsylvania to increase her appropriations for the general welfare after the War for the Union?

2. Do you believe that non-profit institutions such as churches should be exempted from paying taxes? What buildings or institutions in your community are excused from paying taxes?

3. What new features were incorporated in the fourth state constitution? Were these changes improvements?

4. How did the party machine impose its will upon the voters? Who were the party bosses in Pennsylvania? Is it possible for a party machine to dominate voters who are educated?

5. What is meant by reform? Are there any reforms you would like to see enacted into legislation? Why? Have you realized that sometimes desirable reforms may be put into effect only by sacrificing things we cherish even more than the desired change?

6. Is the capitol graft scandal a reflection on the efficiency of the democratic system? How can the people in a democracy protect themselves against dishonesty in government? What advantages do citizens of a democracy have in this respect that citizens under a dictatorship do not have?

7. How does the support which Pennsylvania gave to the Progressive party in 1912 form a part of the political trends in the state and nation?

Chapter XIII

THE AGE OF BIG BUSINESS

The period between the War for the Union and the First World War is often known in our national history as the Age of Big Business. The phrase describes certain changes which took place in the economic life of the nation. These developments in industry and business are almost perfectly reflected by developments taking place within the borders of the great industrial state of Pennsylvania.

At the close of the war, industry in the North was booming. The demands of the war for matériel and supplies had called forth the inventive and organizing genius of American businessmen, as war was to do again in 1917 and in 1941. Mass production on the assembly-line principle as we know it today found its beginning in this period. The breaking-down of the processes used in making a product into a series of standard operations requiring simple mechanical skill made it possible to increase quantity and improve quality at the same time. War contracts had proved profitable, and business leaders found that they had funds on hand for new enterprises. New industries were established and factories poured forth wonderful new products at a price within the range of people of very moderate means. In this way the standard of living was raised and opportunities for employment were greatly increased.

Another trend of the times was the consolidation or combining of industrial enterprises—factories, mines, mills—into ever larger units. The goods used by the average American were now made in huge factories managed by the board of directors of a great corporation, which might control hundreds of factories making similar products, plus mines and forests which were the sources of raw materials, and the steamships and railroads that carried the goods to market.

With this general picture in mind, let us see what happened to the Keystone state's industries during the era of big business.

236

A MODERN COAL MINE
Find the breaker, the culm bank, the railroad siding.

MINING

Coal. Prior to 1920 miners had dug more than six and one-half billion tons of coal from the black caverns under the surface of Pennsylvania soil. This amount was greater than the entire production of coal in the other forty-seven states combined. The greatest year for the Pennsylvania anthracite fields was 1917, when nearly one hundred million tons were mined. The coal-mining industry in the state followed the national trend in organizing into large units. Three fourths of the hard coal mined in Pennsylvania was produced by eight large companies, which were formed during the preceding fifty years by the combination of several smaller companies.

The peak year of soft coal production in the state came in 1918 when more than one hundred and seventy-five million tons were mined. This represented nearly one third of the total production of this type of coal in the entire nation.

Oil. The early settlers of Venango County in northwestern Pennsylvania were puzzled by the scummy substance

OIL TRANSPORTATION IN THE EARLY DAYS

which they found floating on the surface of a stream now known
as Oil Creek. A few enterprising persons collected this substance and sold it as medicine, calling it "Seneca Oil," or "Rock
Oil." During the middle of the nineteenth century, people in the
towns of Titusville and Tarentum began to experiment with
other uses for the oil which they found on the surface of the
streams or that seeped into the salt wells. Lumbermen found
that this natural oil worked better than lard grease as a lubri-
cant for their sawmill machinery. Samples of the oil were tested
in the laboratories of eastern universities. Some of these tests
showed that by refining this oil it could be used as fuel for lamps
which had formerly burned whale oil.

This was all that was known before Edwin L. Drake began
to drill for oil in August, 1859. No oil well had ever been drilled
before anywhere in the world when Drake and his assistants
drove their cast iron pipes into the ground near Titusville. Many
scoffed at the project, calling it "Drake's Folly." After drilling
to a depth of sixty-nine feet, Drake struck oil.

After Drake sunk his first shaft, new wells were soon drilled
in many places in northwestern Pennsylvania. In 1859 two
thousand barrels of oil were sold. During the next twelve years
forty million barrels of oil were produced and sold, and by 1891

wells in the state produced thirty-one million barrels annually. Pennsylvania oil was shipped to all parts of the world. Great fortunes were being made by those who owned land where oil could be produced. Oil prospectors came to the state from all parts of the country, hoping to share in the wealth, but the majority, of course, were disappointed. One example of the rush to the oil fields is the very brief history of Pit Hole City in Venango County. Between May and September of 1865 an ordinary farm suddenly grew into a city of 16,000 people. But a short year later, Pit Hole City had become a "ghost town." The people had moved away because the oil wells which had promised so much soon stopped producing.

The oil industry furnishes an excellent illustration of the development of big business. While the amount of oil coming from the wells was still relatively small, a young Cleveland businessman, John D. Rockefeller, sensed the possibilities and set out to gain control of the refining plants which had sprung up to prepare the crude oil for use. From 1865 to 1870 he worked steadily at buying as many of the plants as he could. In June, 1870, the Standard Oil Company of Ohio was organized. Rockefeller continued to expand and consolidate his position until he became the unchallenged dictator of the entire industry.

MANUFACTURING

Several factors have combined to make Pennsylvania the manufacturing center of the New World. The raw materials are here in abundance; skilled workmen are here. The geographic position of the state is almost perfect, for Pennsylvania is centrally located with respect to the other seaboard states. Furthermore, it is blessed with a system of natural waterways that made it easy for manufacturers to get their products to market even before the railroad had become the common means of transporting freight. In the east, the Delaware River provides an outlet to the ocean. In the west, Lake Erie is a link in the chain of Great Lakes which connects the state with the northwest. The broad arm of the Ohio sweeps westward to the Mississippi, giving Pittsburgh an outlet to the interior and to the Gulf of Mexico. Thus, the state early assumed a commanding position in the manufacture of many products, a position which it continues to hold to the present time. During the era of big business, new enterprises were begun and older industries were combined into larger units with greatly increased production.

The Steel Industry. As the center of the iron industry for the nation, it was only natural that Pennsylvania should become the leading steel producer as well. The great organizer of the steel industry in the state was Andrew Carnegie, who came to the United States from Scotland when he was a boy of thirteen. At the time he began to develop the steel industry Carnegie was already a wealthy businessman. He had been interested in railroad building and for a time in the oil industry. During the War for the Union, Carnegie served as superintendent of military railways. After the war, he founded the Keystone Bridge Works and the Union Iron Works at Pittsburgh. At first, Carnegie was not interested in the new process for making steel from iron that had been invented by an Englishman, Henry Bessemer, in 1856. Soon, however, he came to realize the importance of Bessemer's discovery. In 1868 Carnegie introduced the Bessemer process into his iron works. At the same time that he introduced the new process for making steel, Carnegie set out to increase the number of plants under his control. Soon he acquired the Homestead Steel Works and

—*The Bettmann Archive*

MANUFACTURE OF BESSEMER STEEL IN 1875
What other kinds of steel were, or are, manufactured?

a number of other mills. In 1889 these were united into the Carnegie Steel Company which later, in 1901, became a part of the still larger United States Steel Corporation. At this time Carnegie retired from an active part in the steel industry.

Andrew Carnegie is remembered for the many gifts that he bestowed on charitable and educational institutions. Many small city libraries in the United States owe their existence to endowments from Carnegie funds. He established the Carnegie Institute of Technology, the Carnegie Foundation for International Peace, and contributed to other worthwhile enterprises.

TRANSPORTATION

Railways. The great volume of materials produced in Pennsylvania's mines, forests, farms, and factories created a demand for increased means of transportation. Raw materials must be hauled from the sources of supply to the factories and mills. The finished products must be carried to the stores of the cities where customers can buy them. In 1860 there were 2,598 miles of railroad in Pennsylvania; now there are about 14,000. Great railroad systems tap the industrial areas of the state. Many of these systems resulted from the merging of small independent lines into one large system of railroads. Between 1859 and 1900, the Philadelphia and Reading Railroad Company consolidated with sixty smaller railroad companies. The Pennsylvania Railroad System was also built up by merging smaller lines. It now includes more than one hundred smaller roads which were at first organized independently.

THE TARIFF QUESTION

Because of Pennsylvania's extensive manufacturing enterprises, the problem of protective tariffs has been a matter of interest to the voters of the state for years. The tariffs with which we are concerned are taxes levied upon goods brought into the United States from other countries. If such taxes are high it means that imported goods will cost the consumer more money; if they are low, the retail price of imported goods may be lower than the cost of manufacturing and marketing American-made articles. This may mean in turn that American manufacturers are forced out of business because they can no longer

—Brown in the Chicago Daily News

A PROBLEM FOR THE COOK
How would you solve it?

compete with foreign merchants. For example, let us say that the cost to the consumer of a pair of gloves made in Pennsylvania is three dollars. But a glove manufacturer in Europe can make the same quality of gloves, transport them to America, sell them here at two dollars, and still realize a profit. This may happen for several reasons, such as the lower wages the European manufacturer can pay to workmen or because raw materials are cheaper. If this were to happen, the American glove manufacturer would not be able to sell his products. Instead, he would be forced to go out of business and his workers would lose their jobs. On the other hand, if a tariff of one dollar is placed on the pair of gloves made in Europe, it forces the price of the imported article to three dollars, the same as the price of the American-made gloves. At this price American manufacturers could at least compete on even terms.

The question of high or low tariffs has been a political issue for many years. The Democratic party has generally favored low tariffs, while the Republicans have advocated high levies on imported goods. It was to the advantage of manufacturers to favor the Republican party, and most of the employees of Pennsylvania's industries realized that their jobs and high wages were in danger if tariffs were too low. The success of the Republican party in most of the national elections in Pennsylvania after 1860 grew out of a feeling on the part of the voters that the state's manufacturing interests should be protected.

242

We have seen new industries developing and old industries growing. Coal, "black gold" as it was called, was building great cities at Scranton and Wilkes-Barre; oil was attracting new settlers to the north and west of the state; iron smelting was rearing an industrial giant at Pittsburgh. The population of Pittsburgh almost doubled during the twenty-year period between 1880 and 1900. No other eastern city in America showed such a rapid rate of growth. Altoona, Johnstown, and Tyrone were growing manufacturing centers along the tracks of the Pennsylvania Railroad; Allentown, Reading, and Easton were expanding as steel mills brought new workers to settle there. Erie was the port of entry for iron ore brought from the mines of Michigan and Minnesota for the gaping, flaming furnaces of Pittsburgh. Williamsport expanded as the center of the lumber industry. Chester was building ships, and many smaller communities were hurrying, bustling, and crowded with newcomers seeking their fortunes in the fabulous resources of natural wealth that Penn's Woods contained.

New Hands for Industry. From 1880 to 1914 the United States was admitting hundreds of thousands of immigrants each year. Formerly, most of the new arrivals to America came from northern Europe—from Ireland, the British Isles, Germany, Norway, and Sweden. After 1880 the tide of immigrants came from southern and central Europe. Italians and Poles found work in the coal mines; Hungarians worked as railroad builders and gang workers on trolley car lines; Croatians and other Slavs settled in mining towns. Greeks found their way to the cities to engage in the restaurant business; Russian and German Jews fleeing from persecution in the Old World found a haven here and set up retail business shops.

New Labor Conditions. Most of the new arrivals were unskilled laborers. The old spirit of the independent farmer carving out his own destiny in the virgin soil of a New World was not demanded or desired by the great industrial corporations which were wresting wealth from the interior of the earth. Laborers were needed to work in gangs under foremen, who in turn were supervised by managers. The managers were responsible to boards of directors of great stock companies whose investors were more interested in profits than they were in the

243

—*Drawn after a photograph by W. R. Leigh in Harper's Weekly*

**BURNING THE ROUNDHOUSE AT PITTSBURGH DURING THE PENN-
SYLVANIA RAILROAD STRIKE, 1877**

welfare of the workers. The old friendly relationship between
employer and employee was disappearing as big business ground
the individual worker into a statistic on the company's account
books.

This change in the status of the workingman was not
brought about deliberately by any group. It was a natural result of the new system of production. Unfortunately it led to
misunderstandings between laboring men and their employers
that resulted in bitter industrial warfare—in strikes, lockouts,
and sometimes in acts of violence.

Strikes of 1877. In 1877 a series of railroad strikes caused
disturbances in scattered portions of Pennsylvania as a result of
the railroads' policy of cutting wages. This was during the period
of national depression, and the railroads had heavy fixed expenses which they had to meet. The most serious of these
strikes took place in Pittsburgh, where rioters destroyed a considerable amount of railroad property. Units of the Pennsylvania National Guard were sent to restore order, but they were

subjected to insults and rough treatment by the strikers. Order was restored only when it became known that Governor Hartranft had called upon the federal government for soldiers of the regular army to come into the state. In Reading a mob burned a bridge and trapped a unit of the state militia in a railroad cut. At Scranton during a series of strikes, mobs were broken up by the sheriff and local police, but blood was shed in the process of restoring order.

The Homestead Strike of 1892. Another strike which attracted national attention was the Homestead Strike near Pittsburgh in 1892. In 1889 the Carnegie Steel Company agreed on a three-year contract with the steelworkers union, the Amalgamated Association of Iron and Steel Workers. When the three years had passed, the company refused to renew the contract at the old wage scale, whereas the workers were demanding an increase in wages. Andrew Carnegie was visiting Scotland at the time, and the task of dealing with the demands of the workers fell upon Carnegie's assistant, Henry Clay Frick. Frick refused to listen to the workers, and when violence began, he hired three hundred men from a detective agency to put down the strike. The strikers staged a battle against the detectives, in which ten of the latter were killed and the remainder forced to withdraw. The state government sent all units of the National Guard to the Pittsburgh area. Before the troops could act, an event occurred which doomed the cause of the strikers. An anarchist named Alexander Berkman tried to murder Frick. This act of violence lost the sympathy of the public for the strikers and with it their cause.

The Molly Maguires. During this period the anthracite mining regions were terrorized by a gang known mysteriously as the Molly Maguires. This was a secret organization of miners, made up almost entirely of men who had recently come from Ireland. These men were prepared to take the law into their own hands in trying to get what they wanted from the mine owners. They operated secretly with codes and passwords that were changed from time to time. Foremen or bosses who were not sympathetic to their interests were marked for murder. A member of the organization was chosen by lot to perform each act and the murders were carried out systematically. The Molly Maguires spread terror throughout the hard coal regions of

Schuylkill and nearby counties. Finally, in 1876, a detective engaged by the Reading Coal and Iron Company discovered their secrets and brought many of the guilty persons to trial, breaking up the organization. The experiences of this detective formed the basis for Conan Doyle's story of Sherlock Holmes entitled *The Valley of Fear.*

—Drawn after a photograph by W. F. Snyder in Harper's Weekly

DETECTIVES LEAVING THE BARGES AFTER THE SURRENDER
DURING THE HOMESTEAD STRIKE

—*The Bettmann Archive*

A MEETING OF THE MOLLY MAGUIRES
This meeting was being held for learning new secret signals just received from Ireland.

Coal Strikes. While we cannot condone the actions of men who defy the law, we must remember that working conditions in the mines were very poor and hours were extremely long. Coal operators were often more concerned about showing profits than they were about the safety of the men who worked in the mines and who were always in danger of being trapped by cave-ins, or suffocated by the fumes of poisonous gases which collected in the subterranean chambers of the earth. Usually the miners' families were forced to live in poorly built houses erected by the company on their own property—houses without any conveniences and offering little privacy. Miners' wives were required to shop at the "company store" where prices were often high. As a result, only too frequently the entire wages of a miner went back to the company for goods and rent, yet he and his family could not live decently.

Strikes as a means of collective bargaining in the coal mines began as early as 1868, when anthracite miners demanded an eight-hour day, but without success. Other unsuccessful strikes in the hard coal fields occurred in Luzerne County in 1872 and in Lehigh and Schuylkill counties in 1875. There were strikes in the coal industry during the closing years of the

247

THE COAL STRIKE OF 1902

Conference between President Theodore Roosevelt and J. P. Morgan. What do you suppose Morgan is saying? Why is he present at the conference?

nineteenth century, but none of them won any real relief for the miners. In 1900 the miners in the anthracite fields were organized into a labor union known as the United Mine Workers of America. Later the union organized the bituminous coal miners as well. Sensing that the demands of a united group of a hundred thousand members would be effective, they struck for an increase of pay and for the recognition of their union by the owners as a bargaining agency. This time they won a ten per cent increase in pay, but failed to have their union recognized.

The Coal Strike of 1902. Two years later, 1902, the anthracite miners went out on strike again, demanding the recognition of their union. The strike of 1902 is of national importance because it was the first time that the President of the United States intervened in an industrial dispute. The President, Theodore Roosevelt, was forced to intervene because of the serious situation created by the strike. Many families and industries were unable to buy coal to warm their homes or operate their factories. Nearly a hundred and fifty thousand miners had laid down their tools and demanded not only the recognition

248

of their union, but a further increase in pay, a shorter working day, and a rate of pay based upon the weight of the coal mined instead of on the number of cars loaded. The miners were willing to accept President Roosevelt as arbitrator of the strike, but the owners at first refused. Later the force of public opinion, heavily on the side of the President, convinced the owners that they should accept mediation. In the final settlement, Roosevelt prevailed upon the mine owners to accept a settlement which gave a ten per cent increase in pay, a nine-hour working day, and partial recognition of the union by the mine owners. Strikes by no means ended at this time, and labor problems in the coal mines were destined to disturb the industrial life of the state for many years to come.

The Position of Labor. Strikes and other forms of labor trouble were efforts on the part of working men to make their adjustment to the new industrial system of big business. Laborers learned that they must unite in order to protect their rights; that as individuals they were helpless but that in their unions they possessed strength. They learned another important lesson—that in order to win they must have public opinion on their side and that acts of violence and disregard of public welfare loses sympathy for their cause.

AGRICULTURE

Pennsylvania agriculture felt the impact of the great industrial expansion of this period in several ways. The farmers were quick to avail themselves of new labor-saving machinery built by implement factories. Old methods of plowing, sowing, and harvesting were replaced by power machinery and other mechanical devices.

The Wheat Harvest. Let us consider one farming operation as an example. The average farm of eighty acres ordinarily would have approximately ten acres sown in wheat. Before the invention of the mechanical reaper the services of eight or ten men were required to cut the wheat with sickles or cradles, tying each armful of wheat into a bundle or sheaf. Then the sheaves were placed upright in shocks of ten or twelve sheaves each. These shocks were allowed to stand in the fields until the stalks of wheat and the kernels had thoroughly dried. The

249

shocking was necessary because the harvesting of the wheat had to be started early, before the grain was quite ripe, since several weeks were required to cut ten acres of wheat by hand. If rains happened to soak the standing sheaves they would have to be scattered on the ground and dried before they could be taken to the barn. If there was a prolonged rainy season the sheaves were in danger of rotting or the grains might sprout before they could be threshed. If this happened the crop might be entirely ruined.

Harvest Machinery. When the reaper was invented, the work of cutting the standing wheat was made much easier. Horses pulling a reaper which cut a swath of five or six feet through the standing stalks could mow a ten-acre field in three days. But many hands were still needed to bind the sheaves, or tie the mown wheat into bundles. Early in the present century a new machine was invented known as the binder. This machine not only cut the wheat but tied the sheaves as well. Because less time was needed to mow the standing grain, it was possible for the farmer to wait until his crop was fully ripe before beginning the mowing operation. The shocking of wheat was no longer absolutely necessary. The threshing operation could begin as soon as the sheaves were ready. As time went on, automotive tractors were introduced to pull the binders. Now a ten-acre field could be cut in less than two days and only two men were needed in the operation—one to run the tractor and one the binder. A more recent development is the machine known as the combine which mows and threshes the wheat at the same time, filling bags with grain ready for delivery at the mill. In this way many days of tedious work were saved and risks of spoilage avoided.

From Farm to Factory. We have considered only one farm operation in this example. There were many others which could be used to illustrate the same story. Steam engines, and later gasoline engines, provided the power to drive the whirling cylinders of threshing machines; gang-plows pulled by tractors could turn over several furrow-widths of ground each time they circled a field. It required from ten days to two weeks to plow a ten-acre field with a team of horses; the tractor plow can do this in two days. Other mechanical appliances, such as the cream separator, grain grinder, and milking machine, all operated by gasoline or electric power, help to reduce the drudgery of labor on the farm.

Fewer hands were needed on the farms after the introduction of labor-saving machinery. Boys and girls, no longer needed on the farms, found jobs in the factories of nearby towns and cities. The movement from the farm to the city began during the period between 1880 and 1885 and has continued to the present. At some periods during the years which have passed since that movement began there has been fear that too many of our young people were deserting the farms for other occupations, but it is worth noting that Pennsylvania still has a farm population of 850,000 and ranks second among all of the forty-eight states in the number of people still residing on farms.

SOCIAL LIFE IN THE AGE OF BIG BUSINESS

We have seen that the years between 1865 and 1917 were marked by ruthless business and industrial strife, but there is another side to the picture. It was an age in which the finer things of life were brought to ever-increasing numbers of people. Life for all of us becomes richer as we share in the good things of the earth, although not all of us enjoy the same pleasures. For example, most persons enjoy music, but tastes vary all the way from popular songs to the great classical operas, from the "juke box" to the symphonic orchestra. He who has learned to enjoy his cultural heritage possesses the greatest riches life can offer. Money may sometimes serve as a means to secure the things that enrich life, but there are great stores of cultural wealth that are free to all of us.

It is natural that we enjoy most those forms of culture which are closest to us—the comforts and pleasures to be found in our family, in the church, the school, and the community. As time passes and our experience grows we can expand our interests, absorbing the culture of our state, our nation, and finally the fascinating treasures of the entire world. In the long span of time a human life covers only a tiny fraction of history. That life should be filled with all of the joy that it can find for itself. The fruits of the past are harvested by each generation which must pay its debt to the past by adding in its turn to the common treasury of culture.

Pennsylvanians have many reasons to be grateful to the citizens of their state who have added to the fullness of life. In some cases these men and women have made and are making contributions which enrich the culture of the nation and the world. Others add to the cultural life of their own communities. It would be impossible to mention all of these by name. They are the good citizens, the leaders of thought and action, the men and women who in their gratitude for their inheritance from the past are adding to it day by day, gradually evolving a way of life that becomes ever richer.

Let us look back now at what we owe to the Pennsylvanians of the nineteenth century.

Painting. During the years that Philadelphia was the capital of the United States, many artists had been attracted to the city. Gilbert Stuart worked there in 1794, painting his famous portrait of George Washington. Later, Thomas Sully came to Philadelphia from England. Stephen Girard, the banker, built a large mansion for Sully, equipping it with studio and exhibition rooms. During his lifetime, Sully painted the portraits of Commodore Stephen Decatur, Thomas Jefferson, and other famous Americans. Other Europeans came to Philadelphia to establish studios. There were also many native Pennsylvanians who became painters. Robert Fulton, inventor of the steamboat, studied painting under Benjamin West and painted portraits before he turned his interest to steam navigation. Rembrandt Peale of Bucks County painted famous portraits, including one of Washington. The works of these painters are on exhibit today in art galleries of the state and in famous national galleries.

After the War for the Union, Pennsylvania continued to produce distinguished artists. Edwin Austin Abbey, a Philadelphian, became a well-known painter of murals. He did some of the murals in the state capitol at Harrisburg, showing scenes from the state's history. His work was unfinished when he died in 1911. It was completed by Violet Oakley, of Philadelphia, a mural painter who received her training at the Pennsylvania Academy of Fine Arts.

Other Pennsylvanians who became distinguished as artists were Joseph Pennell, skilled in pen and ink drawing and in etching; John Sartain, the engraver; Maxfield Parrish, the illustrator; William Rush, John Boyle, and George Gray Barnard, sculptors; Thomas U. Waller, William Strickland, Napoleon LeBrun, and Benjamin Latrobe, architects; and Samuel Yellin, one of the world's greatest sculptors in metal.

Music. Philadelphia and Bethlehem, leaders in music during colonial times, continued to be the musical centers throughout the nineteenth century. The Philadelphia Orchestra was organized in the year 1900. It became one of the greatest organizations of its kind in America. At Bethlehem the original Collegium Musicum of colonial days was replaced by the Philharmonic Society in 1820. Late in the nineteenth century, J. Fred Wolle, a native of Bethlehem, studied the music of Johann Sebastian Bach under European masters. Wolle returned to America determined to acquaint his fellow-countrymen with the works of Bach. He organized Bach festivals in California, Missouri, and other parts of the United States before he returned to Bethlehem to found the famous Bach Choir in 1908.

In the western part of the state, the Pittsburgh Symphony Orchestra was organized in 1896 with Frederick Archer as conductor. For some years the conductor of the Pittsburgh Symphony was the famous composer, Victor Herbert. Pennsylvanians have always been fond of band music and many famous bands have been organized in the cities and towns of the state. One of the earliest was the Repasz Band organized in Williamsport in 1831. By 1900 nearly every village could boast of its "Silver Cornet Band." In gay uniforms these bands marched in parades and played at picnics, political rallies, and public gatherings of all kinds. The public parks were equipped with bandshells to improve listening at out-of-door concerts and special celebrations.

Pennsylvania has had her share of distinguished composers. The most famous of these was Stephen Collins Foster, who died in 1864 at the very early age of thirty-seven. In his brief lifetime he wrote plantation songs and lyrics that will live forever. His "Oh Susannah!" which became the favorite of the pioneers moving westward in covered wagons, was written before the author was twenty years old. Second only to Foster as a famous Pennsylvania composer was Ethelbert Nevin, who was born at Edgeworth, near Pittsburgh, in 1862. He too is remembered for his songs such as "The Rosary" and "Mighty

Like A Rose." Charles Wakefield Cadman was the composer of the group of American Indian songs containing the beautiful "From the Land of the Sky Blue Water."

Schools. We have already seen that the Free School Act was accepted by all school districts in the state in 1868. The constitution of 1873 included provisions which firmly established the system of free schools. In 1885 an act was passed fixing the school month at twenty days and prohibiting the holding of school classes on Saturdays. The school term was set at a minimum of six months. A law requiring the school districts to provide textbooks was enacted in 1893. The first compulsory attendance law was passed in 1895, which required that all children between the ages of eight and thirteen must attend school. Six years later the age of compulsory attendance was raised to sixteen. In 1937 the age was again raised, this time to eighteen, with some exceptions. In 1921 the minimum length of the school term was changed from six to eight months for the rural districts and to nine months in the larger communities of the state.

The first public high school in the state was the Central High School of Philadelphia established in 1836. Before the War for the Union, communities were slow in establishing secondary schools, and by 1860 there were only six high schools in the state. Ten years later there were only twenty-six. The chief reason for this slow progress was the attitude held by the public that higher education was a special privilege which should not be paid for out of tax funds. Private schools and academies prepared students for college, and it was felt that parents who wished their children to have advanced training should bear the expense themselves.

This attitude changed, however, when compulsory attendance laws forced children to stay in school until they were sixteen. Moreover, industry began to demand more and more training of the young people seeking employment. Competition for jobs became keener; the use of machinery placed emphasis upon alert minds, trained powers of reasoning and memory, rather than on mere brawn and muscle. As these demands were felt, opposition to public high schools vanished. In its place came an ever-increasing insistence on high school opportunities for all young people. In 1887 the state authorized the building of high schools in all cities, and five years later this privilege was extended to all communities with a population over five thousand. Since 1895 the increase in high schools has been constant.

Science and Scientists. From the small beginnings of the Junto of colonial times have developed a number of famous scientific institutions. The American Philosophical Society, organized before the Revolutionary War, today numbers among its members the most brilliant scholars of the world. The Academy of Natural Sciences, organized in 1812, did pioneer work in equipping expeditions to explore the Antarctic in 1839 and the Arctic in 1853. It was this institution which made it possible for Robert E. Peary, born at Cresson, Pennsylvania, to undertake his successful expedition to the North Pole in 1909. Many other scientific expeditions were sent to remote parts of the world in search of new forms of plant and animal life. The Academy has continued its work right down to the present day. In 1929 there were fifteen expeditions under its sponsorship, engaged in explorations in thirty countries scattered over the globe.

Another institution which owes its origin to the Junto and the American Philosophical Society is the Franklin Institute organized in Philadelphia in 1824. There the mysteries of the heavens were explored, industrial products tested, and the wonders of science—past and present—exhibited. Through the years this institution has furnished important weather data, recorded eclipses, and searched for unknown planets. Chemistry, physics, geology, astronomy—all of the physical sciences—have been studied. In addition, the Franklin Institute sponsored other scientific organizations which were devoted to a specialized field.

The spirit of inquiry is supplied by inspired men. Institutions are merely the agencies through which men may pursue their studies. The list of Pennsylvania's great scientists is far too long to be included here. We should remember, however, that Joseph Priestly, the discoverer of oxygen, made his home in Northumberland, Pennsylvania, when he came to America from England in 1791. John James Audubon, the authority on bird life in America, lived at Mill Grove on the Perkiomen Creek in Montgomery County during a part of his life. Dr.

THE UNIVERSITY OF
PITTSBURGH

Joseph Leidy, one of the most famous research scholars in the field of medicine and anatomy, was a native of Pennsylvania. Other eminent scientists of the state were: David Alter of Allegheny County, who invented a crude telegraph before Morse perfected the instrument; Daniel Drawbaugh of Cumberland County who invented and used a telephone before Alexander Graham Bell successfully demonstrated his invention. These men were pioneers in their fields but failed to attract public attention with their discoveries. Elihu Thompson, a teacher in a Philadelphia high school, patented some seven hundred inventions, including an arc lamp, an electrical transformer, and an electric welding device.

Medicine. Philadelphia remained the medical center of the nation throughout the century. Hundreds of famous physicians practiced their skills in the city founded by Penn, bringing relief to suffering humanity. Great medical schools were established along with hospitals, clinics, and dispensaries. Leadership in this field was not limited to Philadelphia, however. Excellent hospitals were established in most of the larger towns of the state. The Mercy Hospital of Pittsburgh was opened in 1847. The Western Pennsylvania Medical College was founded in 1883, and nine years later it was united with the University of Pittsburgh.

Recreation. Today Pennsylvania offers its people many and varied forms of healthful play. Organized games for public entertainment did not develop until after the War for the Union. The game of baseball was invented in 1839, but it was not until the soldiers in the army took it up that it became popular. Late

—*From a drawing by W. C. Synder.*
Culver Service

AN EARLY BASEBALL GAME

in the nineteenth century the game spread to every village **in** the state, and "batter up!" became a familiar cry heard **on** vacant lots throughout the country. Many Pennsylvania cities organized teams and formed leagues, and not a few of the great national league players learned the game on "home grounds." In his youth, John K. Tener, Governor of Pennsylvania from 1907 to 1911, was a second baseman for the Chicago Cubs of the National League. Basketball was invented in New England in 1891. Football is an adaptation of an English game known as rugby. Through playing these games of skill, Americans learned the essentials of good sportsmanship. President Theodore Roosevelt summed up the spirit of American sports at an assembly of the Central High School in Philadelphia when he said, "Don't flinch, don't foul, but hit the line hard."

Social Gatherings. During the nineteenth century, people delighted in social gatherings which brought neighbors and friends together for amusement. Before the War for the Union and for a number of years thereafter, the entire community turned out for Battalion Day, late in May, when the local militia gathered for roll call and drill. Band music, impressive ceremonies, and public dancing in the town square were the order of the day. Late in the harvest season county fairs were held in the rural sections of the state where farmers proudly exhibited their finest produce and livestock. A number of these annual fairs are still flourishing, particularly at York, Allentown, Williamstown, Kutztown, and Reading.

In the period after the War for the Union, interest in literary societies developed. Public debates were held in schoolhouses and town halls. Traveling lyceums and Chautauqua units visited the towns offering lectures, concerts, and theatrical performances to the citizens. Less pretentious as a form of entertainment, but equally good fun, were the traveling medicine shows that set up their platforms near the center of the village and proceeded to dazzle the crowds with farce and magic in order to sell their wares.

Religious camp meetings attracted old and young a generation ago. Not all of the time at such meetings was spent in worship. Reunions of the Grand Army of the Republic, as the veterans of the War for the Union were called, brought parades and festivities to many communities annually. Fire companies organized street carnivals to raise funds for their organizations. Political rallies with torchlight processions and band concerts enlivened many evenings.

Many of the forms of organized entertainment are enjoyed today in the state. We can still attend a county fair, a public sale, a strawberry festival, or a church social. Amateur theatrical performances, music festivals, historical pageants, and parades are still part of the life of communities in the state.

The Centennial. A great fair held in Philadelphia in 1876 to celebrate the one hundredth anniversary of the nation's birth brought together many things which illustrated the social and industrial progress of the era. The fair opened in Fairmount Park, Philadelphia, on May 10. Many of the great nations of the world sent exhibits, and some of them erected special buildings to house their exhibits. Among the nations contributing to the celebration was Great Britain. This was a splendid gesture of good will. Twenty-eight states of the Union participated in the Centennial. Southern states joined with their northern neighbors, thus generously showing their faith in the Union which only fifteen years before they had fought to destroy.

—*Harper's Weekly*

PRESIDENT GRANT OPENING THE CENTENNIAL EXHIBITION
This building, Memorial Hall, is still standing in Fairmount Park,
Philadelphia.

Ten million people paid more than three million dollars to see
the fair. They came from all parts of America, many of them
riding on trains for the first time.

Among the inventions exhibited were the telephone, which
was new at that time. The great engineering spectacle of the age
was the Girard Avenue Bridge over the Schuylkill River adjoining the fairgrounds. A number of the buildings erected for the
Centennial still stand today in Fairmount Park. Among them
are Memorial Hall and Horticultural Hall. The statues along
the winding driveways of the park were also put there in honor
of the fair.

Woodrow Wilson wrote of the Philadelphia Centennial
that it showed that "the national spirit was aroused, and conscious now of its strength."

X Equals?—The Question Marks of Life. In our study
of algebra the letter x is always the unknown quantity. By processes of reasoning and calculation we find what x equals, and
thereby solve the problem. Life in a democratic state presents
many unknowns. By trial and error we find the answer to x.

259

But, just as it is true in mathematics that by knowing the rules and formulas we find the answer more readily, so, too, in life we can solve new problems more readily and find the correct answer if we know how similar problems were solved in the past.

In this unit we have seen how our parents and grandparents met the problems that grew out of the great industrial development of the state and nation. Some of these problems were solved. Orphaned children were cared for. The needs for more education were recognized and supplied. Steps were taken to insure honesty in elections; machine politics was brought under control.

Other problems were only partially solved, their final solution being postponed by the appearance of new factors from time to time. Labor unrest still perplexes us from time to time; the relations between huge business combinations and the people's government are not always clearly defined. But great progress has been made toward developing a better understanding of these matters. It is to be hoped that the coming years will bring answers to unsolved problems and that our citizens will be equipped to find the x in meeting new problems as they arise.

QUESTIONS FOR STUDY AND REVIEW

1. What natural advantages have helped to make Pennsylvania a great manufacturing state? Name at least ten articles which are manufactured in great quantities in Pennsylvania.

2. What mineral resources are there in your community? What manufacturing enterprises? To what extent do they provide employment for members of your family?

3. Do your local industries need tariff protection? Name some large industries in Pennsylvania which would suffer severely if all tariffs were removed.

4. Show how the development of big business served to intensify labor problems. What weapons can labor use to secure its demands? What forces serve to check unreasonable demands that labor might sometime put forward?

5. What big business has factories, stores, offices, lines, or agents in your town? Can you name any business establishment in your community that is not dependent upon a business place in some other portion of the state or nation? How is this different from industry in colonial days? What changes in transportation influenced this development?

260

6. What school laws affect you? Compare the educational advantage which you have with those of a child of your age in 1880. What debt do you owe to the future as a result of the opportunities offered you in school?

7. How would you account for Pennsylvania's leadership in science? in medicine? in the arts?

8. What forms of healthful and worthwhile recreation does your community offer during the course of a year? Consider all seasons. What are your hobbies?

9. Has the development of big business helped or hindered the living of a full life by the people as a whole? Would you wish to change places with John Evans whom we met in Chapter V, or would you prefer to live in the present century?

PROBLEMS AND ACTIVITIES

1. Who is the state Senator from your district? the Representative? What is the number of your senatorial district? your congressional district?

2. Define inflation; deflation. Show how these terms are related to periods of prosperity and depression.

3. Name at least five other world's fairs held in the United States before or since the Centennial.

4. Why did the immigrants from southern and southeastern Europe find it more difficult to make adjustments in America than did the earlier immigrants?

5. What, if any, limits should be fixed in recognizing the worker's right to strike?

6. Outline the causes of the Spanish-American War. Do you know any veterans of that war?

7. Hold a debate on the following question: Resolved that the right to vote should be given to all persons over eighteen years of age.

8. Prepare a list of institutions which in your judgment are worthy of financial aid from the state. Discuss in class why you believe they should have such aid.

9. You are planning to celebrate the anniversary of the founding of your town. Prepare a program of entertainment and exhibits.

10. What federal laws were passed in the period between the War for the Union and World War I for the purpose of regulating big business? How were these laws enforced? (Look in a standard textbook in American history under anti-trust laws.)

11. Report on the chief provisions of the tariff laws between the years 1896 to 1924. This question may be divided among several students.

12. What advantages does the large company have over the small business firm? Does the general public benefit as a result of large business combinations, or does it suffer?

13. Write a short essay on the history of labor unions in the United States. What are some of the gains which unions have secured for the workers?

14. Show the difference in organization between the American Federation of Labor and the Congress of Industrial Organization.

15. Indicate which of the following articles should have a high tariff, which should have low rates, and which should enter the country free of taxes. Be prepared to justify your answers.

Sugar	Coal	Butter
Flax	Eggs	Silk
Carpets	Lime	Cement
Rubber	Coffee	Cigars
Steel girders	Grapes	Tin

SUGGESTIONS FOR FURTHER READING
Industrial Development

J. W. Coleman, *The Molly Maguire Riots*, Richmond, Va.: Garrett and Massie; Herman L. Collins, *Pennsylvania the Golden*, Harrisburg: Pennsylvania Book Service; P. H. Giddens, *Beginnings of the Petroleum Industry*, Harrisburg: Pennsylvania Historical Commission; Elsie Gluck, *John Mitchell, Miner*, New York: John Day; Frederic A. Godcharles, *Pennsylvania: Political, Governmental, Military and Civil*, 5 vols., New York: American Historical Society; George Harvey, *Henry Clay Frick, the Man*, New York: Scribner's; Burton J. Hendrick, *Life of Andrew Carnegie*, New York: Doubleday; *Industrial Directory of the Commonwealth of Pennsylvania*, Harrisburg: Department of Internal Affairs; Glenn E. McLaughlin, *Growth of American Manufacturing Areas*, Pittsburgh: University of Pittsburgh Press; Ernest C. Miller, *Oil Mania: Sketches from the Early Pennsylvania Oil Fields*, Philadelphia: Dorrance and Co.; Terence V. Powderly, *The Path I Trod: Autobiography*, New York: Columbia University Press; James M. Swank, *Progressive Pennsylvania*, Philadelphia: Lippincott.

Political Developments

County Government and Archives in Pennsylvania, Harrisburg: Pennsylvania Historical Commission; Walter Davenport, *Power and Glory: Life of Boies Penrose*, New York: Putnam's; P. H. Love, *Andrew W. Mellon*, New York: Heath Coggins and Co.; Alexander K. McClure, *Old Time Notes of Pennsylvania*, 2 vol., Philadelphia: John C.

Winston Co.; *Pennsylvania Manual* (published biennially) Harrisburg: Department of Property and Supplies; Samuel W. Pennypacker, *Autobiography of a Pennsylvanian*, Philadelphia: John C. Winston Co.; William S. Vare, *My Forty Years in Politics*, Philadelphia: Ronald Swain; George Woodward, *The Pennsylvania Legislator*, Philadelphia: Harris and Partridge.

Social and Cultural History

Gertrude B. Biddle and Sarah D. Lowrie, *Notable Women of Pennsylvania*, Philadelphia: University of Pennsylvania Press; Katherine Henry, *Back Home in Pennsylvania*, Philadelphia: Dorrance and Co.; *Johnstown Floods*, distributed by Mayor's Committee, Johnstown; E. H. Loucks, *The Ku Klux Klan in Pennsylvania*, Harrisburg: Telegraph Press; Elsie Murray, *Stephen C. Foster at Athens: His First Composition*, Towanda: Tioga Point Museum; *Pennsylvania Cavalcade*, Writers Program of Pennsylvania, Philadelphia: University of Pennsylvania Press.

Fiction

Thomas Bell, *Out of This Furnace*, Boston: Little Brown; Frank L. Benedict, *Miss Van Kortland*, New York: Harper; Edward B. Bloss, *Tales of Petrolea*, Philadelphia: Dorrance and Co.; Katherine Brush, *Don't Ever Leave Me*, New York: Farrar and Rinehart; Taylor Caldwell, *Dynasty of Death*, New York: Scribner's; Taylor Caldwell, *Strong City*, New York: Scribner's; Sir Arthur Conan Doyle, *Valley of Fear: A Sherlock Holmes Mystery*, New York: Doubleday; Garet Garrett, *Cinder Buggy: A Fable in Iron and Steel*, New York: Dutton; Joseph Hergesheimer, *Three Black Pennies*, New York: Knopf; Elizabeth D. Kaup, *Not for the Meek*, New York: Macmillan; John T. McIntyre, *Ragged Edge: A Tale of World Life and Politics*, New York: McClure, Phillips and Co.; Patrick J. McMahon, *Philip; or the Mollies' Secret, A Tale of the Coal Regions*, Philadelphia: H. L. Kilner; Margaret Marchand, *Pilgrims on the Earth*, New York: Crowell; Mary Moss, *Sequence in Hearts*, Philadelphia: Lippincott; Reuben E. Stainbrook, *Flaming River*, Meadville: Tribune Publishing Co.

UNIT VII

MODERN TIMES

In 1914 war began in Europe, which before it ended was to engulf most of the world. America entered the war in 1917, and the Commonwealth of Pennsylvania was called upon to give unsparingly of her skills, resources, and manpower.

In the decade following the war, one fact began to emerge clearly. The problems besetting the American people could no longer be settled on a local or even a statewide scale. With the onset of a serious economic depression in 1929, the trend toward national solutions of national problems accelerated. The following decade was to show that even the nation could no longer exist sufficient unto itself alone. There were many reasons for this state of affairs. Some of them lie outside the province of our story. Others should be clear to the student who reads these pages thoughtfully.

The outbreak of World War II in September of 1939 has required a new perspective of every American citizen. Some of the questions we shall have to face as a result of the war are already clear; others we can only guess. The issue of the war itself was never in doubt, once Americans realized the gigantic task before them and set about doing it willingly and earnestly. To the job of winning the war, Pennsylvania made magnificent contributions worthy of her tradition of service whenever the nation has been threatened.

Every individual is partially what he makes himself to be, and partially the result of his heritage from the past. Pennsylvanians are fortunate that their heritage has been kept alive through the efforts of sincere and devoted citizens who have realized its worth. In this unit we survey the work of those individuals and see for ourselves the debt we of today owe to the future as a result of our gracious past.

Chapter XIV

PROBLEMS OF WAR AND PEACE

The history of Pennsylvania from 1917 to the present includes events which are within the memory of most people now living. Many of the leaders who made that history are still among us and are adding to our history day by day. Often it is difficult to describe recent events properly because the true perspective is not clear at such close range. It is not always possible to see causes or to evaluate effects.

During and after the First World War, business first expanded to great proportions and then slumped into a long depression lasting from 1929 to 1939. Twice within a quarter of a century Pennsylvania, along with the other states of the nation, was called upon to use her material and human resources to wage world-wide war. We shall consider the glorious record which the sons and daughters of the Commonwealth wrote in these conflicts.

WORLD WAR I

How America Became Involved. When war broke out in Europe in 1914, the people of the United States hoped that they could keep out of it. Early in the war, however, the United States became involved in disputes with Germany and Great Britain over shipping rights. Since the early days of our history we had always insisted upon the freedom of the seas—the right of American ships to travel where they pleased without interference. The quarrel with England was never serious because the ships stopped by her were taken into British ports and the owners paid for any cargoes seized. No American lives were lost as a result of British interference with our shipping. With Germany the situation was different. Germany's chief weapon in sea warfare was the submarine. To be effective, submarines must strike quickly and sink the vessel attacked on the spot. In 1915 German submarines began to attack both British and neutral vessels, sinking them without warning. A number of Americans lost their lives as a result of this practice, and the

—Cartoon by McCutcheon in the Chicago Tribune

CAREFUL NAVIGATION REQUIRED TO AVOID TROUBLE

entire nation was shocked over the brutal action. The United States government made bitter protests to Germany, but the protests got few results. Other influences besides the submarine attacks were leading the United States toward participation in the war. The traditional friendship of this country for Great Britain and France exerted a powerful emotional pull on the people. Moreover, as the war progressed, Americans found

266

themselves admiring the heroic stand made by the Allies against German military might. They saw that the war was really a struggle between democratic government and autocratic government and that our own safety depended upon joining Britain and France against the enemies of freedom.

Congress declared war on April 6, 1917. President Woodrow Wilson rallied the people by his declaration that we were entering the war "to make the world safe for democracy." "To such a task," he told Congress, "we can dedicate our lives and our fortunes . . . with the pride of those who know that the day has come when

—*George W. Tyler Collection, Temple University*

A LIBERTY BOND POSTER

America is privileged to spend her blood and her might for the principles that gave her birth and happiness and the peace which she has treasured."

Pennsylvanians in the Armed Forces. At the time the war began, units of the Pennsylvania National Guard were stationed on the Mexican border to help guard American lives and property during a period of border raids by Mexican bandits and revolutionists. These troops were well trained and ready to be sent to European battlefields. But additional men were needed for the great army we planned to build.

The first conscription act, passed in May of 1917, called up men between the ages of twenty-one and thirty-one. In September of 1918 all men between the ages of eighteen and forty-five were required to register. But the latter group was never called into military service, since the war ended in November, 1918, before they were needed. At first men were drafted by lot and given a physical examination. If they passed this examination, they were then given the chance to ask for exemption on the basis of dependents. Those who did not ask for exemption and those whose requests were rejected by local draft boards were inducted into service. During the last months of the war, a National Selective Service Act was put into operation. Under this act men registered in the draft were classified according to their availability for service; that is, men with dependent families and men with important war jobs were placed lower on the list.

Nearly eight per cent of all of the armed forces of the United States during the First World War were Pennsylvanians. Almost 380,000 men answered their country's call. Two divisions of the United States Army that saw the thick of the fighting in France were the Forty-second, or the Rainbow Division, and the Twenty-eighth, known as the Iron Division. Both divisions had large numbers of Pennsylvania men. But divisions to which other Pennsylvanians were assigned also saw action and took part in the great battles at Saint Mihiel, Chateau-Thierry, and in the Argonne.

Soldiers of Production. Pennsylvania's contribution toward our part in the First World War cannot be measured in terms of the number of servicemen only. The great industries of the state—steel, coal, oil, munitions, textiles—were called upon to produce great amounts of war materials. The ship-building plants along the Delaware River performed miracles in constructing vessels for the merchant fleet. At Hog Island, near Philadelphia, a vast area was converted into ways and docks for building ships. By the end of the war these yards were completing one ship each day.

Dollars for Democracy. War bonds, known as Liberty Bonds, were sold in a series of four drives; a fifth drive, conducted after the war had ended, sold Victory Bonds. These bonds were sold at the full face value and were transferable. Children were urged to buy War Saving Stamps which were redeemable for cash, with interest, in 1925. Pennsylvanians purchased nearly three billion dollars' worth of war bonds during the five drives.

The Armistice. On November 11, 1918, came official news that an armistice had been signed. The news arrived during the night when most people were still asleep. There were many celebrations, but they were sober and restrained as befitted a people who realized that though the strain and stress of war was over, there would be new problems to be solved. However, festive indeed were the receptions given to the soldiers who returned home in 1919 and 1920. Today we pause at eleven o'clock on the morning of each November eleventh to pay a silent tribute to those boys who did not return.

Readjustments in Industry. The cancellation of war contracts and the return of soldiers to their peacetime jobs led to a mild depression in the years immediately following the war until industry could reorganize for peacetime production. There was widespread unemployment and in many industries wages were reduced. Workers protesting against wage cuts staged a series of nation-wide strikes in 1919 and in the years following. The most serious of these for Pennsylvania was a steel strike which lasted for several months. Governor William C. Sproul, who had succeeded Governor Brumbaugh, promptly sent units of the National Guard to the troubled areas and no violence occurred. Although the workers did not succeed in maintaining their wartime wage levels, the strikes served to call public attention to unfavorable conditions which existed in the steel industry. A few years later wages were raised and other complaints of the workers were adjusted by the steel companies themselves.

In 1922 the anthracite miners of eastern Pennsylvania left their work because the owners of the mines refused to insert in the new contracts a provision requested by union officials that each miner's dues should be deducted from the pay envelope and turned over to the union. The strike brought about a serious coal shortage in the eastern states. It was adjusted, however, by an arrangement under which the miners agreed to continue work under their former contracts.

There were strikes in the bituminous coal fields in 1922 and 1927. One of the chief complaints leading to these strikes was that the operators held too much control over the civic and personal affairs of the workers. There was resentment against a group of officials known as the "Coal and Iron Police," men hired by the operators to enforce company rules. None of these strikes resulted in clear-cut victory for either side. Labor problems became more complex as time went on.

269

STEEL IS KING IN PENNSYLVANIA
From white hot furnaces comes the molten metal to be cooled and
rolled into ribbons of steel.

Prohibition. One of the results of World War I was to
merge the problems of the state more closely than ever with
those of the nation. Two amendments to the federal constitution
were ratified by the state Legislature in 1919. One of these was
the woman's suffrage amendment; the other, the prohibition

270

amendment. The latter of these, the Federal law prohibiting the manufacture, transportation, and sale of intoxicating beverages, aroused a great deal of opposition. Efforts to pass a prohibition law for the state had always met with dismal failure. Between 1884 and 1914 the state Legislature had passed a series of acts in an effort to control the evils which attended the sale of liquor. When prohibition became law throughout the nation, Pennsylvania experienced the gross violations which were common elsewhere in the United States. Bootleggers and others defied the law and reaped a rich harvest. People who had formerly favored prohibition were disturbed to see how the flagrant violations of the law tended to break down respect for all laws. When public opinion forced the repeal of prohibition in 1933, the state established a system of state liquor stores under the control of a state Liquor Board. In this way the sale of liquors is being regulated.

Progressive Legislation. Gifford Pinchot, elected governor in 1922, brought a truly progressive spirit into the state government. Boss rule came to an end when Senator Boies Penrose died in 1921. Pinchot had always opposed machine politics. As a close friend of President Theodore Roosevelt he had shared the latter's liberal views. In the days of the Progressive party, Pinchot had joined in the revolt against the Republican machine and throughout his political career had maintained an independent position. It was only natural, therefore, that as Governor he would endeavor to make reforms in the state government.

The first Pinchot administration established a fine record of achievement. In 1923 a new code was drawn up for the reorganization of the state government. Under this code many of the administrative offices were combined into several departments, thus guarding against overlapping of authority and duplication of work. State finances were improved by the creation of a state budget which planned in advance how funds were to be spent. Pinchot found the state treasury in debt by twenty million dollars. In the first two years of his administration this debt was wiped out, and there was a surplus in the treasury when his term ended. During this administration the state tapped new sources of revenue by taxes upon gasoline which were used to pay the costs of road building.

271

Pinchot's interest in reform extended to many fields of activity. Laws were passed preventing the sale of worthless stocks and bonds; a pension system was established for state employees. Because of his training as a forester, the Governor gave his support to laws for the protection of the forests.

Prosperous Years. John S. Fisher, elected to succeed Pinchot in 1927, served during years of prosperity. The state treasury was well-filled and the Commonwealth found it possible to undertake a vast highway building program. More than four thousand miles of new roads were built and many old roads repaired. Although the state spent more than $600,000,000 in the four years of the Fisher administration, there was a substantial surplus in the treasury at the close of his term.

THE NATIONAL DEPRESSION

The years of national prosperity came to a sudden end in the autumn of 1929 when the stock market crashed and the value of stocks and bonds came tumbling down. There had been warning signs for some time that all was not well in industrial life. Because more and more machinery was used in factories, unemployment had been increasing even during the prosperous years. Certain industries—chiefly agriculture, textiles, and coal—had never shared in the boom. For example, in the farming areas of the nation, banks had been failing at a dangerous rate ever since 1921. But the immediate cause of the financial crisis of 1929 was the wave of speculation in stocks and bonds which had spread through the land. As a result, the prices of most stocks and bonds kept soaring far out of proportion to any real value they might have had.

When the price of stocks fell suddenly, many banks were forced to close because they did not have the funds to pay the long lines of depositors who wished to withdraw their savings; industries were forced to discharge their workers because the demand for the goods they sold diminished. At first, the effects of the crash were not felt very keenly by people who had not invested in stocks, but as conditions grew steadily worse nearly every home in America was affected by the prolonged depression which lasted with varying degrees of severity from 1929 to 1939. Millions were unemployed and faced starvation because they had no means of earning a living.

—*Keystone View Co.*

QUEUES OF UNEMPLOYED, LOOKING FOR JOBS
The problem of full employment during peace times is yet to be solved.

In 1931 Gifford Pinchot was elected Governor for the second time. His administration was faced with the many problems resulting from the depression. The most serious was providing relief for the unemployed. In 1931 there were nine hundred thousand unemployed in the state. The depression was nationwide in scope, however, and no state could hope to solve its problems alone.

The Democratic Tidal Wave. In the elections of 1934 the Democrats elected their first governor of the state in the twentieth century. George H. Earle, an ardent supporter of the policies of the national administration, came into the office in 1935. The Democratic party also won control of both houses of the state Legislature. In the election of 1936, a Democratic presidential candidate carried the state for the first time since 1856, when Franklin Roosevelt received the state's electoral vote.

Interpreting the votes of the citizens of the state as approval of the program of social legislation that was being enacted

273

in the national capital, the Governor and the Legislature set to work to pass laws improving working conditions and establishing social and economic security for workers. In passing these laws, it was probably unavoidable that some ill-considered and poorly constructed legislation found its way into the statute books. But most of the laws passed at this time have proven their worth. Minimum wages were fixed for women and children; the forty-four hour work week was established; the affairs of companies that furnished services necessary to the public—such as light, telephone service, and transportation—were placed under the direction of a Public Utilities Commission. A Teacher's Tenure Act was passed protecting teachers from being dismissed from their positions without cause.

Unemployment Problems. At first the burden of providing relief for the unemployed fell upon the state. Later, however, the federal government took over the task of providing work programs and granting relief to those who were unable to work. The work programs of the federal government usually were based upon the willingness of the states and cities to furnish part of the money needed for constructing public buildings and other projects for improvements in local communities. Thus, the state was required to help by adding its own funds to federal funds. New sources of revenue were required to meet these increased expenses. Cities and counties were permitted to borrow money against future tax collections. Some cities in the state reached the limit of their borrowing power in an effort to take advantage of all opportunities to provide work for their people. These measures helped to reduce the number of unemployed.

In their desire to make changes quickly, the state officials found themselves hindered by provisions of the state constitution of 1873. There was talk of calling a convention to form a new constitution, but instead, in 1937, the voters were asked to approve or reject several amendments to the constitution. Only one of the proposed amendments was passed. This permitted the granting of pensions to the blind and aged. One amendment earnestly sought by a number of Philadelphians was defeated. The amendment called for a change in the Philadelphia city charter which would have made possible the adoption of a city manager plan of municipal government.

Close of Earle's Administration. As Governor Earle's term of office neared its close, charges of dishonesty were made against his administration. The accusations were made by the Attorney-general, one of Earle's advisors who presented formal charges to the District Attorney of Dauphin County. Fourteen state officials, including Governor Earle himself, were accused of dishonesty. The District Attorney of Dauphin County ordered a grand jury investigation of the charges.

The situation was a difficult one for the Democrats because it was an election year (1938), and they feared that a grand jury investigation might be used to embarrass the candidates of the Democratic party. In an effort to keep the grand jury from acting, Earle summoned a special session of the Legislature. Laws were passed promptly which were designed to prevent a grand jury investigation. At the same time, a committee of the state House of Representatives was appointed to make its own investigation of the charges.

The state Supreme Court quickly declared the laws limiting grand jury investigations to be unconstitutional, and the investigation proceeded. The committee of the House of Representatives made its report a few days before the November election. They stated that the charges against Earle and his associates were without foundation. Later the grand jury concurred in these findings.

Although Governor Earle and his administration were cleared before election day, the Democrats suffered embarrassment in their campaign as a result of the charges against Earle's administration. The Republicans were able to win a clear-cut victory. Arthur H. James, the Republican candidate, was elected by a large majority.

Debt Reduction. With the inauguration of Governor James in 1939, the Republican party returned to power in Pennsylvania. Pledged to reduce taxes and at the same time to provide for the needy, the James administration found itself faced with a huge debt created by the previous Democratic administration. Measures were taken to reduce the expenses of the state government. By the time the United States entered World War II, the debt had been substantially reduced. The improvement in the finances of the state reflected not only the economies introduced in the state government, but also the improved business conditions which developed when the United States began to rearm for national defense.

WORLD WAR II

In September, 1939, Germany invaded Poland and for the second time in this century plunged Europe into a devastating war. Although they hated the dictators who had brought on the conflict, Americans again hoped that our country would be spared the sacrifice and human misery of war. The conquest of Holland, Belgium, and France by Germany in the spring of 1940 was a rude shock to such hopes. The success of the airplane as an instrument of destruction demonstrated that there was no safety in distance. Prudence required that we prepare to protect ourselves against the Axis nations, Germany, Italy, and Japan, who were clearly bent on world conquest. Modern war equipment required months, even years, to build. Men needed to be trained to operate it. Wisely our government inaugurated an extensive program of rearmament.

Throughout 1940 and most of 1941 we were able to maintain a position of neutrality, even though by now the vast majority of Americans were openly opposed to the Axis countries. On December 7, 1941, Japanese airplanes attacked the American fleet stationed at Pearl Harbor in Hawaii. The nation was shocked by the event and by the scheming treachery of the Japanese. The attack on Pearl Harbor was made at a time when Japanese representatives were in conference with our officials in Washington to arrange a peaceful settlement of our disagreements with Japan. Immediately after the attack, Japan declared war on us. Her partners, Germany and Italy, followed a few days later.

Pennsylvania's Part in the War. The first unit of Pennsylvania's soldiers to be called into active service was the National Guard, 17,000 strong, mustered into service in February, 1940. On October 16, 1940, the first registration for Selective Service was made. Men between the ages of twenty-one and thirty-five were registered. The state was divided into local draft boards, and advisory committees were established in each county. Later registrations included men from eighteen to sixty-five. The state now had almost two and a half million men registered for service.

According to figures released by the War Department in February, 1943, Pennsylvania led the entire nation in marine enlistments, and was third in the number of volunteers in the other branches of the armed services. More than half a million Pennsylvania men and women were then in the armed forces.

Newly inducted selectees were frequently sent to the New Cumberland Reception Center in Cumberland County. Indiantown Gap, near Lebanon, the training camp of the Pennsylvania National Guard, was used as a training base for troops from all parts of the nation.

Pennsylvanians as Military Leaders. Next to the President of the United States, who is Commander in Chief of the armed forces, the most important military post is that of Chief of Staff of the United States Army. General George C. Marshall, the present Chief of Staff, is a native of Uniontown, Fayette County; General Joseph McNarney of Erie, is second to Marshall, as Deputy Chief of Staff. General Henry Arnold of Montgomery County is Commander in Chief of the Army Air Force. In command of the European Air Force is Major General Carl B. Spaatz of Boyertown, Berks County. Lieutenant General Jacob Loucks Devers of York, Pennsylvania, served as commander of American forces stationed in Great Britain. General Dwight D. Eisenhower's ancestors migrated to Kansas from their Pennsylvania home in Elizabethville, Dauphin County. Admiral Harold R. Stark, Chief of Naval Operations, is a native of Wilkes-Barre, Luzerne County. Major General Dawson Olmstead, Chief of the United States Army Signal Corps, calls Corry in Erie County his home.

Pennsylvania Heroes. The term hero could properly be applied to hundreds, perhaps thousands of Pennsylvanians who have distinguished themselves in the service of their country. In listing the heroes of the Keystone State we select a few "firsts," the names of those who won distinctions for valor and sacrifice early in the war. The first American sailor to lose his life was Iral William Stoltz, of Spangler, Cambria County, who died when the *U.S.S. Kearny* was struck by a torpedo near Iceland on October 17, 1941. The first American paratrooper killed was W. Edwin Sprenkle of Fawn Grove, York County; Miss Anna Bernatitus of Exeter, Luzerne County was the first navy nurse known to have escaped from Corregidor; Lieutenant

Colonel Boyd Wagner of Johnstown was one of the flying heroes of Bataan. Four Pennsylvanians were among those who helped General Douglas MacArthur to reach Australia in safety. Their names are Richard A. Regan of Upper Darby, Delaware County; John Shambora of Bethlehem; Paul Eichelberger of Shippensburg, Cumberland County; and Harry G. Keith of Lancaster.

The Home Front. All of the human resources of the state were mobilized for war. Some of the services were organized into units such as the Civilian Defense Organizations, the Victory Corps in the high schools, and many other associations. But there were many persons who served without belonging to any organization. They were the great host of blood donors, volunteer workers, nurses' aides, and many more who silently and bravely gave of their time and themselves. Servicemen's organizations were scattered throughout the state. The agencies of the United Service Organization (USO), which included the Y.M.C.A., Y.W.C.A., the National Catholic Community Service, the Jewish Welfare Board, the Salvation Army, and the Travelers' Aid Society, were devoted to the welfare of the servicemen. The people, realizing that this was everybody's war, responded nobly to the many calls for service on the home front.

QUESTIONS FOR STUDY AND REVIEW

1. Why did we insist on the "freedom of the seas" during the early years of World War I? Can you find other instances in American history when America took this stand?

2. Explain what President Wilson referred to when he spoke of the "principles that gave her birth."

3. Why was there a period of industrial unrest when the First World War ended?

4. What evils was national prohibition expected to correct? What new troubles developed? Is the issue a settled one today?

5. What were the underlying causes of the national depression from 1929 to 1939? How was Pennsylvania affected? What relief measures were taken? Were they successful?

6. How did we become involved in World War II?

Chapter XV

THE ARSENAL OF AMERICA

When the United States began to rearm in the spring of 1940, President Roosevelt declared that America would become the "Arsenal of Democracy." This sentiment was echoed by Governor Arthur H. James, who promised to make Pennsylvania the "Arsenal of America." It was a large order, but the industrial powers of the state were great and its natural resources were abundant. Years of training and experience made Pennsylvania's workmen skilled and ready to face the new and difficult tasks which the burden of war work imposed. Quickly Pennsylvania became one of the most important war production centers in America. By July of 1941, six months before we entered the war, more than twenty per cent of the total industrial output of the state was in the form of war materials. One year later, July, 1942, Pennsylvania manufacturers held war contracts totaling nearly five billion dollars. This does not include many other kinds of war services, such as transportation and telephone communications, which cannot be recorded in terms of contracts but which are vital to war production.

As a result of wise laws regulating the use of the state's natural resources, our mineral, field, and forest wealth has been conserved so that today our mines, oil wells, forests, and farms are yielding the materials so much needed in war production.

WAR PRODUCTION

Coal for the Furnaces. During the years of depression after 1929, coal production steadily declined. The increase in use of oil in industry and the closing of factories were chiefly responsible for the decrease in demand for coal. As a result there was severe unemployment in the coal-producing areas of the state. In the anthracite region the depression years saw the development of a practice known as "coal bootlegging." The term was applied to miners who tried to eke out a living for themselves and their families by digging coal on lands owned

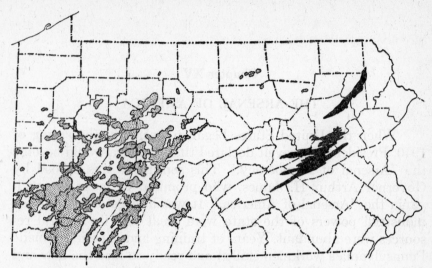

MAP OF COAL FIELDS IN PENNSYLVANIA
The solid black areas on this map show the location of anthracite in
Pennsylvania; the dotted areas represent bituminous coal deposits.

by large companies and selling it to consumers in nearby towns
and cities. Of course the mine owners objected to this practice
because the "bootleggers" were not only taking coal from their
property, but by offering "bootleg" coal for sale at a cheaper
rate they cut down the prices which the operators had been
asking for their coal.

All of this changed, however, when the World War II
began. The demand for coal, both hard and soft, became so
great that miners again found regular employment in the
mines. Working in the mines which were operated on a business
basis was much safer than digging in the dangerous pits and
in abandoned mines where coal "bootleggers" had to work.

The production of anthracite had fallen to fifty-four million
tons in 1936, but in 1942, sixty million tons were mined. In
contrast to the 108 million tons of soft coal mined in 1936 were
the 130 million tons mined in 1942.

Oil for the Wheels of Production. The yield of oil from
Pennsylvania wells diminished during the years of depression.
In 1930 the output was only 13 million barrels, but spurred by
the demand for oil for war machinery, in 1942 some 18 million
barrels of crude oil were produced. Almost all of this was converted into heavy lubricants, as Pennsylvania oil excels in this

280

use. Today McKean County is the largest producer
Venango County ranks second, and Warren County,
Even though the state no longer leads the country in the
duction of crude oil, Philadelphia remains the greatest
refining center. Transcontinental pipe lines pump oil to
eastern seaboard and huge tankers bring millions of barrels
crude oil to the refineries along the Delaware River.

Other Minerals for War Production. Pennsylvania
leads the nation both in the total quantity of minerals produced
and in the variety of ores mined. Glass sand quarries are
operated in the western counties, and the city of Pittsburgh is
the center of the plate glass industry. Zinc is mined in Lehigh
County. One of the largest makers of zinc products in the world
is a plant in Palmertown in Carbon County. Lehigh County
adds greatly to the wealth of the state by producing the ingredi-
ents for manufacturing cement. Thirteen per cent of the clay
products made in the United States are made from Pennsylvania clay. More than one half of the slate quarried in the
country is produced in this state. Lehigh and Northampton
counties are the chief contributors to this industry.

Manufacturing for War. The great manufacturing centers of the state are engaged in production for the nation's war
effort. For heavy castings and for delicate precision instruments,

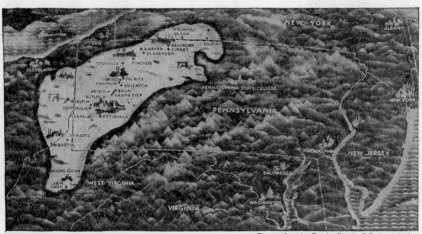

—Pennsylvania Grade Crude Oil Association

PENNSYLVANIA OIL DEPOSITS
The irregular white area enclosed with black shows the Pennsylvania oil
deposits. What states are part of this oil field?

for textiles, leather goods, cement, candy, to name only a few articles, Pennsylvania is the producing center. In this state is made the best armor plate for battleships, the largest engines, locomotives, and ships for the navy and merchant marine.

The steel industries of the state lead all other types of production. In 1942 the Pittsburgh mills alone produced twenty million tons of steel for war needs. Other steel cities lie along the western borders of the state, and moving eastward we find steel manufactured in Johnstown, Lewistown, Harrisburg, Steelton, Coatesville, and Bethlehem.

Highways. The increase of motor transportation has led to an ever increasing demand for improved highways. In 1937 there were nearly 100,000 miles of public highways in Pennsylvania. This includes township roads, city streets, and state-owned highways. Of the latter, more than 30,000 miles have been surfaced.

On October 1, 1940, the great Pennsylvania Turnpike, sometimes called the Superhighway, was added to the already

—*Luke Swank and the Philadelphia Museum of Art*
A MODERN BLAST FURNACE IN PITTSBURGH

A PENNSYLVANIA INDUSTRIAL PLANT FLYING THE ARMY-NAVY "E"
What is meant by the Army-Navy "E"? What message do you think the
letter contains?

excellent transportation system of the state. A 160-mile stretch
of concrete extending from near Carlisle westward to Irwin
near Pittsburgh, the Pennsylvania Turnpike passes through
seven mountain tunnels and skirts the edges of cities along the
route. Federal funds were supplied to aid in building the Superhighway. Tolls will be collected until the road has been paid for.
It is now a vital link in the transportation system of the state
and nation, carrying the war materials quickly and efficiently
from mines to factories and from factories to munitions plants.
The Pennsylvania Highway system has become an important
channel for the nation's inland commerce.

    True to Our Past Record. In every major war in which
America has been engaged, Pennsylvania has been one of the
chief sources of supply for our armed forces. We remember that
General Braddock and General Forbes relied upon the Province
of Pennsylvania for horses and wagons during the French and
Indian War; that Pennsylvania ironworkers and rifle makers
helped the colonies to win the Revolutionary War; that Pennsylvania farms fed the armies of the North, and Pennsylvania
soldiers fought with their comrades of other states to win the

day at Gettysburg during the War for the Union. So, too, in World War I and in World War II reliance was placed once again upon our industries and skills.

OUR FOREST RESOURCES

The Forest Commission. Sensing that our vast forest resources were in danger of depletion, the state took steps to check the danger by appointing a Forest Commission, which began its work in 1895. The state began to purchase forest areas from private owners, creating reserves in which only scientific timber cutting is permitted; fire stations were established at various peaks in the mountains to check forest fires; new forest areas were planted on denuded hillsides; and abandoned farms were planted with young seedlings which will some day pay rich dividends in the form of marketable timber.

As a result of these steps the forest area of the Commonwealth increased by one million acres between 1900 and 1921. The largest state forests are located in Potter and Clinton counties, but there are state-owned forest areas in thirty-seven other counties. Every county in the state contains forests—the largest in Clearfield and Lycoming and the smallest (877 acres) in Philadelphia.

Wild Life in the Forests. It may come as a surprise to learn that Pennsylvania has more game animals and birds than it had during the days of the Indians. Half a century ago, however, it would not have been possible to make such a statement. Heedless of future needs, hunters had killed off most of the wild birds and animals. In 1895 public-spirited citizens successfully urged the creation of a Game Commission to provide refuges and bird sanctuaries and to restock the woods with wild birds and animals. The real sportsmen welcomed this far-sighted move and co-operated by observing the fish and game laws. As a result of this splendid teamwork, we now have an abundance of wild life.

The wild life of Pennsylvania supplies approximately fifteen thousand tons of meat for the tables of its citizens, or three pounds per person a year. This is a valuable addition to our food supply. The pelts of fur-bearing animals contribute additional wealth. Conservation of Pennsylvania's wild life is big business.

Unfortunately, the efforts to protect the fish in our inland waters have not proved as successful as the efforts to increase the game supply. Repeatedly fish life is destroyed by the pollution of streams as a result of pouring chemical wastes into creeks and rivers and of the unwise disposal of sewage in our streams. Fines have been imposed upon offenders, but this has not stopped such practices. The state has established hatcheries in Erie, Bedford, Wayne, Philadelphia, Forest, and Cumberland counties where fish are hatched from eggs for restocking the streams of the state. Sportsmen have co-operated in the attempt to protect fish life by observing open and closed seasons, limiting their catch, and using only permitted kinds of tackle. But so long as mass execution of fish occurs in poisoned waters no great strides can be made.

AGRICULTURE

Farm Lands. The number of individual farms increased steadily until 1900 when there were more than 224,000 farms in the state. Since then there has been a steady decline, to 169,000 farms in 1940. Some of the decrease can be accounted for by the consolidation of small farms into larger units, but the total acreage devoted to farming has also decreased. In 1920 sixty per cent of Pennsylvania was farmland. Today, barely fifty per cent is cultivated. Most of the decrease is reflected in the growth of the forest area of the state. The Census of 1940 showed that the average size of a Pennsylvania farm is eighty-six acres and the average value is $5113. Lancaster County, often called the Garden Spot, leads the state with 8,446 farms valued at over seventy-two million dollars.

There was also a decrease in the value of farm crops during the decade from 1930 to 1940. This fact must be considered in the light of two important developments which took place during the depression. The first of these was the sharp decrease in prices for farm produce. The second was the program of the federal government to reduce the national surplus by limiting the number of acres farmers were permitted to plant. Under this program farmers were asked to take some of their fields out of production. In return they received cash refunds for money spent in converting these fields into pasture and protecting them from erosion.

285

SPECIALIZED FARMING IN PENNSYLVANIA
One of the largest dairy farms in eastern Pennsylvania.

Farm Crops. Corn is the chief field crop in Pennsylvania. More than fifty million bushels are produced annually. In terms of money value, tobacco ranks second, oats third, and potatoes fourth. In average years Pennsylvania leads all states in the production of buckwheat and ranks third in the production of potatoes and peaches, fifth in grapes, sixth in hay, seventh in wheat, ninth in rye, and tenth in apples. In recent years the great canning companies in the state and in neighboring states have contracted with Pennsylvania farmers to purchase tons of tomatoes, beans, and other vegetables suitable for canning. Many farms are changing from diversified farming—that is, the growing of many things—to specialized farming, concentrating upon the production of a few major crops.

Specialized Farming. Specialized farming tends to increase the efficiency of farm labor and machinery; therefore, usually a greater farm income per acre is possible. There are many kinds of specialized farming: in fruit, field crops, vegetables, livestock, dairy products, wool, eggs, and lesser-known products such as herbs, nuts, and honey. For the four-year period from 1939 to 1942, Pennsylvania was first among all of the states in the money value of eggs produced. The livestock wealth of the farms has remained fairly constant during recent years. There are fewer horses and mules, but more dairy cattle. The dairy cattle are of superior quality than those formerly raised on our farms. Better breeding methods, careful inspection, and tuberculosis testing have improved the stock, and

286

scientific feeding has increased the milk production of most of the herds.

Although the period we have been studying covered two wars and ten years of economic depression, these misfortunes did not hinder cultural and social progress within the nation. Let us see how Pennsylvania was able to enrich the lives of its people during these years.

Education. The schools of the state made many strides forward in the twenty-year period between the two world wars. Teaching standards were raised and broader opportunities were offered to the young people of the Commonwealth. In the larger cities there are specialized high schools—vocational, academic, technical, manual, and commercial. In smaller communities having but one school a great variety of courses are offered in the same building. Many towns have organized junior high schools which combine the seventh and eighth grades and the first year of high school. The senior high school course in such

—*Luke Swank and the Philadelphia Museum of Art*
A FARM IN LANCASTER COUNTY
Here we see evidences of diversified farming, plus intelligent use of the land.

287

cases runs for three years. Today there are more than thirteen hundred high schools in the state, with approximately one-half million students enrolled in them.

The Consolidated School. One of the greatest changes in the organization of the public school system is the disappearance of the one-room district school, which is rapidly being replaced by large consolidated schools. These schools draw upon large areas of population for their student bodies. Improvements in transportation—school buses and better roads—have made this development possible. There were many excellent features about the "little red school house" remembered by the parents and grandparents of students now in school, but the greater efficiency and economy offered by the consolidated school justifies the change.

Higher Schools. Today there are sixty-six accredited colleges and universities in the Commonwealth. In addition, there are many professional schools of excellent standing. There are eighteen theological seminaries, five law schools, seven medical colleges, three dental colleges, four colleges of pharmacy, and other schools for technical training. Many of these are attached to the universities of the state.

Special Schools. The Commonwealth owns and operates schools for deaf children in Philadelphia and in Scranton; a school known as the Pennsylvania Soldiers' Orphan School is located in Scotland, Franklin County, and the state-operated Thaddeus Stevens Industrial School is in Lancaster. State aid is granted to other schools, such as the National Farm School in Bucks County, the Philadelphia Nautical School, the Pennsylvania Institution for the Deaf at Mt. Airy, Philadelphia, and the Downingtown Industrial and Agricultural School in Chester County.

We have mentioned by name only those special schools which are either state-owned or partially supported by the state. There are many other special schools conducted independently. One of the most famous of these is the International Correspondence School of Scranton, the largest institution of its kind in the world. Equally famous is Girard College in Philadelphia established by Stephen Girard in his will.

Care of Unfortunates. Pennsylvania has been a leader among the various states in caring for its mentally unfit persons.

AIRPLANE VIEW OF THE WEST CHESTER TEACHERS COLLEGE

Hospitals for the insane are established in many sections of the state. The first of these was opened in Harrisburg in 1851. Since then the Commonwealth has built and operated hospitals at Allentown, Danville, Farview, Norristown, Torrence, Warren, and Wernersville. The state gives aid to other hospitals which care for unfortunates, such as epileptics and feeble-minded persons. Medical and surgical hospitals owned and maintained by the state are located at Ashland, Blossburg, Coaldale, Connellsville, Hazelton, Locust Mountain, Mercer, Nanticoke, Philipsburg, Scranton, and Shamokin. A state soldiers' and sailors' home is located in Erie, and the federal government maintains hospitals for war veterans at Aspenwall, Coatesville, and Valley Forge. The state also gives some financial support to institutions which care for the blind, the aged, the crippled, and others who suffer physical or mental defects.

Religion. From the beginning of her history, Pennsylvania has had people of widely different national origins. These racial groups usually brought with them the forms of worship which they had cherished in their homelands. The faiths established by the pious settlers of colonial times grew and flourished. Throughout the nineteenth and twentieth centuries, the Commonwealth continued to be a melting pot in the New World. Emigrant groups coming to the state brought with them the religious faith they had known in the Old World and set up their churches here.

The Religious Census of 1936 showed that Pennsylvania was leading other states in the number of church establishments. In that year there were 13,461 churches in the state with memberships of approximately five and one-half million.

The Pennsylvania State Sabbath School Association estimated in 1941 that one-eighth of the Sunday schools of the nations are in Pennsylvania. In that year there were almost 11,000 Sabbath schools with a membership of over two million. The religious development in the state brought with it the establishment of many religious societies. Foreign missions were sent to many parts of the world; young people's societies such as the Luther League, Epworth League, and Christian Endeavor attracted large numbers; the Y.M.C.A., Y.W.C.A., and Y.M.H.A. were organized in many cities; Scout troops and Campfire clubs were organized throughout the state; summer camps sponsored by religious groups are found in many parts of Pennsylvania.

DISTINCTLY PENNSYLVANIA

The lines are fallen unto me in pleasant places; yea, I have a goodly heritage. *Psalm 16:6.*

Pennsylvania has been discovered three times: first, when the white men came; second, when the wealth of mineral resources was tapped; and third, when her own rich culture was recognized and added to that of the nation and the world.

Horizons Grow Wider. The introduction of motion pictures, early in the present century, served to bring a much greater variety of outside entertainment. The development of the automobile and the building of roads provided greater opportunity for travel. The radio widened the scope of human experience even more. One effect of the opening of these vistas of culture has been to make Pennsylvanians more conscious of the value of the things they have at home—the beauty of their wooded hills, the fertility of the soil in the valleys, the historic shrines, the varied European cultures living peacefully and happily side by side in the land of William Penn. Comparison with the other sections of the world brought to them by the screen, the auto tour, or the radio, has given citizens of the Commonwealth an appreciation of the fine things of their own and a desire that they be preserved and refined.

Public Interest Develops. Beginning in 1890, many counties organized societies for the study of local history. At first these organizations were supported by a few persons whose love for the study of history brought them together. But as more and more persons became interested in the development of their communities, these societies expanded. Today nearly every county can boast of a historical society, usually located in the countyseat. Many of the societies publish magazines in which events from the past are recaptured by the study of members. Forward-looking men and women have collected books and relics which are housed in libraries and museums for all to study. In most sections of the state, monuments and tablets have been erected to mark the location of historic spots. The Department of Public Instruction of the Commonwealth has published pamphlets on the history of the state. Junior historical associations have been formed in many high schools. The state Department of Commerce and Industry has supplied information on the economic history of the state to newspapers throughout the Commonwealth. The state Historical Commission has helped in co-ordinating the work of local historical societies.

Novelists Find Settings in Pennsylvania. The awakened interest in the history of the state has encouraged the development of a distinct literature. Novelists have gained inspiration for stories in the varied cultures to be found in Pennsylvania. Neil Swanson writes charming stories about the western region. His books, *The First Rebel* and *The Judas Tree,* have won him a high place in contemporary literature. Conrad Richter in *The Free Man* describes the part played by the Pennsylvania Germans in the Revolutionary War. Colonel Henry W. Shoemaker of McElhattan has collected the songs and folklore of the mountaineers of central Pennsylvania. Elsie Singmaster has won world-wide renown for her books and stories in Pennsylvania settings. Hervey Allen revives the life on the Pennsylvania frontier in his novel, *The Forest and the Fort.* Joseph Hergesheimer of West Chester is famous for his stories into which he has woven incidents from the history of the state. Cornelius Weygandt paints colorful word pictures in his *Red Hills* and *The Dutch Country.* The motion pictures have found background for great productions, such as "Black Fury," a story of the coal regions. There are many other writers who have found themes within the boundaries of the Commonwealth.

Sculptors and Artists Portray Scenes of the State. The quaint mode of dress of the Plain People has captured the fancy of artists. William A. Swallow of Allentown, a sculptor, has gained recognition for his models of the sturdy men and women who maintain their ancient culture in the midst of modern surroundings. In recent years Marguerite deAngeli, Katherine Milhous, Ella Mae Seyfert, and Clinton DeWitt have written and illustrated children's books, drawing upon the same theme for colorful portrayal of scenes distinctly Pennsylvanian. Among contemporary painters there is Walter Emerson Baum of Sellersville who specializes in painting farm and village scenes observed in the eastern part of the state. This trend is characteristic of the work of most of the painters of Pennsylvania today. They, too, like the writers, are helping to crystallize our Pennsylvania heritage.

Americans All. The state Folk Festival and the various county festivals have served to draw attention to the many European and African cultures which have been transplanted to America. These festivals portray the dances, songs, and customs of many groups, ranging from the war dances of Chief Fireway, a Pennsylvania Indian, to the songs and customs of the most recent immigrant groups that have found shelter and happiness in the Commonwealth. Greeks, Hungarians, Croatians, Hebrews, Negroes, Irish, Italians, Spaniards, and many others—Americans all—bring the Old World to life again as they frolic together, each adding to the treasure house of American culture.

Sports. There are many Pennsylvanians who find escape from their daily routine by hunting for deer along the Juniata, for bear in Bradford County, or cast lines hopefully into fresh water streams for trout or into Lake Wallenpaupack in the hope that a pickerel will flash in the sunlight as the rod and reel bring it protestingly to its captor. The pleasures of scenic beauty, mountain climbing, camping, and out-of-door sports of all types are available to the citizens of the state.

Handicrafts. The state Department of Commerce has encouraged the development of crafts and skills, both old and new, and has urged that the skills brought to the state by the

RECREATIONAL OPPORTUNITIES IN PENN'S WOODS
A glimpse of one of the many vacation spots in the state.

colonial settlers be preserved. Pottery-making has been revived in several parts of the state, notably at the kiln of Mrs. C. Naaman Keyser, who specializes in reproducing Pennsylvania German pottery; the art of spinning on the spinning-wheel, almost forgotten for two generations, has been revived; needlework, patchwork quilts, embroidered linens, hand weaving, and similar handicrafts which had almost disappeared as a result of the factory system have been revived as recreational activities and as worthwhile hobbies. Two museums featuring Pennsylvania arts and crafts are the Landis Valley Museum in Lancaster County and the Bucks County Historical Museum in Doylestown. There are other societies and museums in many parts of the state that have sensed the value of preserving the mementos of earlier days.

The Past Is Made To Live Again. The interest in Pennsylvania history has led to the restoration of many historic sites. During the administration of Governor Pinchot a portion of the old Delaware Canal near New Hope in Bucks County was restored in order that future generations can see how the canals were operated. The buildings of the Ephrata Cloisters,

293

the Mill Hotel near Pottstown, and Pennsbury Manor in Bucks County are also being restored.

As Yet Unrevealed. What of the future? That cannot be recorded here. Much depends upon the zeal and wisdom with which the young people now in our schools will tackle the problems which will arise. Oncoming generations can profit by guarding against the mistakes of the past and applying the lessons they have learned. In meeting new problems we can confidently expect the future leaders in Pennsylvania to serve the state as nobly as did the men and women of the past.

QUESTIONS FOR STUDY AND REVIEW

1. What problem for the future may develop as a result of the drain upon our mineral wealth? What can be done to offset the depletion of the state's natural resources? What can you do?

2. What is meant by conservation of forests? of wild life? of soil?

3. Show how the factories and mills in your community depend upon nearby natural resources. Is a river a natural resource? the fish in the river? a harbor? a silo? a stone quarry? wild game? fertile soil?

4. Account for the development of interest in state and local history.

5. Have you read any novels or stories about your own community? Can you think of some historical fact or some exciting incident which might be used for the basis for such a story?

6. Suggest improvements which you would like to see developed during your lifetime. How would you prepare yourself to become a leader to bring them to pass?

PROBLEMS AND ACTIVITIES

1. Show how the following incidents helped to involve us in World War I: the sinking of the *Lusitania;* the Zimmerman note; the U-boat.

2. Perhaps your local American Legion post will co-operate with you in planning a program, featuring events, popular songs, and souvenirs of World War I.

3. The following generals of World War I had Pennsylvania backgrounds: General John J. Pershing, General Hunter Liggett, General Peyton C. March. Perhaps you will be able to prepare short biographies of these leaders showing their Pennsylvania heritage.

4. An interesting project may be developed by reporting what your parents and grandparents can remember about Armistice Day, November 11, 1918.

5. Compare the methods used to fill the army quotas in World War I with methods used in World War II; the kinds of war bonds and stamps; home front services.

6. Prepare a program for a folk festival in your county. What national groups should be represented?

7. Read the eighteenth amendment of the federal constitution. What was the Volstead Act?

8. Interview businessmen to learn how the depression of 1929–1939 affected your community. Did the factories and mills shut down? Did banks fail? Was there widespread unemployment? What relief measures were taken?

9. Can you identify any public buildings, roads, bridges, parks or other public improvements which were built as a result of work programs to relieve unemployment?

10. What war industries are located near your home? Why were they situated there, rather than elsewhere?

11. Prepare an essay on the topic, "My Town (or County) as the Home Front."

12. Prepare a brief summary of the work which your school has done in such units as the Victory Corps, Junior Red Cross, Junior Historians, bond sales, salvage drives, or any others. Is there something more that you could do?

13. The following are Pennsylvanians of national fame. See how many of them you can identify: Charles Brockden Brown; Ida M. Tarbell; Stephen Collins Foster; Ethelbert Nevin; Marian Anderson; Robert Peary; Kate Douglas Wiggin; Owen Wister; Thomas Buchanan Read; Bayard Taylor.

14. Can you find any skilled handicrafts which are still carried on in your community? Try to learn about one of these handicrafts.

15. Write a short story using a historical event in your community as the setting or background.

16. If a relative from a different state came to visit you, what sights would you show him in your community? How would you explain their importance?

World War I

Sidney B. Fay, *Origins of the World War*, New York: Macmillan; *Pennsylvania's Participation in the World War*, Harrisburg: Pennsylvania War History Commission.

Pennsylvania Politics in the Twentieth Century

R. D. Bowden, *Boies Penrose, Symbol of an Era*, New York: Greenburg; Water Davenport, *Power and Glory: The Life of Boies Penrose*, New York: Putnam's; Frederic A. Godcharles, *Pennsylvania:*

Political, Governmental, Military, and Civil, 5 vol., New York: American Historical Society; P. H. Love, *Andrew Mellon*, Baltimore, Md.: Heath, Coggins Co., William S. Vare, *My Forty Years in Politics*, Philadelphia: Ronald Swain.

Brief biographical sketches of public officials can be found in the biennial editions of the *Pennsylvania Manual*, Harrisburg: Department of Property and Supplies. For statistics on population, industrial production, and agricultural wealth see the annual edition of the *Bulletin Almanac*, Philadelphia: Philadelphia Evening Bulletin. For an excellent review of Pennsylvania in the first year of World War II, see: *Pennsylvania's First Year at War*, Harrisburg: Pennsylvania Historical Commission.

Agriculture

Henry F. James, *Agricultural Industry of Southeastern Pennsylvania*, Philadelphia: Geographical Society of Philadelphia; Walter F. Kollmorgen, *A Study of a Contemporary Farm Community* (U. S. Department of Agriculture Bulletin, Rural Life Series, No. 4) Washington, D. C.: Government Printing Office. Bulletins of the Pennsylvania Department of Agriculture and of Pennsylvania State College will also be found useful.

Distinctly Pennsylvania

W. K. Dorman and L. S. Davidow, *Pennsylvania Dutch Cook Book*, Reading: Culinary Arts Press; Edwin M. Fogel, *Proverbs of the Pennsylvania Germans*, Philadelphia: University of Pennsylvania Press; Mildred W. Keyser, *Home Craft Courses*, Plymouth Meeting: the Author; Earl F. Robacker, *Pennsylvania German Literature*, Philadelphia: University of Pennsylvania Press; Henry W. Shoemaker, *Addresses and Papers Pertaining to Pennsylvania History and Customs of the People*, Altoona: Times Tribune Press; Henry W. Shoemaker, *Some Stories of Old Deserted Houses in Central Pennsylvania Mountains*, Altoona: Times Tribune Press; Cornelius Weygandt, *Dutch Country*, New York: Appleton-Century; Cornelius Weygandt, *Red Hills*, Harrisburg: Pennsylvania Book Service, Cornelius Weygandt, *The Plenty of Pennsylvania*, New York: H. C. Kinsey.

Fiction

Philip Barry, *The Philadelphia Story*, New York: Coward-McCann; M. Struthers Burt, *Along These Streets*, New York: Scribner's; Arista E. Fisher, *Requiem*, New York: John Day; Helen Martin, *Porcelain and Clay*, New York: Dodd Mead; Elinor Cowan Stone, *Fear Rides the Fog*, New York: Appleton-Century; Mary D. Thayer, *Foam*, Philadelphia: Dorrance.

APPENDIX

GOVERNORS OF PENNSYLVANIA, 1790 TO 1944

Thomas Mifflin, 1790 to 1799: Thomas Mifflin of Philadelphia was the last president of Pennsylvania under the first state constitution. He was also the first governor under the second state constitution. He served three full terms in succession.

Thomas McKean, 1799 to 1808: Thomas McKean was one of the signers of the Declaration of Independence and a member of the Delaware delegation to the Second Continental Congress. At the time of his election he was Chief Justice of Pennsylvania. He was twice re-elected, serving three consecutive terms of three years each.

Simon Snyder, 1808 to 1817: Simon Snyder was the first person of German descent to hold the executive office in Pennsylvania. He had been a delegate to the convention which formulated the state constitution of 1790. He had been a representative and the Speaker of the state House of Representatives. He, too, was elected for three successive terms.

William Findley, 1817 to 1820: William Findley of Mercersburg in Franklin County had been active in the affairs of the state for many years. At the time of his election to the Governor's chair, he was the state Treasurer.

Joseph Hiester, 1820 to 1823: Joseph Hiester had gained distinction during the Revolutionary War as a recruiting officer. Later, he had served in the Pennsylvania convention for the ratification of the federal constitution. He had served in the United States House of Representatives as a representative of Berks County for fourteen years.

John Andrew Schulze, 1823 to 1829: As a young man, John Andrew Schulze had served in the Lutheran clergy until a protracted illness had prevented him from continuing his duties. After recovering from his illness, he had entered into business. He also had served several terms in the state House of Representatives and in the state Senate.

George Wolf, 1829 to 1835: Before George Wolf's election as Governor he had held a number of offices in Northampton County and had served in the United States House of Representatives from 1824 to 1829. He was governor for two successive terms.

Joseph Ritner, 1835 to 1839: Joseph Ritner had served several terms in the state House of Representatives (1820 to 1826) and had been the Speaker of that body from 1824 to 1826.

David Rittenhouse Porter, 1839 to 1845: Prior to his election as Governor, Porter had been trained as a lawyer, had been a businessman, and had represented his district, Huntingdon County, in the state Legislature. At the time of his election as Governor he was a member of the state Senate.

Francis Rawn Shunk, 1845 to 1848: Before serving as Governor, Francis Rawn Shunk had been a school teacher, a private in the War of 1812, and a clerk in the state House of Representatives. In 1838 he had become Secretary of the State under Governor Porter. Shunk was re-elected for a second term, but in July, 1848, he resigned his position because of illness.

William Freame Johnston, 1848 to 1852: William Freame Johnston became Acting-governor for three years upon the resignation of Governor Shunk. He had been a Senator in the state Senate at the time of his election.

William Bigler, 1852 to 1855: William Bigler had served as the Speaker of the state Senate from 1843 to 1845 and then had continued to serve in the state Legislature until 1849. At the time of his election as Governor, he was one of the Revenue Commissioners of Pennsylvania.

James Pollock, 1855 to 1858: James Pollock had served in the United States House of Representatives from 1844 to 1850. In 1850 he was appointed a President Judge. He was engaged in the private practice of the law at the time of his election as Governor.

William Fisher Packer, 1858 to 1861: Packer had served as Auditor-general of the Commonwealth under Governor Porter. He had also served many terms in the state Assembly, both as a member of the House of Representatives and as Senator.

Andrew Gregg Curtin, 1861 to 1867: A former lawyer, Andrew Gregg Curtin had been appointed as Secretary of the Commonwealth in 1854. In 1863 he was a candidate for a second term and was re-elected. He was not eligible to succeed himself in 1867 because he had already served two consecutive terms. In 1869 he was appointed Minister to Russia.

John White Geary, 1867 to 1873: John White Geary had been Assistant Superintendent and Engineer of the Allegheny Portage railroad, had served in the Mexican War, and had been active in the campaign to bring California into the Union as a free state. He had served as Governor of the Kansas Territory. In the War for the Union, he had been promoted to the rank of Brigadier-General, then to Governor of the military district of Savannah, Georgia, and finally to Major-general of the Volunteers. He served two terms as Governor.

John F. Hartranft, 1873 to 1879: John F. Hartranft had distinguished himself as an officer during the War for the Union. After the war he had served as Auditor-general of the Commonwealth for two terms. He was re-elected as Governor in 1875.

Henry M. Hoyt, 1879 to 1883: Henry M. Hoyt had served as Colonel of the Fifty-second Pennsylvania Regiment. After the war he had served as a judge in Luzerne County and as chairman of the Republican State Committee.

Robert E. Pattison (First Administration), 1883 to 1887: Robert E. Pattison had been a lawyer from Philadelphia before his election as Governor. His two administrations were marked by strict economy in government spending.

James A. Beaver, 1887 to 1891: James A. Beaver had served throughout the War for the Union, attaining the rank of Brigadier-general. At the time of his election as Governor he was engaged in a law practice in Belleville.

Robert E. Pattison (Second Administration), 1891 to 1895: After an interval of four years, Pattison was eligible for re-election. His campaign was successful.

Daniel H. Hastings, 1895 to 1899: Daniel H. Hastings had been active in the Pennsylvania State Militia, rising to the rank of Adjutant-general in 1887. He had taken a prominent part in the relief work following the Johnstown flood.

William A. Stone, 1899 to 1903: William A. Stone had served in the Federal Army during the War for the Union. He had also served as United States District Attorney for the Western Judicial District, and had been a member of the United States House of Representatives for eight years prior to his election as Governor.

Samuel W. Pennypacker, 1903 to 1907: After a number of years spent in legal practice in Philadelphia, Samuel W. Pennypacker had been appointed as judge of the Court of Common Pleas in that city, and had served as President Judge from 1896 until his election as Governor.

Edwin S. Stuart, 1907 to 1911: Edwin S. Stuart had served as president of the Young Republicans until 1891, when he was elected mayor of Philadelphia.

John K. Tener, 1911 to 1915: John K. Tener was born in Ireland, his family coming here in 1871. From 1885 to 1890 he had played professional baseball as a member of the Chicago team of the National League. He had been elected to the House of Representatives of the United States Congress in 1908.

Martin G. Brumbaugh, 1915 to 1919: Martin G. Brumbaugh had served as County Superintendent of the Schools of Huntingdon County, as President of Juniata College, and as first Commissioner of Education in Puerto Rico. At the time of his election as Governor, he was Superintendent of Schools of Philadelphia.

William C. Sproul, 1919 to 1923: A former newspaper publisher and businessman, William C. Sproul had served as state Senator for six terms.

Gifford Pinchot (First Administration), 1923 to 1927: Gifford Pinchot was America's first professional forester, holding the office of Chief of the United States Forestry Department from 1898 to 1910. Later he had founded the School of Forestry at Yale University. As Governor he was known as a reformer.

John S. Fisher, 1927 to 1931: John S. Fisher had been a lawyer and had been active in many civic groups during his lifetime. The most important office he held prior to his election as Governor was to serve as chairman of the committee appointed to investigate frauds in connection with the building and furnishing of the state capitol.

Gifford Pinchot (Second Administration), 1931 to 1935: Gifford Pinchot's second administration occurred during a severe economic depression, and was fraught with many difficulties.

George Howard Earle, 1935 to 1939: Prior to his election as Governor, George Howard Earle had served with the armed forces during the First World War and had also served as United States Minister to Austria.

Arthur H. James, 1939 to 1943: Arthur H. James had been District Attorney of Luzerne County from 1919 to 1926, when he resigned to become Lieutenant Governor of Pennsylvania, holding office from 1927 to 1931. In 1932 he was elected Judge of the Superior Court of Pennsylvania, which position he resigned when he became Governor.

Edward C. Martin, 1943 to ——: Edward C. Martin had served in three wars, the Spanish-American, World War I, and World War II. He was Commanding General of the Twenty-eighth Division of the Pennsylvania National Guard when it was inducted into federal service in 1941. The public offices held by Martin during the peace years, 1919 to 1941, were Auditor-general of Pennsylvania and state Treasurer.

300

VISUAL AIDS

For the convenience of teachers we list the titles of lantern slide sets which portray various phases of Pennsylvania history. The State Museum, through its Visual Education Section, maintains a circulating library of 100,000 educational slides, covering all school subjects. The slides are sent free, upon request, to any part of the state—to schools, churches, clubs, adult education, or other groups. The borrower pays transportation. Address: Lantern Slide Department, Pennsylvania State Museum, Harrisburg, Pennsylvania.

PENNSYLVANIA ARTISTS

	Number of Slides
Edwin Austin Abbey's State Capitol Murals	12
Violet Oakley's State Capitol Murals	18
John W. Alexander Carnegie Institute Murals	6
Group of Pennsylvania Artists and Their Work	54
Benjamin West	14

BIOGRAPHY AND HISTORY

Benjamin Franklin	66
Founding of Pennsylvania	30
Pennsylvania	92
Harrisburg	69
Philadelphia—Points of Historic Interest	30
William Penn and His Neighbors	21

OTHERS

The Arts and Crafts of the Pennsylvania Germans

The Pennsylvania Dutch Folk

Early Swedish Settlements of Pennsylvania

SPECIAL DAY SLIDES

	Number of Slides
Flag Day	54
Franklin's Birthday	66
Independence Day	29
Penn Day	44

FAMOUS PENNSYLVANIANS

Brown, Charles Brockden Cenotaph, Laurel Hill Cemetery, Philadelphia	2
Franklin, Benjamin	6
Harbaugh, Henry Birthplace, near Waynesboro	1
Grave, Mercersburg	1
Mifflin, Lloyd Portrait	1
Home, "Norwood," Columbia	1
Read, Thomas Buchanan Birthplace, "Korner Ketch,"	1
Taylor, Bayard	7
Van Dyke, Henry *The Other Wise Man*	38
Wiggin, Kate Douglas *The Birds' Christmas Carol*	21

GEOGRAPHY OF PENNSYLVANIA

	Number of Slides		Number of Slides
Pennsylvania, General	64	Juniata	9
Pennsylvania, Scenic	59	Lackawanna	11
Gettysburg National Park	40	Lancaster	36
State Capital	46	Lehigh	9
Pennsylvania by counties:		Luzerne	6
Adams	54	Lycoming	6
Allegheny	31	Mercer	3
Bedford	12	Mifflin	1
Berks	7	Monroe	16
Blair	9	Montgomery	23
Bradford	1	Montour	3
Bucks	7	Northampton	11
Cambria	6	Northumberland	6
Cameron	4	Perry	7
Carbon	6	Philadelphia	57
Centre	6	Delaware River Bridge	50
Chester	8	Pike	8
Clinton	2	Potter	10
Columbia	1	Schuylkill	2
Cumberland	31	Snyder	1
Dauphin	43	Somerset	1
Delaware	10	Sullivan	17
Erie	10	Venango	2
Franklin	21	Warren	5
Huntingdon	19	Westmoreland	2
Indiana	3	York	1

PENNSYLVANIA MUSIC AND MUSICIANS

	Number of Slides		Number of Slides
"Battle Hymn of the Republic"	15	Life of Stephen Collins Foster	
"Columbia, the Gem of the Ocean"	18	Early Life to Eighteen Years	25
"Hail Columbia, Happy Land!" (Hopkinson-Roth)	1	Eighteen to Thirty Years	29
"Silver Threads among the Gold" (Danks)	1	Thirty Years to His Death	33
"Whispering Hope" (Hawthorne)	2	Life of Ethelbert Nevin	5
		"Mighty Lak' a Rose"	1

Many other forms of visual aids are distributed by art museums and the visual education departments of school systems.

INDEX

303

305

Oil, 238, 280–281
Oruktor Amphibolis, 177
Overseers of the Poor, 158

Paine, Thomas, author of *Common Sense*, 110
Painting, 252
Palatine Germans, 32–33
  oaths of allegiance, 33
Paoli Massacre, 117
Paper money
  printed by Commonwealth, 128
  printed by Provincial Assembly, 52
Pardons, Board of, 222
Parker, William, 197
Parrish, Maxfield, 252
Pastorius, Francis Daniel, 31
"Paxton Boys," 63
Peale, Rembrandt, 252
Peary, Robert E., 255
Penn Charter School, William, **76**
Penn, Fort, 59
Pennell, Joseph, 252
Penn Estates, 128–129
Penn, John, governor, 64
Pennsylvania Academy of Fine Arts, 252
Pennsylvania Antislavery Society, 194
Pennsylvania Canal, 175–176
Pennsylvania "Dutch," 36
Pennsylvania Gazette, 77
Pennsylvania Germans
  buildings and furniture, 83, **84**
  fractur art of, 85–86
  peoples, 33–35
  schools of, 94
Pennsylvania Historical Commission, 234
Pennsylvania Hospital, 72
Pennsylvania, how named, 18
Pennsylvania Institution for the Deaf, 288
Pennsylvania Line, 113
Pennsylvania Navy, 113
Pennsylvania Railroad Company, 176, **178, 241**
Pennsylvania's claim
  on Maryland, 46
  on New York, 48
Pennsylvania Society (Pennsylvania Society for Promoting the Abolition of Slavery and Relief of the Negroes Unlawfully Held in Bondage), 193

Pennsylvania Soldiers' Orphan School, 288
Pennsylvania State Police, 232
Pennsylvania Turnpike, 282–283
Pennsylvania University, 76
Penn, William
  advertisements for settlers, 30
  conversion to Quakerism, 17
  dealings with Indians, 24–25
  Delaware, proprietor of, 19
  disagreement with Lord Baltimore over boundary, 45–46
  early years of, 16–17
  establishes religious freedom, 20–21
  founds Pennsylvania, 21
  Holy Experiment, objectives of, 20–21
  Indian policy, 24–25
  interests in west New Jersey, 18
  later years of, 28–29
  loss of money in Pennsylvania, 28–29
  loss of proprietorship, 27
  proprietor of Pennsylvania, 20
  receives charter for Pennsylvania, 18
  restoration of proprietorship, 27
  return to England, 26–27
  sale of lands, 26
  second visit to England, 28
Pennypacker, Governor Samuel W., 231–232
Penrose, Boies, 227, 231
Perry, Commodore Oliver H., 151
Perry County, 223
Philadelphia, 22, 69–77, 120–121, 132, 139, 258–259
Philadelphia and Reading Railroad, 177–178, 241
Philadelphia County, 126
Philadelphia Dispensary, 74
Philadelphia, Germantown, and Norristown Railroad, 177
Philadelphia Library Company, 72
Philadelphia Nautical School, 288
Philadelphia Orchestra, 253
Philharmonic Society of Bethlehem, 253
Physical features, 3–5
Pinchot, Governor Gifford, 271, 273
Pitt, Fort, 61
Pittsburg Gazette, 149
Pittsburgh, 146, 148–149, 243, 244, 246, 281, 282
Pittsburgh, Greater, 232